A Year of Flowers

Other Gardening Books by
Peter Loewer

The Indoor Water Gardener's How-to Handbook
Bringing the Outdoors In
Seeds and Cuttings
Growing and Decorating with Grasses
Growing Plants in Water
Evergreens: A Guide for Landscape, Lawn and Garden
The Garden Almanac: For Indoor and Outdoor Gardening
Gardens by Design
The Annual Garden
American Gardens

with Bebe Miles: *Wildflower Perennials for Your Garden*

A Year of Flowers

Peter Loewer

Rodale Press
Emmaus, Pa.

Library of Congress Cataloging-in-Publication Data

Loewer, H. Peter.
   A year of flowers : your house and garden in bloom, from January to December / written and illustrated by Peter Loewer.
     p.   cm.
   Bibliography: p.
   Includes index.
   ISBN 0-87857-817-X (alk. paper)   hardcover
   1. Flower gardening. 2. Flowers. I. Title.
SB405.L83 1989
635.9—dc19   88-39615
                                     CIP

2 4 6 8 10 9 7 5 3 1 hardcover

Photo Credits

Front Cover: Photograph, Sally Shenk Ullman; Styled by Barbara Fritz; Design by Denise Mirabello

Back Cover: January–May, July, October by author; June, Rodale Press Photography; August, December by Margaret Skrovanek; September, T. L. Gettings; November, Alison Miksch; Design by Denise Mirabello

Interior Photo Credits (t = top, b = bottom)
Author: 15, 16t, 17t, 17b, 19t, 19b, 21, 56t, 56b, 58b, 60t, 60b, 61t, 61b, 102t, 167, 169, 171t, 171b, 172, 173t, 173b
Rodale Press Photography: 16b, 57b, 62t, 174t, 174b
Yoder Brothers: 18
Alison Miksch: 20t, 57t, 59
Margaret Skrovanek: 20b, 102b
Patricia Lynn Seip: 22t
Tovah Martin: 22b
T. L. Gettings: 55, 62b, 168b, 170t
Joe Griffin: 97b
Dutch Gardens, Inc.: 95, 96, 98, 100t
American Daylily & Perennials: 97t
Park Seed Company: 99, 101t
John P. Hamel: 100b
John Hawkins: 168t
Diane Petku: 170b

God Almighty first planted a garden. And indeed it is the purest of human pleasures. It is the greatest refreshment to the spirits of man; without which, buildings and palaces are but gross handyworks: and a man shall ever see that when ages grow to civility and elegancy, men come to build stately sooner than to garden finely; as if gardening were the greater perfection. I do hold it, in the royal ordering of gardens, there ought to be gardens for all the months in the year . . .

Bacon, *Of Gardens*

Contents

Preface

As I write this preface, the yellow swallowtails are bouncing about on the purple lilac blossoms in our front yard. We've just had twelve straight days of rain coupled with temperatures in the mid 50s, then five days of hazy sun with highs in the 90s. Tonight is a blue moon, the last night of May, 1988, and the deer have eaten all the blossoms on the quince tree, so I look upon the butterflies as something special and I hope they augur well for the months to come in the garden.

For nothing in the world reflects the changes of nature better than a garden, whether it's only a shelf of African violets in a small city apartment, a plot of vegetables in the suburbs, a perennial border in the country, or a window greenhouse with a few small pots of narcissus that looks out on a wall of sleet or snow.

Here in the country we watch the seasons come and go surrounded by flowers in our home and in our gardens. Every month brings new bursts of color as the plants change with the seasons. In the dark days of winter, cyclamen, camellias, hyacinths, and narcissus light up the house with their flowers. Then, as the snow begins to melt, the early-blooming bulbs push their blossoms into the chilly air, happy signs of things to come. As spring melds into summer, the flowers in the garden reach their yearly peak, presenting a wave of color that both brightens the garden and our spirits. Summer's journey into fall doesn't stop the floral display, it just adds new characters to the cast of bloomers, as the mums and New England asters open to the clear blue skies. I find that I trace the circle of the year as much by the flowers that bloom as by the days and months that pass.

During my 20 years as a gardener I have grown and enjoyed hundreds of flowering plants both indoors and out in the garden. In this book I am highlighting many of my favorites and a number of plants that have been among the best performers. Throughout these pages you'll find annuals and perennials, bulbs and wildflowers, and flowering trees and shrubs. Some may be familiar to you and some you may be encountering for the first time. For all of them I am providing the growing instructions that I have followed with success. My hope is that you will be inspired to surround yourself with flowers, just as I do, all year-round.

Once again, thanks must go to my wife, Jean; my agent, Dominick Abel; my editors at Rodale, Suzanne Nelson and Claire Kowalchik; Nancy Land, who turns thought into type; and all the people in the world who love flowers and the gardens in which they grow.

Peter Loewer,
Cochecton, NY

Introduction

Once there was a front porch on our country house; a place where the original owners sat and rocked at the end of their day in the fields and watched the sun set over the back 40. Then for years the house sat vacant and wildlife moved in and wildlife moved out until we finally found it, began to renovate, and moved from the city for a life that revolved around green instead of gray. When we began to remodel the house we discovered that that wonderful front porch was infested with carpenter ants and the only cure was to tear it down. It was then that I decided to build a greenhouse—a story in itself—not only to provide the winter protection that the old porch did, but to give me an opportunity to garden all year-round.

As a result of installing that greenhouse we now have a big living room window that no longer looks out on the fields, the woods, and the pond, but instead looks into the greenhouse and all that it contains. Except for three months in summer when the view is one of green bamboo blinds installed to cut the sun's glare and heat, that window is a window full of flowers, blossoms that begin with the plants brought in from a summer in the garden, followed by the fall-flowering bulbs, then the Christmas plants, then orchids, and finally the flowers of spring. This book is about these flowers and suggestions on how to select them for your garden—both indoors and out—and how to keep them flourishing.

The Importance of Flowers

Flowers are a part of everyone's life. For a special dinner we put a vase of flowers on the table. When embarking on our first formal date or as a gift on many holidays, we either give or receive flowers. Weddings are awash with flowers. Parade floats are literally made of flowers. Even people who dislike the imperfections of life will still surround themselves with artificial flowers. If greeting cards, for example, could not use flowers, if roses and forget-me-nots were somehow in the same league as crabgrass or algae, Hallmark and Norcross would have very little left to use to gussy up a birthday or valentine greeting.

In winter we wish for flowers; in spring we greet the flowers; in summer we delight in flowers; and in fall we say farewell to flowers. Flowers are involved with many human ceremonies: When the ship leaves the dock, we get baskets of flowers or when we finally leave this earth, we are surrounded by an explosion of flowers. Whether one perfect rose or a dozen, a bunch of violets or an exuberance of orchids, the language of love and human affection revolves about flowers.

I hope that by using this book the reader will wind up surrounded by flowers throughout the year and find them, as I do, a truly valuable part of his or her life.

Making Sense of Plant Names

As you page through this book you will come across both the common and botanical or Latinized names for flowers. I do this not to confuse or impress you, but to make it as clear as possible which plants I am discussing.

Although it's true that many plants can be recognized by their common names, many more cannot. There are, for example, 17 different plants found in commerce that have the word snake in their name. Among these serpent appellations are: snake plant (often called mother-in-law's tongue), snakehead, Sampson's snakeroot, Seneca snakeroot, Snake's-head, snake vine, snakeweed, and snake-mouth.* All these names are in general use. Now imagine the local variations on these eight names across the fifty states and Canada. Then picture the resultant confusion that would arise when one snakeroot plant is confused with another by someone in a nursery order department who has a headache and hates plants to begin with.

* The Latin names for these plants are (in the same order as above): *Sansevieria trifasciata, Chelone glabra, Gentiana Catesbaei, Polygala Senega, Fritillaria Meleagris, Hibbertia scandens, Polygonum Bisorta, Pogonia ophioglossoides.*

To prevent such confusion, all plants known to man have been given Latin or scientific names—each unique—that are easily understood throughout the world, whatever native language is in use. In the 1700s, when the present system began, Latin was the international language of scholars and seemed the obvious choice to botanists. The words are derived from Renaissance Latin with a great many terms appropriated from ancient Greek. The man primarily thought of as the founder of the system is Carl Linnaeus (1707–78).

If you are worried about pronunciation, don't be. Very few people today can speak these names aloud with impunity. The English, for example, have rules for Latin pronunciation that are at odds with most of the rest of the world. Just muddle through, the best that you can, and speak the words syllable by syllable. Besides, you will generally be using them in the written sense alone.

A Gardener's Guide to Names

Scientific or botanical names may contain four terms which are in general use: genus, species, variety, and cultivar. All reference books, most gardening books, nearly all responsible catalogs and nurseries, and even the majority of seed packets list the botanical name just under the common.

In print, the *genus* and *species* are set off from the accompanying text by the use of *italics*. *Genus* refers to a group of plants that are closely related, while the *species* suggests an individual plant's unique quality, color, or even habit of growth. Either one of the names often honors the person who discovered the plant. For example, the botanical name given to the shoo-fly plant consists of the genus *Nicandra*, named in honor of Nikander of Colophon, *c.* A.D. 150, who wrote on medicine and botany, and the species *physaloides*, which is from a Greek word meaning the seedpods resemble a bladder. The *Genus* has an initial capital and the *species* is all in lower case, at least most of the time. One of the major references for botanical names used in this book is *Hortus Third*, and its authors will, on occasion, begin the species with a capital letter when it has been derived from a former generic name, a person's name, or a common name. I have followed that style.

The third term is *variety*. It is also italicized and usually preceded by the abbreviation "var.," set in roman or regular type. A variety represents a noticeable change in a plant that naturally develops by chance and breeds true from generation to generation.

The fourth term is cultivar. This represents a variation that appears on a plant while it is in cultivation—and thus could be a change either by chance or design. The term was first introduced in 1923 by L. H. Bailey from *cult*ivated *var*iety, and is distinguished in print by being set in roman type inside single quotation marks. Strangely enough, many garden writers and nursery folk frown upon the term cultivar as being an ugly-sounding word but never object to such cultivar names as 'Itsy-Bitsy', 'Big Daddy', or 'Eenie-Weenie'. It is not necessary for a cultivar to breed true from seed, but many do. Most gardeners and nursery catalogs interchange the terms variety and cultivar with ease in general use.

To see how all these terms fit together, here's the real-life example of the flowering inch plant with variegated leaves. The botanical name is *Tradescantia albiflora* 'Variegata', where the genus is named in honor of the great English plant explorer, John Tradescant, the species name means the plant bears white flowers, and the cultivar name refers to the markings on the leaves.

It should be noted that many flowers listed in catalogs have scientific names that are woefully out of date. This is because the catalog writers know the public recognizes the name *Lisianthus* but is unfamiliar with its current name of *Eustoma*. To accommodate both the correct and the popular designations, many of the entries in this book list more than one name.

Raising Flowers Naturally

The following information is not meant to be a primer on organic gardening practices since that would be impossible to do in a book this size. Instead here are some general guidelines on soil, fertilizers, watering and pest controls. More specific growing details for individual flowers are provided throughout the book.

Soil Mixes

For many plants I have given recipes that include recommendations for a good commercial potting soil, peat moss, sharp sand, and composted manure.

Sharp sand is the term used for the type of sand sold by lumber yards for mixing cement. "Sharp" simply means that the sand grains are rough to the touch, as opposed to soft sand, which is too fine to be useful. Never use beach sand: It is too soft and contains salt.

Composted manure (either cow or sheep) is usually for sale in 20 and 40 pound bags at local garden centers, nurseries, and other outlets for plant supplies. It is much easier (and neater) to use than regular animal manure.

Fertilizers

The composted manures added to the various soil mixes will usually provide sufficient nutrients for most plants between pottings. But if a plant is known to be a heavy feeder and is outside in a small pot, continually subjected to rains and waterings, or I suggest in the text that you provide additional plant food, use one of the fish emulsion concentrates. These are natural, nonburning formulas derived from sea-going fish. Be sure to look for the deodorized product especially if you're planning to use it indoors.

Self-Watering Pots

There are pots that have been on the market for some years that feature reservoirs to hold additional water. They allow you to provide moisture-loving plants with just the proper amount of water without getting the soil or the plant roots too wet. They are also great for taking care of plants while you are on a short vacation.

In addition, you may purchase water wicks to draw water from a container into the soil to match the demands of the plant. You also may make your own out of strips of fiberglass or cotton wicks made for kerosene lamps. Bury the wick in the plant's container so that one end extends from the drainage hole (or over the side in pots without holes). Put the free end of the wick into a reservoir of water that is set below the level of the plant pot. Capillary action draws the water up through the wick to keep the soil evenly moist.

Pests

Most gardeners are aware of the rich smell of chemicals that hits their nose upon entering the typical garden center. Anything that potent, packed in bottles with colorful labels warning you to use gloves and providing a toll-free number for help, can't be that great around the house. Thankfully there are alternatives.

Pest control on the home horticultural front starts with good soil, good fertility, adequate watering, and good housekeeping practices. Never allow diseased or decaying plant material to lie about. And remember that a healthy plant can fight off many attacks of pests or disease that will kill a weaker cousin.

Our worst problem is the slug, simply one of nature's most disgusting creatures. These are snails that have given up their shells and glide about at night on a trail of self-generated slime and chew holes in just about everything. I've tried slug traps baited with beer —we cannot use the poisoned bait because of possible danger to garden cats (who effectively take care of any rabbit problem)—but have never found them to be as successful as taking a flashlight out into the night. There we spotlight the slugs, and by sprinkling a few grains of salt on their tender bodies cause the chemical process of reverse osmosis to begin and effectively "do them in."

Japanese beetles are also a trial. I pick them off individually and drop them in a can of high-concentrate soap water; the resulting liquid is buried deeply in an out-of-the-way place when the can is full. There are also traps on the market that use the beetles' own lust to lure them to one-way bags where they die of thirst and can eventually be buried.

Insects like flea beetles and aphids are controlled by spraying with an insecticide derived from dried flower heads of the pyrethrum daisy (*Chrysanthemum cinerariifolium*), a plant that resembles the common field daisy. The active ingredients are removed with solvents and the result is either a powder or a liquid concentrate. The one problem: Pyrethrum is readily broken down chemically by the action of light, often in a matter of hours. So apply the product in the late afternoon to prolong its bug-controlling effects.

Rotenone is another plant-based insecticide, manufactured from the roots of the tuba root (*Derris elliptica*) and the lancepods (*Lonchocarpus* spp.). It can cause severe irritation to humans if inhaled, so care is warranted. It is sold as a dust and is an extremely potent control for many insect species, but the killing action is slow. Like pyrethrum, rotenone breaks down in the environment (but not as quickly).

There are new insecticidal soaps on the market that will effectively control aphids, mealybugs, whiteflies, scale, and spider mites. Read the directions and remember to treat these soaps and all insecticides—even if organic—with care.

For those gardeners who have the inclination to carry the war directly to the enemy there are firms who now supply the eggs of ladybugs (*Hippodamia* spp.), praying mantises (*Mantis* spp.), and green lacewings (*Chrysopa* spp.). After hatching, these troops wage the war for you.

Despite all your best efforts, there will always be times when it seems as if the forces of Nature are conspiring against you and your flowers. Don't give up; just remember that gardens are living things and never perfect.

How to Use This Book

This book is written as a month by month guide to many of the glorious flowers you can enjoy in bloom both in and out of the house. It covers annuals, perennials and bulbs, as well as wildflowers, trees and shrubs. Over the years I have grown all of the plants that appear in these pages, so I'm able to share with you my firsthand experiences.

The book is arranged by the month and contains the descriptions of over 150 plants noted for their floral displays. Special directions on starting from seed, planting, watering, and other instructions on care are given, when needed, to help you get the plants started, and keep them thriving and eager to bloom.

Appendix 1 covers the construction of various types of greenhouses and other places to grow plants.

Appendix 2 discusses an interesting variety of shrubs that can be potted up and forced for a glorious display of flowers in winter and early spring. There's also a special feature on forcing individual branches you've clipped from shrubs and trees in the yard.

Appendix 3 lists a number of mail-order sources for plants. I have dealt with all the firms on the list and found them to be run by kind and generous people who love what they do. For those who wish to read further about the fine art of flower gardening, there is an annotated bibliography.

If you have exceptionally good luck with a plant from this book, or for that fact, especially bad luck, please write me at Rodale Press, Inc., 33 East Minor Street, Emmaus, Pennsylvania 18098. I promise to answer your letters.

Announced by all the trumpets of the sky,
Arrives the snow, and, driving o'er the fields,
Seems nowhere to alight: the withered air
Hides hills and woods, the river, and the heaven,
And veils the farm-house at the garden's end.
The sled and traveller stopped, the courier's feet
Delayed, all friends shut out, the housemates sit
Around the radiant fireplace, enclosed
In a tumultuous privacy of storm.
                     Ralph Waldo Emerson, *The Snow-Storm*

Often when we become lost in the limbo that exists between the days of Christmas and the wakening spirit of the Easter season, when skies are often overly dark with most of the window views of America showing barren branches whipped by bone-chilling winds, we can easily forget the values of the seasons. But stop and think for a moment about a garden that is forever green and growing, producing brilliant dots of color every day of the year, a garden that is never at rest. There would be no time to plan, no time to quietly sit and reflect on the triumphs and failures of the preceding seasons, no time to delight over catalogs and the joy of over-ordering seeds and plants.

Grass would always need cutting and weeds would never stop in their advances. And, too, those special muted colors of winter would be gone. We would miss that time of the year when the landscape resembles a sheet of paper and all upon it the dark lines of pen and ink, with only here and there a watercolor touch of faded brown or that particular orange of a winter's setting sun when it lights the final twilight glow along the horizon.

Left, the flowering maple is called 'Clementine'. After blooming all summer long in the garden border it is now brightening the greenhouse for the winter.

Flowers in the Living Room

Even though the surrounding countryside is a drift of white from one end to the other, the indoor landscape is full of color. Our living room is full of flowers including three poinsettias; two I hold over year after year and the third is one of the new varieties with bracts in a bright shade of pink. Over in the corner by the sofa is a plant stand that holds a decorative pot with a large chenille plant, its hot red, drooping catkins always bringing forth comments from visitors. Cyclamens, red, white, and white edged with pink, sit on the table underneath the window that looks out to the greenhouse and to one side of the large table at the room's end (a catch-all area for dining, holding the day's or more often the weeks' mail, and piles of books and magazines) is a pot of bright red flamingo flowers (*Anthurium Scherzeranum*). Just behind is a pot of variegated flowering maple (*Abutilon* spp.) that I bought at the Philadelphia Flower Show of 1987, which has been blooming on and off for the past year.

The Flowering Maples

Flowering maples or Chinese lanterns belong to the genus *Abutilon* (from an Arabic name for a species of mallow) and have been in cultivation for some 150 years. Over that span of time so many different hybrids and cultivars have arisen that the species name is now given as *hybridum*. During the Victorian era these plants were in every parlor and were only outdone in the world of flower decoration by the aspidistra or cast iron plant. A well-grown flowering maple can reach a height of 2 to 3 feet in the first year.

The name refers to the shape of the leaf which is decidedly maplelike, but they are not named in honor of a hockey team from Canada. Most of the original plants came either from China or Brazil. Bell-shaped flowers will appear at anytime during the year but peak in late spring and summer. Some hybrids will bloom all year long, without stop. Colors include yellow, pink, rose, red, yellow, white, orange, and various combinations in between and there are various cultivars with variegated leaves.

Seeds may be started in February or March with a soil temperature of 60°F. Pot the seedlings on when four to six leaves have appeared, using a soil made of equal parts of loam, peat moss, and sharp sand, for even though these plants need a lot of water, they require good drainage. A mature plant is usually happy in a 7-inch pot. Flowering maples should begin to blossom by August and be ready for a winter of bloom in the house. Since these plants can get scraggly, remember to pinch back plants in the spring. Cuttings can

The leaf of a variegated flowering maple.

be rooted at any time of the year, but for blooms the following winter take cuttings in March.

All flowering maples delight in fresh air and sunlight and if grown indoors need a greenhouse, a sunporch, or a sunny window. And don't stint on the water; in fact, these plants are perfect candidates for self-watering pots. At least five hours of sun and night temperatures of between 50 and 60°F are needed for the best winter flowers.

During the winter the soil should be kept a bit dryer as the plants are often resting, but if the stems start to shrivel, it means they need more water. For fertilizing I feed mine only during the summer every two weeks with fish emulsion.

Not only are these plants a marvel because of blooming in the winter, they make great plants for the perennial border in frost-free climates where they can be grown permanently out-of-doors. In areas where frost defines the growing season, you can still enjoy the plants outdoors. I move mine outside for a summer in the sun, after the last frost dangers are past, where their nodding bells give an exotic touch to the garden. They come back inside before the first frost of autumn.

The Amaryllis

Surely the queen of the winter window is the amaryllis, a family of flowering bulbs with more than 70 members that hail from tropical America (with one member from Africa), belonging to the genus *Hippeastrum. Amaryllis* is the old genus name, no longer used. In the new genus, *Hippeus* means knight on horseback and refers to the leaves which in botanical terms are *equitant* or overlapped, and *astron* means star, referring to the flowers. The star is easy to figure, the knight is not. It shows just how far botanical Latin can go.

The bulbs can be left out-of-doors in the southern tip of Florida, a bit of southern Texas (where it touches Mexico and the Gulf), and a few small areas of California. Elsewhere this is a potted houseplant that usually spends its time indoors except for a sojourn to the backyard during the heat of summer.

If your first bulb is a gift, fully packaged and/or potted when you receive it, follow the directions on the package and repot it in the autumn that follows blooming, after the leaves turn yellow and begin to die back.

If yours is a naked bulb, plant it in a soil mix of potting soil, sharp sand, and composted cow manure, one third each. Place the bulb halfway into a pot that is no more than 2 inches larger in diameter than the bulb. Firm the soil but leave the top part of the bulb—about one-third—uncovered. Keep the soil moist but not wet. After the leaves appear, feed the plant every month during growth. Give the bulb at least four hours or more of full sun with about 50°F at night and 70°F or more during the day. Every summer after the first year, replace the top inch of soil with fresh potting mix, and pot on every three years. In time a healthy bulb can produce many flowers and attain a circumference of some 14 inches.

From late October to mid-December, keep the bulb slightly drier and allow it to rest in a cool, dark place. When you wish to start bloom, bring the pot into a warm room and place it in a dim or dark spot. When the emerging flower stalk is about 6 inches high, set the plant in a sunny window. Remove the flower after blossoming is over unless you wish to set seed.

Starting your own amaryllis plants from seed is always an interesting thing to do. You can cross-pollinate two plants by taking pollen from the anther of one flower and using a watercolor brush, dabbing it on the stigma of another flower. When the pods ripen and burst, black seeds will appear, stacked like slices of bread within the pod.

Right, the amaryllis is known as 'White Christmas'. This bulb has bloomed every winter and is now four years old.

Sow the seeds in spahagnum moss or a prepared growing mix, covering the seeds lightly. With growing temperatures of 65°F seeds should germinate within two weeks. When the seedlings are large enough to handle, place ten in a 6-inch pot and keep them at 60°F. When the leaves are 6 inches long, pot them up individually in 4-inch pots. Seedlings will bloom in three to four years after germination.

Among the newer amaryllis cultivars are: 'Appleblossom' with soft pink and white petals; 'Orange Sovereign', a deep orange; and 'Vera', a light pink.

The Chenille Plant

I never thought that I would count among my favored plants one that in bloom closely resembles the type of bedspread found in the Bates Motel. Red-hot cats-tail, or more popularly, the chenille plant, has such a flower. The botanical name is *Acalypha* (a name used by Hippocrates for the nettle, which the flowers of this plant somewhat resemble) *hispida*. First introduced from New Guinea in the late 1800s, this tropical shrub is so proficient a bloomer that even a rooted cutting will seem to be stirred by the bleak view of a January scene and soon produce flowers.

Give the plant a sunny window, keep the soil evenly moist—this plant is a good candidate for a self-watering pot—and keep it warm, usually around 70°F. (However, there may be exceptions to

this rule: Although my studio is often 55°F on cold winter nights, my chenille just keeps on blooming.) These plants are delighted to spend the summer out on a patio, but give them protection from the sun at high noon. Acalyphas also like a moist atmosphere so keep a mister handy. This action helps to prevent an attack from spider mites, a pest that is particularly fond of this genus.

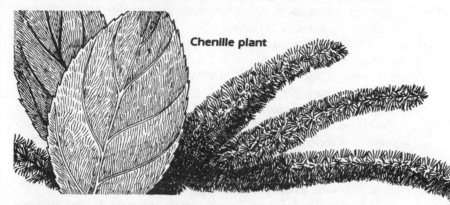

Chenille plant

The Flamingo Flower

This tropical plant also will flower for most of the year if conditions are to its liking. Known in the flower trade as flamingo flower or pigtail plant, the botanical name is *Anthurium* (*anthos* means flower and *oura* is tail) *Scherzeranum*. The single leathery blossom of lipstick red—not really a petal but a spathe—surrounds a scarlet spadix that is made up of dozens of tiny flowers only clearly seen when under a lens. These blossoms are admittedly strange, quite artificial in aspect, and were very popular in floral arrangements during the 30s when two or three were often seen in combination with a twisted stick, all in a copper vase. The plants grow by adding another leaf to a rosette of leaves and flowers, and these leaves are quite tough.

Anthuriums must have a humid and warm atmosphere at all times, easily provided by misting whenever you pass by. They like morning sun but should be protected from hot afternoon sun as they are really plants from the deep jungles. Any well-drained potting mix will do, and if the plants are grown in the good light they prefer, give them fertilizer once a month. Anthuriums prefer warm temperatures in the 70s like the chenille plant.

These plants are also climbers and will eventually lift themselves above the pot. Wrap the new roots in moist sphagnum moss and eventually you can repot the plant up to the level of the new bottom leaf.

Left, the flamingo flower is another tropical plant that blooms in the winter if given adequate light and heat.

Flower Feature: The Charming Cyclamen

The first rays of dawn were reflected through foot-long icicles that clung to the greenhouse eaves—the result of a short January thaw the previous two days. The cold light glistened on some 30 blossoms that hovered on now bending stems over a pot of florist's cyclamen (*Cyclamen persicum* 'Giganteum') that I've been growing since my wife gave me the plant back in the winter of 1972. Last winter it bore over 120 flowers.

Of all the flowering plants of the Christmas season, this is my favorite. If you are unable to find a cool place for this plant, never buy one and if yours is a gift, enjoy the flowers while you can, then give it away to a friend who lives in cooler surroundings. Since the original plants came from the mountains of Persia where the climate is cool and the skies are blue and bright, warm rooms where temperatures are above 60°F shorten flower life and prevent immature buds from ever opening. You can try moving the plant closer to a window, where temperatures are always cooler, but the plant will eventually wear itself out from heat.

Most garden books tell a cyclamen owner to dry the tuber—the corky surfaced, brown "bulb" that sits like a rounded potato on the soil's surface—after winter flowering is over, allowing it to dry out completely for the summer. The pot then sits on its side under a bench in a greenhouse until early autumn when the plants are top-dressed or repotted and the watering cycle starts again. The problem with this approach is that a summer in the Northeast is too hot and I've lost a lot of plants this way.

The secret is to store the potted tuber in a cool room (below 60°F) until the weather has warmed up outside. Then starting in May (here in Zone 5), the pots are set under a canopy of white pine branches at the shady end of the garden where the soil is lightly moistened about every two weeks.

In early August the dormant tuber should be lifted and the soil replaced by a fresh mixture. I prefer sterilized potting soil, composted cow manure, and sharp sand, one-third each. Carefully position the tuber half in and half out of the soil with the tuber's slight depression on top. Water the plant and place it under the shade again. New shoots will soon sprout, with more appearing as the cooler weather approaches.

Soil should never be allowed to completely dry out or the whole plant will wilt, both leaves and flowers quickly drooping over the edge of the pot. If this happens to you, don't despair. Take newspaper sections and completely surround the pot, slowly and gently propping

Right, the cyclamen pictured at the top of the drawing is called *Cyclamen hederifolium*. The flowers in the vase belong to the cultivar 'Giganteum'.

the stems in an upright position, much like a florist wrapping a bouquet. Fasten the paper with tape, clips, or string and immediately soak the soil. Before the day is out, the stems should absorb enough water to hold themselves up. Never wait too long for this emergency procedure or the plant will die back. This watering forces it to produce new leaves, which will sap its strength for more flowering until next season. A self-watering pot or water wicks (you will need more than one wick for a large plant) are a big help.

Water should never be poured directly on or into the slight depression on the tuber's top as it could produce a case of rotting. This doesn't mean that an occasional few drops will destroy the plant, but it's a good habit to take care in watering. Give plants morning and late afternoon sun, the best spot being an east or west window. When removing dead flowers or leaves, give the stems a sharp twist before pulling them away from the tubers.

Starting from Seed

Seed of the various hybrid forms of C. *persicum* take up to two and a half months to germinate, and the plants should begin to bloom within eighteen months. Soak seeds in warm water (70°F) for 24 hours before sowing in mid- to late summer. Use the standard cyclamen soil mix, sowing seeds 2 inches apart and about 1/4-inch deep; darkness is needed for germination. Maintain the temperature at 65°F, as higher temperatures can prevent germination.

Once the leaves have appeared, give the seedlings plenty of bright light but keep temperatures below 60°F; a spot in a cool room near a window is best. When the seedlings have two leaves move them to new flats, and space the plants about 1 inch apart. Transplant them again when the leaves begin to touch. Usually by April the plants are big enough for individual pots. Pot them on as roots fill the containers, each plant eventually ending up in a 5-inch pot.

The Miniature Cyclamens

Miniature cyclamens have been developed by hybridizing various forms of C. *persicum* with a hardier member of the clan, C. *purpurascens*, a very fragrant form from central and southern Europe with lovely rose-pink, carmine, and magenta flowers. This species blooms in late summer and fall.

Not only are the new miniatures half the size of the typical Persian hybrid, but they are not as fussy about heat, they will bloom for months without stopping (just seven months after germination), and their flowers have a noticeable fragrance. They come in shades of salmon, lilac, scarlet, purple, white, and various shades in between.

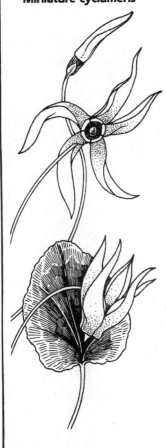

Miniature cyclamens

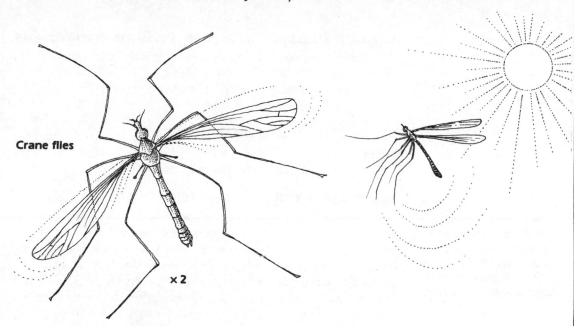

Crane flies

× 2

The January Thaw

It is difficult to believe that winter has at least six weeks to go when the January thaw presents itself. That warm sun in a clear blue sky can lull you into a false sense of security, especially when the snow level starts to fall. Mouse prints enlarge as their moulded edges pull away with the melt (and dog prints loom as large as a bear's); snow fleas (*Achorutes nivicolus*) bounce across the sparkling surface; and one peculiar variety of crane fly (*Trichocera* spp.) suddenly appears outside the kitchen window, bobbing up and down in the warming air.

It's hard to believe that winter still poses a threat to your plants, faced with so many signs of impending spring. But the combination of warm days and frigid nights first melts the snow, then freezes it again. Many plants with shallow or immature root systems (not to mention all those plastic plant labels) rise out of the ground. It is then up to the gardener to push them gently back so they will not die of exposure by early spring.

Another good idea is to mulch your flower beds with pine branches left from your Christmas tree or a light covering of hay. The idea here is to keep the ground frozen under the mulch and protected from melting by the warming sun, especially if you live in an area of the country that has sparse snow cover. For contrary to popular belief, mulching is not meant to keep plants warm but instead, comfortably cold and dormant.

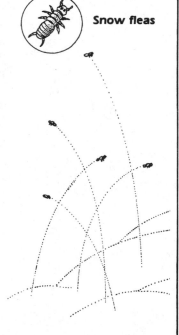

Snow fleas

Garden Plan: A Window of Flowering Bulbs

Nothing can warm a cold winter's heart more than a window full of blooming bulbs. Whether narcissus, tulips, daffodils, or hyacinths, the fragrance and sprightly aspect of these flowers will lift your spirits and put a spring in your step.

Among the bulbs that will do well in a pot are crocus (*Crocus* spp.), 'Paperwhite' narcissus (*Narcissus Tazetta* 'Paperwhite'), *Narcissus* 'Tete-a-Tete', *Hyacinthus* 'Anna Marie', lily-of-the-valley (*Convallaria majalis*), and white calla lilies (*Zantedeschia aethiopica*).

Hardy Bulbs That Need a Chill

Right, the drawing on the opposite page shows a pot of yellow crocus and 'Soleil d'Or' narcissus growing in bird gravel and water.

These directions will get you started with tulips, narcissus, hyacinths, and crocus. Special directions for tender bulbs and lilies-of-the-valley follow. The only requirement you will need for forcing hardy bulbs to bloom early in the season is a cool room, cellar, or garage that maintains a temperature of between 45° to 50°F. If you have no objection to a bit of grit in the fridge, the refrigerator is a good spot to root bulbs since temperatures usually run about 40° to 45°F around the crisper.

Use 6-inch clay pots—I dislike plastic pots because they are too lightweight and their composition prevents the passage of air through the wall of the pot—planting between three to six bulbs per pot. And if planting hyacinths, be sure the clay pots are used and not new. For some reason, unknown to me, new pots and hyacinths do not mix.

For a soil mixture use equal parts of potting soil, sharp sand, and peat moss, plus a little composted cow manure if you have it. Crock the drain hole and fill two-thirds of the pot with the mix. Tamp it down, then set the bulbs carefully on the medium about an inch apart. Do not twist the bulbs as that motion can easily damage the basal plate and interfere with root formation. Fill the spaces around the bulbs leaving just the tips of the noses uncovered.

Now soak the pots in a bucket of water or sink until the mix is thoroughly wet. As you immerse each pot hold your hand over the mix or it will spill up and out. Next drain the pots. The mix should be wet but not dripping.

Put the bulbs in a box and cover it with newspapers or cardboard; anything to prevent light from reaching the surface of the soil. Move the bulbs to an area where the temperature is cool and constant. It should take about eight to twelve weeks for the bulbs to develop root systems. Check to see that roots are peeping through the drainage holes. If you don't have an appropriately cool spot indoors, place the potted bulbs outdoors in a cold frame or a pit and

cover it over with leaves and straw. Remember if left outdoors, the bulbs must not be allowed to freeze. If they do, they will not bloom.

Nothing in life is perfect but if you follow the above instructions, the tulips should root within 12 to 14 weeks, the narcissus between 10 and 12 weeks, and the hyacinths and crocus between 6 and 10 weeks.

Once the roots are formed, bring the pots indoors to a cool window (about 60°F), away from any artificial heat. When the new shoots turn green and are about 4 to 6 inches high, move the pots to a sunny window for blooming. Never let the medium dry out.

After flowers fade, cut them off close to the bulbs. Keep watering the hardy bulbs, allowing the leaves to mature and die naturally, then transplant to the garden in the spring for future blooming.

Tulips are not as easy to force as other hardy bulbs but I've always had good luck with *Tulipa Fosterana* 'Red Emperor'. When planting these bulbs use six to a pot and place the flat side toward the edge of the container. This flat side is the spot where the first leaf will emerge, growing gracefully over the edge instead of toward the center.

Spring-flowering crocus, grape hyacinths (*Muscari armeniacum*), star of Bethlehem (*Ornithogalum umbellatum*), and *Iris reticulata* are all easy plants to bloom in winter.

Precooled Bulbs

Many nurseries now offer precooled hardy bulbs specially prepared for early bloom. Such bulbs should be planted immediately upon receipt and can go directly into a favorite dish or container, stored between four and six weeks at 50°F for some root development, then brought into a warm room for immediate bloom.

Tender Bulbs

'Paperwhite' narcissus, 'Soleil d'Or', and Chinese sacred lilies (*Narcissus Tazetta* var. *orientalis*), are the usual varieties of tender narcissus bulbs offered. They often come preplanted or you can pot them up in your own container using a bowl at least 3 inches high. Pebbles, gravel, or prepackaged bulb mixes will keep the bulbs stable. Fill the container with 2 inches of mix and add water until the mix is thoroughly wet. Place the bulbs on top and surround them with more stones to keep them upright, leaving their top halves clear. Place the bulbs in a cool (45° to 50°F), dark, well-ventilated spot until the emerging leaves are about 3 inches tall. Rooting time is between two and three weeks for 'Paperwhite' and four to five

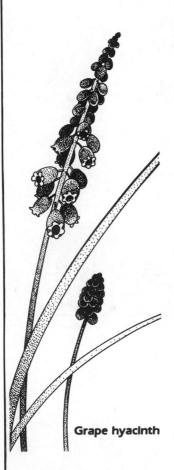

Grape hyacinth

Winter

   If a bee were to wake in January and enter our living room,
flaming red amaryllis blooms would certainly vie for its attention.
The photo above gives the bee's-eye view just before the pollen
ripens and begins to fall.

Two flamingo flowers rear up and give the other flowers in the greenhouse a haughty stare. These blossoms bring a truly tropical look to any plant collection and the plants are even attractive when not in flower.

It's too bad that kalanchoes do not have a common name. But their cheerful winter bloom makes up for any problems in pronunciation. Time of flower is keyed to the amount of light the plants receive.

The blossoms of a new cultivar of common stock called 'Dwarf Stockpot' produce fragrant and silky flowers that begin to open seven to nine weeks after sowing. Colors are rose, purple, white, and red.

Flowering maples provide almost continuous bloom either in the greenhouse or in front of a sunny window. The cultivar shown is called 'Moonchimes' and produces large yellow blossoms, perfect for hanging baskets.

Hibiscus are tender but as long as the roots do not freeze, they can tolerate a touch of frost. Plants bloom almost continuously— indoors or out—as long as they are in very bright light or a sunny, warm location. The flower above is from a new cultivar called 'Vista'.

A pink camellia called 'Debutante', pink Persian cyclamen, and an impatiens cultivar called 'White Gardenia' form a line of bloom in the winter greenhouse. The succulent to the right is called pearly moonstones.

Cymbidiums are tropical orchids that are terrestrial in habit and will tolerate temperatures as low as 40°F without being harmed. The flowers at left will look fresh for up to six weeks.

Christmas cactus will bloom
during the darkest days of the
year. In nature these plants all
grow in the crevices of tree
branches, up in the air like many
orchids and bromeliads.

They're not just common old African violets any more. Today's
cultivars come in an endless array of colors and petal shapes and
will brighten up a windowsill most of the year.

Christmas cactus, florist's cyclamen, and Persian cyclamen brighten the greenhouse until well into March. The large plant in the rear is a cabbage palm that summers in the garden. Note the wire baskets lined with sphagnum moss used for the cactus.

Freesias are excellent plants for winter flowers. The only requirements for bloom are cool temperatures and bright light. They come in an endless line of colors and their perfume is delightful.

Chenille plants are also called red-hot cats-tail and were first introduced from New Guinea in the late 1800s. Even a rooted cutting will soon produce flowers.

weeks for 'Soleil d'Or' and the sacred lilies. Move the pot to a lighted area for three or four days, then set it in the sun. Remember to rotate the containers so the plants do not lean and keep watering. Discard the bulbs after blooming is finished.

Lily-of-the-Valley

When ordering bulbs, don't forget to include some prepared lily-of-the-valley pips. They are usually available in a special mix and all you add is water. You can, however, save a bit of money and get more attractive containers by buying the pips and planting them yourself. They can be potted in almost any mix that holds water, but the basic mix given for hardy bulbs is as good as any. The roots are planted in 3-inch pots with the buds just above the surface. Water thoroughly and place them in a dark, well-ventilated spot for about two weeks. When the flower stems are well developed bring the plants into more light.

Red Emperor tulips bloom in a sunny window.

In every year there are days between winter and spring which rightly belong to neither; days when the round of seasons seems to be at a standstill, as though the inner impulse which held on visibly enough through the worst of the hard weather has failed just when it should begin to quicken towards the first of the better times . . .

There are evenings . . . when the world is nearly unlovely as it ever can be under natural conditions: the air cold with a sodden chill that bites worse than frost; land and sky wrapped in a dim cloud without form or motion; the year altogether at its worst, foul from the winter, frostbitten, flood-swept, sunk in a sapless lethargy when it is more than time for the stirrings of the yearly miracle of repair.

Anonymous, Corners of Old Grey Gardens, 1912.

February can be bleak, it's true, but the month always seems mercifully short, a combination of the everlasting dim and dark days and the actions of the Emperor Augustus who, wishing to make his birth month of August longer, took a nip out of February.

From the gardener's point of view, there is much to be done: it's high time to finally sit down and plan the new additions to the backyard garden and orders for both the next season's seed and plants wait for completion.

Left, a pot of goldfields brightens up a sunny living room window seemingly unaware that it's the middle of February.

A Window of Bloom

The living room window that looks into the greenhouse is ablaze with flowers today. Even though outdoors a wicked chill wind is blowing from the west and the sky has the color of very dirty cotton batting, there is a feeling of spring—at least as long as the furnace continues to work.

The Christmas poinsettias are still bright; the hibiscus is opening at least one flower a day; the goldfields are bright dots of sunshine yellow; the cyclamen continue to unfold new flowers; the spring bulbs are still on display; the calla lilies are ready to welcome Katherine Hepburn; and the camellias and gardenias are blooming to beat the band.

Charming Goldfields

Goldfields are a native flowering annual from California. The genus is *Lasthenia* (named in honor of a Greek girl who attended Plato's lectures in man's clothing) and the species is *glabrata*. The flowers are bright yellow daisies about an inch across that bob and weave on long thin stems, making them perfect candidates for a hanging basket.

The marvelous thing about these plants is the speed with which they flower, making the trip from germination to blossom in just about six weeks. Once they begin to bloom, they seem to go on forever, especially if you remember to remove spent flowers so the plant never gets the message to stop producing.

Use a standard potting mix of potting soil, peat moss, and sharp sand, one-third each. Lightly scatter the seeds on a moist soil surface and cover with a sprinkling of spagnum moss. Place the container in a warm spot, preferably using a heating cable to provide constant bottom heat. Set in a sunny window after the first of the true leaves develop. Seeds started the first week in January will bloom by mid-February since germination occurs within a few days.

Wallflowers in February

Some years ago I bought a packet of wallflower seeds of mixed colors (*Cheiranthus Cheiri*) from a seed company display in our local general store. There was a lovely color picture on the front and the label identified it as a biennial but not hardy in our Zone 5 climate. I planted the seeds in early February, hoping to have flowers by September. I had first seen the vibrant colors of these flowers and smelled their rich fragrance when walking in England's Kew Gardens. In fact, most of the London of April and May is bedecked with window boxes bursting with these blossoms.

Mine did not bloom the first year but the plants were about 2 feet tall with heavy, woody stems forming at the base, so I put them in the cool greenhouse for the winter. By January the plants had lost a few leaves but looked green and healthy.

Then around the first of February, I noticed that buds were forming in the hollow between the newest leaves, at the tips of the

Wallflowers

now 3-foot branches. Each day the buds grew and on February 22 the flowers opened and the perfume reached to every corner of the room. Petals unfurled of the deepest velvet purple, brilliant orange, sunshine yellow, and a mixed white, as well as petals striped with orange on white, and creamy white. They continued to bloom for two months as I removed the dead flowers before they set seed.

In their native haunts of southern Europe, these plants grow in stone walls and sandy soil, so I used a soil mix of equal parts of potting soil and sharp sand. A 6-inch pot worked well for my exuberant plants. Once established the plants are perennial and will bloom in late winter. The secret is the temperature. When kept in a spot with 60°F or slightly less, the plants will set buds. Then when the buds are mature, the temperatures can be warmer. Let the soil dry out between waterings and give the plants full sun.

The Everblooming Hibiscus

The genus *Hibiscus* (from an ancient Greek name for the marsh mallow) bears flowers that were often seen in 40s movies, artfully placed in the free-flowing hair of native heroines, who were casually dressed in patterned sarongs and usually seen climbing to the lip of the nearest volcano.

One of the many bright and colorful cultivars of H. *Rosa-sinensis* is usually offered for the home gardener at garden centers and in catalogs. Plants are tender but as long as the roots do not freeze, hibiscus can tolerate a touch of frost without expiring. They will bloom almost continuously—indoors or out—as long as the plants are in very bright light or a sunny, warm location. After a blossom has opened the petals fold up and within a day or two, drop off the plant. But there are always more flowers to come.

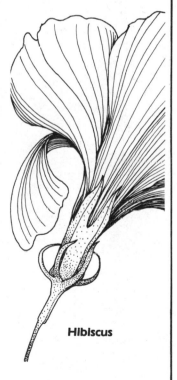

Hibiscus

The length of resting time needed by the plant depends on the time of year, the amount of light the plant receives, and a combination of day and night temperatures. In order to have midwinter bloom, I bring my plants indoors before the first frost and put them in a back corner of the greenhouse where the light is not too bright and temperatures average about 55°F. The plants rest for October and November. In December, I bring them into bright light and increased warmth and soon they begin to bloom.

The soil should be moist at all times and I feed once a month from spring to fall with a liquid fertilizer. They are at home in an 8-inch pot and plants can be pruned in the spring. The only pest is the spider mite, but that can be controlled by misting the plants daily. Bud drop usually means there is not enough intensity of light to develop the flowers.

The Classic Calla

Calla lilies look to me like the kind of flower that graced the scene when Fred Astaire and Ginger Rogers were dancing. These classic blooms belong to the genus *Zantedeschia* (named in honor of an Italian botanist of the early 1800s, Giovanni Zantedeschi) and can easily be brought into flower at any specified time of the year.

There are four general species found in cultivation: the white calla, *Z. aethiopica* from the Transvaal; the pink calla, *Z. Rehmannii*, from South Africa; the spotted calla, *Z. albomaculata*, from Zambia, bearing leaves dotted with white specks; and the golden calla, *Z. Elliottiana*, also from South Africa and also bearing leaves spotted with white.

Unlike many flowers, callas are not dependent on day length or temperature in order to initiate flower production. Flower buds form and develop under the conditions that favor vegetative growth.

In order to have flowers for mid-February, pot up the rhizomes towards the end of November. Any good soil mix is adequate but I use the old standard of potting soil, sharp sand, and composted manure, one third each. Use a 6-inch pot, keeping the roots about 2 inches below the surface of the soil.

Callas like a lot of water and are good candidates for self-watering pots. Dormancy is brought about by lack of water and if not allowed to go dormant, plants will flower for many months at a time.

If started on November 25 and kept in a warm spot with temperatures averaging 70°F, plants will bloom about February 15. If kept in temperatures of 60°F, plants will bloom the first week in March.

From September to June, callas do best in full sunlight, but during the hot days of summer, they should be given shade in the afternoon. In frost-free parts of the United States, calla lilies are perfect for the perennial border.

Kenilworth Ivy

The ivy-leaved toadflax, another common name for Kenilworth ivy, arrived in England sometime in the early seventeenth century. According to Geoffrey Grigson in his charming book, *The Englishman's Flora*, William Coys, one of the best amateurs of the time, appears to have grown it before anyone else in his garden at North Ockendon, in Essex.

"Garden walls, park walls, boundary walls," wrote Mr. Grigson, "went up apace in the seventeenth, eighteenth and nineteenth centuries, so it was a good time for a rock species in search of new terri-

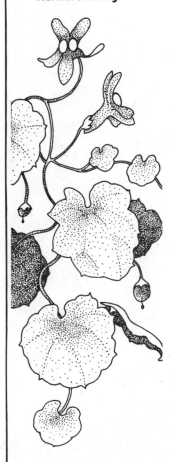

Kenilworth Ivy

tory. By 1640 *Cymbalaria muralis* . . . was much planted up and down the country, it must have made separate escapes over and over again. By 1724 it was growing on walls round about the Chelsea Physic Garden [in London], and the Oxford plants may have escaped on to the walls from the Botanic Garden. In just over three centuries it has conquered most of the walls of Great Britain. It must now come to a halt in the age of fences and barbed wire."

The genus name of *Cymbalaria* refers to a pair of cymbals and nobody today knows the original application; *muralis* means to grow on walls. Other popular names for this plant are creeping Jenny, mother of thousands, Oxford weed (from the numbers found on Ox-

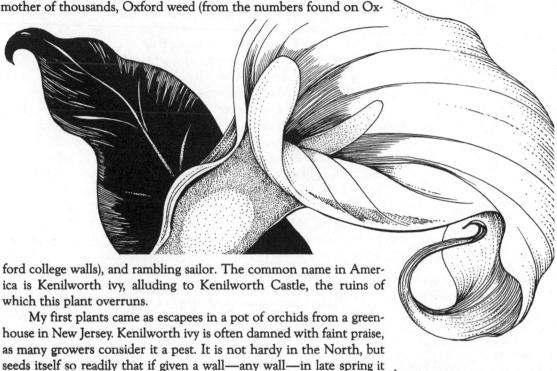

ford college walls), and rambling sailor. The common name in America is Kenilworth ivy, alluding to Kenilworth Castle, the ruins of which this plant overruns.

My first plants came as escapees in a pot of orchids from a greenhouse in New Jersey. Kenilworth ivy is often damned with faint praise, as many growers consider it a pest. It is not hardy in the North, but seeds itself so readily that if given a wall—any wall—in late spring it will make itself known and wink its pretty blue snapdragonlike flowers at you all summer long.

Calla lily

If planted in a 4-inch pot in late December, you will have a blooming basket plant by late February that will delight in a sunny window when given plenty of water and a soil of at least one third sand. When summer comes, you can either keep it in the pot or plant it out in the garden, preferably at the top or edge of a wall or embankment. There are cultivars now available including 'Alba' with white flowers and 'Maxima' with larger than average flowers.

Flower Feature: The Camellia

In 1936 when M.G.M filmed the beautiful Greta Garbo walking into a Parisian floral shop for a nosegay of camellias and holding the flowers to her nose to inhale their sumptuous fragrance, they made a major mistake: The popular *Camelia japonica* does not have a fragrance. If it did, this would be the flower for all seasons, for all of the world, outdistancing even the gardenia and the rose. Unfortunately, its fame must rest with its beauty alone.

Popular for over a thousand years in the orient—Japan alone is said to possess over 900 cultivars—the history of the camellia began with tea, since C. *sinensis*, the tea plant, is a close relative. In the early 1700s some crafty Europeans, wishing to grow tea on their own turf, bought some plants from the Chinese. But the crafty Chinese had no wish to spread the wealth around, and sent instead plants of C. *japonica*. It was hopeless for making a brew but the flowers captivated the Europeans' imagination and the search for more camellias began.

By 1739, two flowering camellias—one a single white and the other red—were bought by Lord Petre of Thornden Hall. Within two years his gardener had a hybrid form with double red flowers. Then in the late 1700s the East India Company brought more camellias into Europe and England and in the first 15 years of the nineteenth century, 12 varieties were grown in England.

Meanwhile in 1797, the first camellias arrived in the United States at the exotic port of Hoboken, New Jersey and became a star attraction with wealthy greenhouse owners up North and every plantation owner in the South.

In 1847, a beautiful French courtesan named Alphonsine Duplessis died at the age of 27. She loved camellias more than anything and her grieving lovers are said to have covered her coffin with a pall of white camellias. Alexandre Dumas *fils*, became enchanted with the story and wrote *La Dame aux Camélias*—mistakenly translated into English as Camille. In 1852, a play was produced and the rage for camellias swept the continent. By the end of the nineteenth century the rage had passed and when popularity again picked up, the interest was in outdoor cultivation.

Cultivating Camellias

In Zones 7 and up, the camellia is hardy outdoors. Some cultivars can even take short spells of −5°F, but in the North, the place for camellias is in the home or greenhouse, with summers in the garden.

These are slow-growing plants and will bear flowers when very young. All during February my C. *japonica* 'Debutante' bore long-

Right, two different camellias bloom in the February window. The larger flower is pink and called 'Debutante'; the smaller is the deep red 'Yuletide' belonging to the species *Sasanqua.*

lasting, large pink flowers of unsurpassed beauty. Yet the shrub had only two stems, the longest only 2 feet high.

To make sure your plants keep blooming for you follow this regimen: Remove the flowers after they brown. To keep the plants within bounds, cut back by a third after they flower. The sheared branches can be rooted to form more plants. By late spring set plants outside in a sheltered spot with filtered sun. Make sure you remember to water your camellias because the soil must never be allowed to completely dry out. Check the pots daily. If you keep your plants indoors, give them a window with sunlight. Feed once a month with a liquid fertilizer like fish emulsion. Repot every two years using potting soil, sharp sand, and peat moss, one third each, and pick a pot 2 inches larger than the old one. Bring plants back indoors just before the frost.

Now about temperature. Camellias want to be kept cool. They will thrive if temperatures range between 40° and 60°F. They detest heat! Bud drop is caused either by keeping plants too dry or a sudden change in temperature.

Outdoors: Winter Begins to Fade

February is not one of the better times outside, especially in Zones 6 down to 1. Temperatures are usually wicked and snow covers the ground. But the following two flowers will often bloom by month's end if your area happens to have a mild winter, with little or no snow and the ground never freezes except for a slight crust on the top. If the winter is bad, look for these flowers to appear by the middle of March.

Coltsfoot

Coltsfoot

The first is the coltsfoot or *Tussilago Farfara* (from the Latin *tussus*, referring to a cough), one of the earliest flowers to bloom in the spring. The yellow daisylike flowers appear first along the sides of country roads, where the late winter sun melts the snow, growing in soil that is usually nothing except road dust and sand. The leaves are large, round, and indented, resembling a colt's foot. It is a creeper and can be as invasive as bamboo, so has no place in the formal garden unless the rhizomes can be contained. Either plant them in a submerged plastic tub or surround the plants with buried metal edging or a plastic guard at least a foot high. But for the wild garden these cheerful sunny flowers are perfect.

Coltsfoot tea, coltsfoot syrup, and coltsfoot "rock," a candy, have been used for generations to relieve coughing from colds and the leaves have been employed as a herbal tobacco to help in cases of asthma.

Japanese Butterbur

Japanese butterbur is used as a vegetable in Japan. The botanical name is *Petasites japonica* var. *giganteus* and the genus is from the Greek word for hat, a reference to the large and broad leaves that can easily keep your hair dry if you are caught in the garden during a sudden downpour.

Like the coltsfoot, this plant blooms first before the leaves appear. The flowers are many on a short spike and look for all the world like a small mop that has been dyed chartreuse. The flowers will, like snowdrops, appear in the midst of a few inches of snow. If winters are hard, butterbur blooms in mid-March.

By mid-summer, the leaves are up to 3 feet in diameter and create a spectacular accent plant in a damp area. Unfortunately, butterbur is also aggressive, so be careful to keep the wandering roots in an out-of-the-way spot or use a container.

The leafstalks are tasty either boiled fresh from the garden or pickled for use as a green for soup. The flowerbuds are picked and eaten when green for their slightly bitter yet agreeable flavor. The Japanese are said to use the hollow stalks as walking sticks by inserting a firm rod for added support.

Garden Plan: Growing Bulbs in Water

Up until a few years ago, the idea of planting bulbs in water was considered old hat, something of little value that the fusty Victorians enjoyed. But nothing can be quite as lovely and encouraging to the spirit as the sight of spring flowers glowing in containers full of water on a windowsill.

For this particular arrangement use the tender 'Paperwhite' narcissus, 'Soleil d'Or', or the Chinese sacred lilies and the precooled hyacinth bulbs. You may also use the Devil's-tongue (*Sauromatum guttatum*), crocus corms, and even amaryllis bulbs.

Fill containers (the illustration shows some of the available types) with water so that the bottoms of the bulbs barely touch the wet surface. Then place the containers in a cool place (50°F) with total darkness. Check to see that the water level is kept up and wait for the white roots to form, a process that usually takes about a month.

When the twining roots have filled the glass container, remove the plants to a cool, shady area for about five days. Then you can place them in a sunny window (still in a cool room), rotating the containers

Japanese butterbur

***Below,* the flowers
are, from the left,
a hyacinth, crocus,
an avocado,
Devil's-tongue,
'Paperwhite' narcissus,
and an amaryllis.**

daily so the flower stalks remain reasonably straight as they grow.

If the hyacinth should start to bloom before the buds are away from the bulb, cover the bulb with an inverted paper cone until the stem is long enough.

The amaryllis will only bloom once with this water treatment. After the leaves have matured and died back, I repot the bulb in soil and treat it as described under January. The Devil's-tongue should be allowed to dry out in October and kept dry over the winter at a temperature of about 50°F, then used as a houseplant. I throw away the other bulbs.

Now that spring is in the winds and ready to move to stage left and thoughts of winter's gloom seem to recede from view, it's time to get ready for another year in the garden and the great outdoors. Unfortunately, it's also time for the developers to gear up their machinery for another assault on the land that is still open to the fields, still covered with woods.

Three years ago I received a call from a local lawyer that the house next door to him was soon to be torn down and it and the garden in back were to become a parking lot. I got there in time to dig up well over 25 old-fashioned hostas that now are at home under the white ash tree in our backyard.

If you are interested in creating a wild garden that features the flowers that abound in field and forest, keep your eyes open for that developer; you might be able to rescue an endangered species or a little-known fern before it's buried under a ton of mediocre planning. To be on the safe side, always ask permission to dig. You might be branded a conservationist, but there are worse things to be called.

Left, **clivias, or Kaffir lilies, bloom in March. Even without blossoms the plants are beautiful and become very large over the years.**

A House of Flowers

That window in our living room looks out on the camellias; a geranium held over from last fall; a poinsettia that still holds forth; cymbidium orchids; primroses; oxalis; Hermannia or honeybells; tiny drabas; the Kaffir lily; cyclamen; schizanthes or butterfly flowers; drunkard's dream; the hibiscus; one of the climbing jasmines, *Trachelospermum mandianum*; freesias; and the wirilda or willow-leafed acacia, *Acacia retinodes*.

The Kaffir Lily

Twelve years ago this month—I know because I do keep records on some plants—I bought a plant by mail. It was a puny thing with two straplike leaves and three white roots all in a plastic pot, doubled over with the weight of polyethylene and the two-week transit of the even then deteriorating postal service.

The plant was called a Kaffir lily, named after a province in South Africa. The botanical name is *Clivia* (in honor of a Duchess of Northumberland, *née* Clive, who died in 1866) *miniata*. A member of the Amaryllis Family, the Kaffirs consist of a radial growth of thick leaves—from 1 to 2 feet in length. They are tropical, evergreen, and make perfect houseplants, especially since they tolerate a wide range of temperatures from 50°F up.

Ranunculus

Two years passed while my plant added a few leaves and struggled to fill a 4-inch pot. Then *voilà!* It began to take off and threw out leaf after leaf, soon splitting asunder a 5-inch pot, then a 6-inch pot, winding up for now in a 14-inch wooden pot that sits in a saucer on wheels, since it is too heavy to move about with any ease.

Every spring, around the middle of March, the flowers appear: large, funnel-shaped affairs, with throats of the brightest yellow that gradually changes to the brightest of orange at the tip of each petal. There are 12 to 20 blooms clustered atop each thick and flattened stem. This is a spectacular plant, worthy of being in every plant collection.

During and after flowering, they require copious amounts of water and, if potbound, a good deal of fertilizer. Soil should once again be a mix of potting soil, sharp sand, and composted cow manure, one-third each. Kaffirs need repotting only when they literally burst the sides of their containers; an annual topdressing of fresh soil is usually enough. The plants need at least eight hours of bright light, but protect them from summer sun if they're left outside for the summer months.

The Kaffirs rest for most of the winter, wanting neither too much heat nor light, and no water at all, except an occasional spritz to keep the soil from becoming dust.

The Frilly Ranunculus

The florist's ranunculus (*Ranunculus asiaticus*) are lovely blossoms that resemble buttercups with double or triple the number of petals. The name is old and is based on the Latin word *rana*, or frog, as many of these plants delight in moist places. Their roots are also splayed and could be thought to resemble a frog's foot.

'Superbissimus' is the cultivar usually offered by the trade. The flowers are of mixed colors—usually red, orange, pink, yellow, and white—and a pot of these beauties could melt a below-zero heart.

Use a soil mix of equal parts potting soil, composted manure, and sharp sand and plant three sets of the tuberous roots per 6-inch pot. Soak the roots for three hours in warm water before potting. Plant the roots claws down, 2 inches deep, scattering some sand over them before covering with the potting mix. Water well. Place the pots in a dim, cool spot, keeping the soil dry until growth begins, then increase waterings. Growth should start in 4 to 6 weeks when pots should be moved to a cool, sunny window.

When the foliage dies back, the tubers can be lifted from the soil and stored in a box of sand. Place in a dry, cool place over the summer and pot up again in the fall.

The Drunkard's Dream

This interesting member of the cactus family has a fascinating trio of common names: drunkard's dream, dancing-bones, or the spice cactus. The first and second refer to the shape of the branchlets and the third I cannot fathom.

The botanical name is *Hatiora salicornoides* (*Hatiora* is an anagram for the sixteenth century botanist, Thomas Hariot, who discovered the plant). The jointed stems are tan to green and strongly resemble small bottles, with smaller bottles growing from the caps. Under strong light, tiny purple spots appear along the stems with no regular pattern. The spines are reduced to minute patches of fuzz at the bottle cap position.

Usually in March, the plants blooms with butterscotch-yellow flowers at the stem ends. The blossoms have a waxy shine and never fully open unless in full sunlight. Fruit will occasionally develop; it's a translucent white with a shiny red tip, like a nose (another reference to the common name).

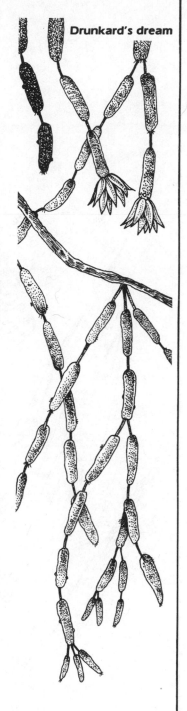

Drunkard's dream

In nature, these plants grow in trees, sending roots out in all directions. So when confined to a pot, the soil must be well drained. Even though it's a cactus, this plant needs a moist, almost junglelike atmosphere, so water well, and cut the potting soil by half with sharp sand. Drunkard's dream wants partial shade during the hot months of summer; to accommodate it I hang the pot under a tree.

Fan Iris

The Poor Man's Orchid

What a lovely flower this is. And what a mouthful for a botanical name. *Schizanthus pinnatus* (from the Latin *schizo*, to cut, and *anthos*, flower, referring to the deeply cut petals) is an annual from Chile. The common names of butterfly flower and the poor man's orchid are perhaps easier to deal with.

When the cultivar 'Hit Parade' is described as: "Large, orchidlike blooms in salmon, light pink, carmine, scarlet, lilac, violet, and purple, with exotic throat markings," it's one of the few times that the catalog writer is not exaggerating in the least, but telling it like it is.

Seeds may be sown from August until late in January, with the earlier sowings providing flowers during March, although last year I planted seeds of 'Dr. Badger' in mid-December and had blossoms by mid-March. Seedlings should be moved to 4-inch pots when they start to get crowded, and pinched once to force branching. They like night temperatures around 50°F and full sun. Use a soil mix of equal parts of potting soil, sharp sand, and composted manure and never let the soil dry out. If deadheaded, the plants remain in flower most of the summer.

Poor man's orchid

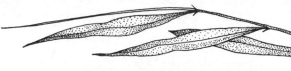

The Willow-Leafed Acacia

Acacias are shrubs or small trees belonging to the Mimosa Family, with many coming from Australia where they are called wattles. There are a number of these plants available from commercial greenhouses, but my favorite for continuous blooming is the wirilda, willow-leafed acacia, or *Acacia retinodes* (the genus is an old Greek name for a thorny tree found in Egypt).

According to Pizzetti and Cocker's marvelous book, *Flowers*, this particular plant was introduced from the state of Victoria in Australia, around 1656. Starting out as a rooted cutting—acacias root easily—in a hanging pot, it will quickly bloom, bearing dozens of tiny fragrant yellow balls of gold along the stems, each beginning at a diameter of a sixteenth of an inch and winding up about a quarter of an inch across. Plants eventually become small trees.

Use a standard potting soil mixed one half with peat moss. Keep the soil on the dry side and try for a winter temperature of 50° to 55°F. Indoors give them as much light as possible and during the summer give them the benefit of being outdoors in full sun.

Willow-leafed acacia

The Twelve Apostles

Known as fan iris, walking iris, twelve apostles, toad-cup, or false flag, the genus *Neomarcia* (meaning new Marcia) contains two species long grown as houseplants for their winter bloom.

Neomarcia northiana has 2-foot leaves arranged like fans with flowers appearing on a leaflike peduncle or flower stalk which stands well above the plant. The blossoms are 3 to 4 inches across and are very fragrant. They are followed by young plants that will eventually root as the leaves bend to the earth. The name twelve apostles refers to the belief that twelve leaves are said to form before one turns brown. *Neomarcia gracilis* is smaller than N. *northiana*, both with leaf and flower, the latter being about 2 inches across.

The flowers on both plants are fugacious, meaning they last only a day but are followed by others. Twelve apostles need daily watering except when resting, and must never be allowed to dry out while blooming (I grow mine in a self-watering pot). Propagate by planting the tips after the flowers are through.

Potting mix should contain potting soil, peat moss, and sharp sand, one-third each with a cup or two of composted manure added. These plants prefer partial shade except during the winter, when they want all the light they can get. They like temperatures in the 60°F range.

Honeybells Scent the Winter Air

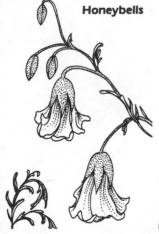

Honeybells

What can I say about a plant of demure habit that in early to mid-March smothers itself with little yellow flowers like bells with fluted edges, flowers that smell of the sweetest honey? Nothing except perhaps to make a wish for more plants like this particular gem. The common name for this African plant is, appropriately enough, honeybells, and botanically called *Hermannia verticillata* (named in honor of a professor of botany, Paul Hermann, 1646–95).

These perennial plants are best in a hanging basket with a well-drained mix of equal parts of potting soil, composted manure, and sharp sand. They prefer bright sunlight and night temperatures from 35° to 55°F to produce the crop of flowers. Let the soil dry between waterings. The flowers appear for about a month and sometimes a second crop appears in early fall.

Flower Feature: The Cymbidium Orchid

Whether flounced across the corner of a suite in Trump Tower, or artfully draped over the edge of a Mies van der Rohe chair in a Princeton architect's office, or precariously perched on the edge of an outrageously expensive marble table, its arching sprays of tinted blossoms in direct contrast to gold frames hanging above on tapestried paper, the cymbidium orchid reigns supreme in today's world of high-priced flowers for decorating. But did you know that many of those fabulous pots of orchids are rented for the length of their period of bloom then returned to greenhouses for, as the army used to call it, R and R? The plants are so strong that even after being rented out—often to people who have no empathy for any plant—they recover to bloom again.

Not only is their popularity due to the appeal of the flowers but also to their incredible length of bloom, one plant often flowering for up to three months. In fact, orchid authorities suggest that flower spikes be removed from the plants after six weeks—they can then be used as cut flowers—thus giving them an extra chance to produce new growth to be used with the next year's flowering.

The genus *Cymbidium* was founded by the Swedish botanist Olof Swartz in 1800, the name being derived from the Greek word for boatlike and referring to the look of the flower's lip. The first hybrid was registered in 1889 and over the next 20 years, 14 more hybrids were registered.

I have two 14-inch pots, one containing *Cymbidium* 'Lewes', featuring white flowers with the lip marked with red and a beautiful pink variety, 'San Francisco'. They were a gift back in 1975 and they have bloomed every year since.

Caring for Cymbidiums

These orchids are terrestrial in habit and do quite well in a good potting soil mixed with peat moss. They need fertilizer and plenty of water during the summer months when they sit outdoors under a large white pine tree, shaded from the worst of the noonday sun. Indoors they need a sunny window, weekly waterings, and continual misting.

For a few hours they tolerate temperatures as low as 40°F—one year when the greenhouse heater failed, a short spell of 31°F didn't phase them—but they prefer 45° to 50°F as the winter norm.

All of today's hybrids are derived from original plants discovered in the mountains of Vietnam, Thailand, Burma, and northern India. In order to guarantee flowering it is important that there is a substan-

Overleaf, the orchids are cymbidiums and the cultivar is 'Lewes'. These plants produce bloom, often over a period of two months.

(continued on page 46)

tial drop in temperatures on summer nights. Since our house is some 1,300 feet up in the Catskill Mountains, even days that see 90°F will cool off to the 50s and 60s at night, so my bloom is almost guaranteed.

When the roots grow and the pseudobulbs (the bulblike swellings at the bottom of the leaf) start to crowd each other, it's time to divide and repot. The best time is in the spring after the flowering is over. Usually I cut the plant in half, using a sterilized knife, removing all the decayed roots and worn out soil.

Each individual blossom can be plucked from the stem, wrapped in a small piece of damp tissue paper, then with a bit of aluminum foil, to become a charming corsage.

Outdoors: The First Signs of Spring

The following description was written on the afternoon of March 31, 1981:

A warm wind is blowing and there's been a promise of rain since early in the morning. But there is a wrongness to the day; the warm air does not belong with trees that are barren of leaves, or to brown fields that are still dashed with snow—fields without the hum of bees or the whir of bird wings.

Out in the backyard, the yellow crocuses have been in bloom for more than two weeks. In fact, their bright petals are already worn and torn from late winter winds.

The snowdrops (*Galanthus nivalis*) that always bend their three-petalled heads to the ground are doing so with a greater fervor than usual; they are on familiar terms with snow and the chills of early spring, but today is much too warm and they begin to wilt.

Russian mustard

Russian Mustards in Bloom

On the top of the ridge behind the house, I've planted draba, or Russian mustard, *Draba lasiocarpa* (from a Greek name for a kind of cress). These are tiny plants from the Arctic Circle of the steppes of Central Asia that are usually at home only on higher mountain peaks. They open their bright yellow, four-petalled blooms only after melting the surrounding snow with self-generated heat. No snow today, and they, too, seem exhausted by the air. Their usual sweet smell, so noticeable on chilly days, is missing this day. A few flies are there, but drawn by the bright color that sings against the background of gray stone and brown grass, not by perfume. The bees have yet to awaken.

There are many species of these plants available. They are perfect for the rock garden and can also be dug just prior to flowering and brought indoors in a small pot.

The Ubiquitous Sedge

Today is one of those days in early March when everything you see is best exemplified by Rita Hayworth's remark to Jack Lemmon in the movie, *Fire Down Below*: "Armies have marched over me!" For even the country snow has a used and smutty look and as for city snow, that is best left undescribed.

Determined to find a symbol of better times, I put on my boots and went for walk in the garden and saw my Japanese sedge grass (*Carex Morrowii* var. *expallida*) pushing its variegated leaves through the low mounds of snow. A few leaf tips had been burned by the freezing temperatures of January when snow cover was poor, but the others were still healthy and glowing with color, truly evergreen in character.

Japanese sedge grass

As a pot plant, Japanese sedge is a good choice as long as you keep it in a cool place and use the standard potting mix of soil, sharp sand, and peat moss, one third each. They like moist soil with plenty of bright winter light and will generally bloom in mid-to late March. If left outside the plant will bloom in April. The flowers are not grand—they look like camel's hair watercolor brushes dipped in golden pollen—but very welcome in winter.

In the garden, plants prefer a shaded spot in moist soil. North of Zone 5 they need winter protection if snow cover is absent.

Garden Plan: The Dependable Early Bulbs

Winter aconite, snowdrops, crocus, and glory of the snow are all marvelous spring flowers that bloom in our Zone 5 climate from mid-March to early April. The following plan is a suggestion for planting these lovely blossoms, hopefully close to a window so you can enjoy the show on an inclement day.

They all should be planted in the fall and ask little except soil that is well-drained and a spot in full winter sun. The marvelous thing about these plants is that by the time the majority of trees leaf out, the bulbs have almost vanished from sight, their leaves naturally drying up after enough energy has been stored for another season of bloom. If you can hold off mowing the lawn, they are great for naturalizing in a sea of grass.

Winter aconites or *Eranthis* (from the Greek for spring flower) *hyemalis*, are members of the Buttercup Family that bloom about a week to ten days before the crocus ever gives a thought to opening, carpeting the ground with a golden glow, and really only effective when planted in dozens, not singly. Fortunately, they are not expensive. Soil should be rich in woodsy humus, and unlike many spring bulbs—they are really tubers—aconites will thrive in the shade. Plan on about 180 tubers per square yard, or portion thereof.

Snowdrops or *Galanthus* (from the Greek for milk flower) *nivalis*, also bloom earlier than the crocus. Like aconites, they like a shady spot with a good, woodsy, well-drained soil. You will need a number of these bulbs to make a decent floral display. Plant new bulbs in the fall, but when the plants become crowded, dig them up in the spring, during flowering or right after, divide them and immediately replant in their new homes. This procedure does not harm the plants at all. Research recently reported in *The Garden* (the magazine of the Royal Horticultural Society) suggests that bulb roots form in August and digging them at that time will be fatal. But in the spring, everything is fine. Plan on about 180 tubers per square yard.

Crocus are members of the Iris Family famous for spring and fall flowers and except for *Crocus sativus*—the source of saffron used to color and flavor foods (*Crocus* is the Greek name for that saffron)—they are mainly decorative garden subjects. (For the autumn crocus, see October.) There are two types: the species crocus and the hybrid crocus. Of the two the species will bloom earlier. Also remember that the species are smaller and you will need more corms to make a good display of flowers. They want the same good soil that the other spring bulbs require and in order to have flowers the next year, the foliage must be allowed to ripen and die on its own accord.

For species crocus look for the celadine crocus, C. *Korolkowii*, with bright yellow flowers and hardy to Zone 5. C. *Tomasinianus* is silver gray in bud, opening to reveal a cobalt-violet interior. The Scotch crocus, C. *biflorus*, has white flowers with purple stripes, is hardy to Zone 6, and has been in cultivation since 1629. Use about 180 corms per square yard for all these species.

The hybrid crocus bear larger flowers so use 125 per square yard. 'Peter Pan' has ivory-white flowers with orange stigmas; 'Pickwick' is striped violet on a blue-white background; and 'Yellow Mammoth' means what it says with big, yellow flowers.

Glory of the snow or *Chionodoxa* (from *chion*, snow, and *doxa*, glory) do bloom in the snow. They are especially attractive growing along the top of a rock retaining wall, where their colors do well in combination with lichen-encrusted rock. Use 125 per square yard. The kinds usually offered are C. *Luciliae*, with bright blue flowers with white centers; a cultivar 'Alba', with flowers of pure white; and 'Pink Giant', with eight to ten blush-pink flowers per stem.

Winter aconite

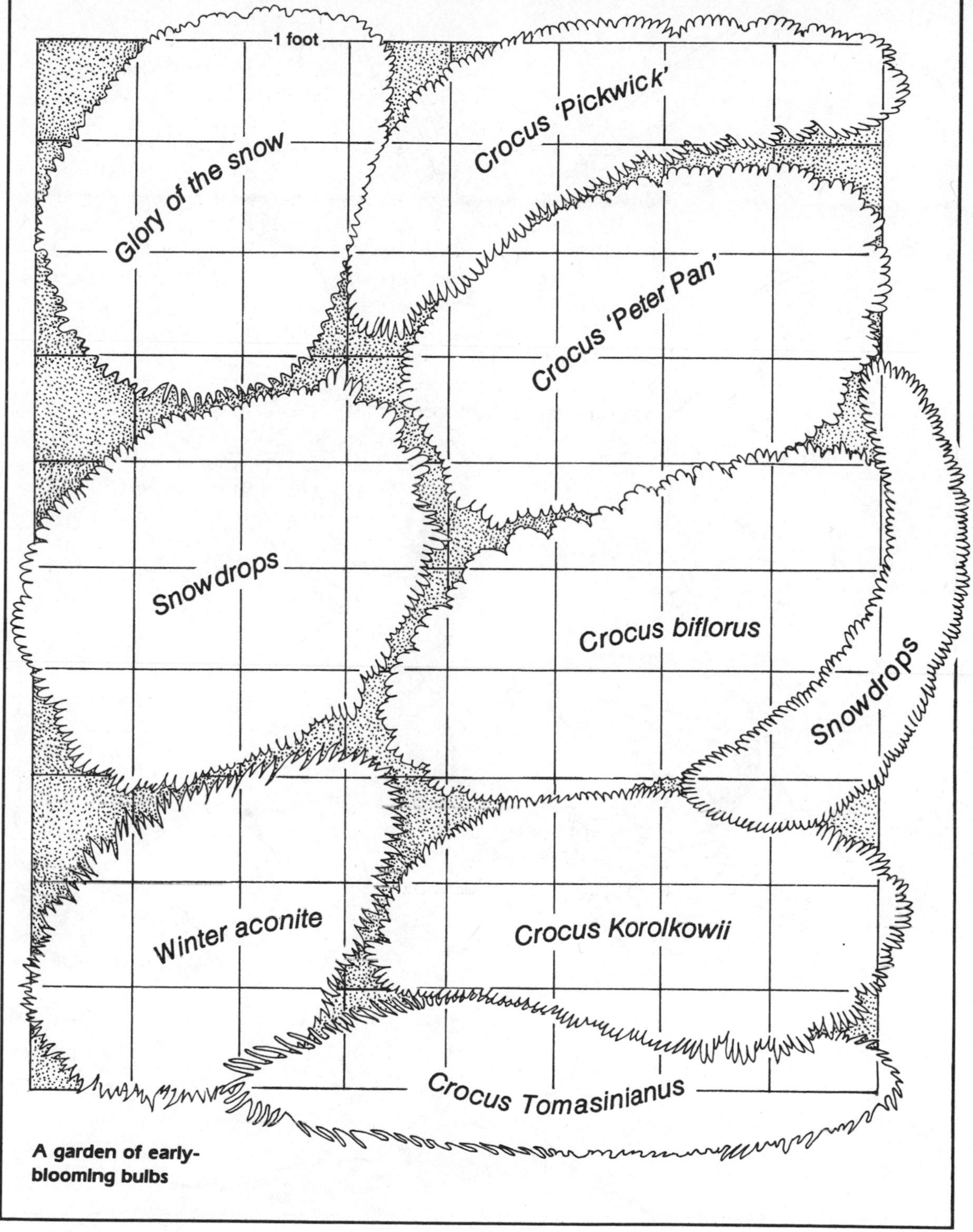

1 foot

Glory of the snow

Crocus 'Pickwick'

Crocus 'Peter Pan'

Snowdrops

Crocus biflorus

Snowdrops

Winter aconite

Crocus Korolkowii

Crocus Tomasinianus

A garden of early-blooming bulbs

A man really in love with a garden is perhaps safer from the usual human temptations than any other . . . woman has no seductions for the man who cannot take his eyes from his magnolias.

A gentleman who is responsible for one of the cruellest wars in the history of the world is known to have a passion for orchids—though those who see something evil and abnormal in the orchid, in spite of its beauty, will perhaps see a certain fitness in his taste . . .

. . . steal out sometimes after sunset and walk up and down between the home end of the garden and the wild end and listen to the sound at each . . .

R. LeGallienne, *Corners of Old Grey Gardens*, 1912

After one has been a gardener for a time, the urge to collect more than plants becomes apparent and the plantsman* turns to books about gardening, books to while away the nonproductive hours far from the yard, to entertain the intellect, to bring pictures to the mind's eye.

The quotes at the beginning of this and some other chapters come from an old book entitled *Corners of Old Grey Gardens*, first published in 1914, residing for a time in an old New York City bookstore, thence to the Garden Club of Cleveland as a gift, on to the Cleveland Garden Center, then deaccessioned and given freedom, and finally winding up in my care, tattered and torn, but charming and full of the pleasures of the garden, a lifeline from one garden era to another.

* "A *plantsman* is one who loves plants for their own sake," wrote Mr. David McClintock. "This concept may include a botanist: it certainly includes a host of admirable amateurs . . ." It is also a generic term, not sexist, and any gardener who wishes to be called a "plantsperson" gets exactly what he or she deserves.

Left, **the lilies in the drawing are Madonna lilies. This species has been in constant cultivation for over 3,500 years.**

Perhaps the woman of today would prefer not to be compared to a magnolia; I'm unable to fathom the name of the infamous warlord of pre-1914 who loved orchids; and there are parts of the book that describe a time in the history of the world that will never live again, but, ah! The thoughts of the home end of the garden . . .

What's Blooming in the Window

The cymbidiums are still in full display, leaves and arching sprays of blossoms swaying back and forth in the slight breeze that results from the opening of the greenhouse and sunporch skylights, necessary because the spring sun is shining with more intensity every day. The poinsettias are still blaring forth and the cyclamens continue to open new flowers. The hanging bromeliads are starting to produce blossoms and the lilies, primroses, and pots of linaria and stocks plus a black-eyed Susan vine are all doing the same and in profusion. Even if it's still chilly outside and patches of snow remain in the deep woods, spring is definitely here.

The Lovely Lily

Everyone knows the lily. The Madonna lily (*Lilium candidum*), for example, has been in constant cultivation for over 3,500 years and this Mother's Day probably will mark 3,501. But in addition to homage to mother, the lily fulfills a number of jobs in the house and garden. It is terrific in pots both in the house, the greenhouse, and on the terrace; marvelous in the woodland garden; beautiful in the border; delightful along a garden path; wonderful when peeking out from the shrubbery; and great as a cut flower.

To grow lilies in pots for outdoor use, see the entry in June. For forcing flowers to use in early spring in the house use the following instructions.

Buy the bulbs in the fall, and pot them up as soon as you receive them. If that's not possible, store them in the refrigerator until needed. If they are sold to you as precooled bulbs, they will bloom in about 120 days after planting; if unprepared, allow 180 days until blooming. This schedule, by the way, is not always accurate but only a rule of thumb. After blooming, lily bulbs never really go into a dormant phase like many other bulbs do, so handle them with extra care. This means they should be in soil whenever possible and be careful not to carelessly remove any of the scales that make up the bulb.

Use a deep 6-inch pot for each bulb or a 10-inch pot for three or more. Prepare a planting mix of one part potting soil, one part composted manure, and a half-part sharp sand and put a layer of stones or crocks at the bottom of the pot. Lilies like moist soil but resent wet!

For the Madonna lily first add soil to the bottom half of the pot. Then add the bulb, broad base down, and fill the pot to within an inch of the top. The Easter lily (*L. longiflorum*) is a stem-rooting lily —it will actually send out roots from the stem section above the bulb—so add soil to the bottom third of the pot, add the bulb, then fill it to within an inch of the top. Once the bulbs are potted they need temperatures around 40°F to force blooms. Put the pots in a cold frame, if you have one, and cover them to keep from freezing while the roots develop. I use the sun porch but any unheated area like a cellar or garage will do as long as the bulbs do not freeze.

After this cooling-off period bring the pots indoors to the window garden or the greenhouse. Give them full sun and a temperature of about 60°F. Keep the soil moist. After the flowers open, carefully clip off the pollen-bearing anthers to prolong the life of the flowers. Let the foliage mature and eventually yellow. Repot in the fall and start the bulbs again.

Oxypetalum Blue

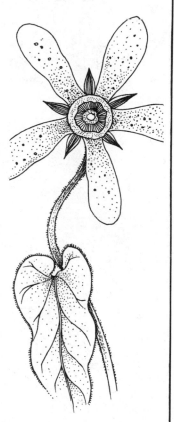

Oxypetalum

There are very few flowers that are pale blue in color. One of the most attractive of this limited assembly of plants is called southern stars or *Oxypetalum* (from the Greek for sharp-petalled, of which this species is not). *O. caeruleum* is also called star-of-the-Argentine as it's a perennial native of Argentina. While not a commercial rage the plant appears to have some value as a cut flower for corsages and bouquets because of the color. About 1 inch across, the five-lobed flowers start out as pale blue, turn purple as they age, then fade to lilac tones as they wither.

A perennial in its native haunts, this vining sub-shrub can be grown as a pot plant that will start to bloom in April. Or when started from seeds sown in January, oxypetalum can be used as a border annual that will bloom from late July to frost. Soil should be a mix of good potting soil, composted manure, and sharp sand that's kept moist. Plants prefer a minimum temperature of 65°F and full sun.

For a pot plant start seeds in September and move to individual pots when seedlings are about 2 inches high. For the garden start seeds eight weeks before your last frost and plant outside when frost danger is past, spacing plants 8 inches apart.

The Delicate Puschkinia

Count Apollos Mussin-Puschkin (1760–1805) left Russia in the year 1800 for the loftier regions of the Caucasus in search of mineral wealth—the first Russian to take a portable laboratory into the field for on-the-spot assays—and died in the mountains after mentioning that the plague was particularly bad that season, especially among members of the expedition.

He had written to Sir Joseph Banks in England and offered to send seeds and natural history specimens in return for seeds of American trees that he hoped to naturalize in the mountains. I have no idea what American plants he introduced to the Caucasus or what mineral wealth he found for the czar, but I do know of one flowering bulb that the count introduced to the gardeners of the world: the striped quill, or *Puschkinia scilloides*. The genus has only two species of which only the one mentioned is in cultivation. They bloom from mid- to late April in Zone 5 and the count could have no finer namesake.

The flowers resemble hyacinths, but while the hyacinth stem is crowded with big and often vulgar flowers and drenched with powerful perfume, puschkinias are a delicate and pale pastel blue, with each petal bearing one pale blue stripe and no heavy perfumes—nothing vulgar here.

Stems rarely reach above 6 inches and the only requirement is that the soil be of a reasonable well-drained nature, easily accomplished by adding sand to the existing soil or planting the bulbs in a rock garden setting.

Puschkinias can be forced indoors by following the directions for the other hardy spring bulbs, given on page 12.

Puschkinias

Spring

After a winter of gray the glistening petals of a bed of red and white tulips in concert with clusters of grape hyacinths should lighten the hardest of hearts. Even the glummest of personalities should be brightened by these flowers.

Spring daffodils will be "fluttering and dancing in the breeze," as the April sun climbs higher in the sky. The cultivar above is called 'King Alfred' and has been popular for naturalizing for over eight decades.

White forsythia is not a forsythia at all but is limited to one genus of shrubs found in Korea in 1924 and first imported to the United States in 1955. It is hardy in Zone 5.

Grape hyacinths are both odd and beautiful at the same time. 'Heavenly Blue' is an especially attractive cultivar for the spring garden.

The typical iris flower is arranged in multiples of three with each of the three outer petals termed a fall. These iris are called bearded because of hairs found on the haft of the fall.

Nothing spells spring like a bed of blooming crocus pushing up through the snow. Crocus require a sunny spot in the garden and well-drained soil.

Tree peonies are spectacular flowers. When they bloom all other flowers must take a back seat. The cultivar above is 'Howki', a double that flowers in May.

Lily tulips have graceful flowers with curved, pointed petals on tall, sturdy stems. They were considered to be the most perfect form of tulip in sixteenth-century Turkey. The cultivar above is 'Arcadia'.

Puschkinias resemble hyacinths but are more delicate in appearance and do not exude a heavy perfume. Stems rarely reach above 6 inches and flowers open in early spring. They originally came from the Caucasus.

Unlike most hybrid tulips, a bed of wild or species tulips will come up every spring year after year with little care. *Tulipa Eichleri* has flowers on 8-inch stems and the individual petals are an intense scarlet.

Oriental hybrid lilies are the result of crossings between speciosum lilies from Korea and the auratum lilies of Japan. They bloom from August into September and are very hardy.

A border of spring bulbs containing narcissus, daffodils, tulips, and along a line of lichened stones, a mix of brownish-purple and white fritillarias.

Columbines will bloom for weeks if the gardener removes the spent flowers. They are found in a wide array of colors. The taller cultivars are perfect for mixed borders and the shorter types are at home in the rock garden.

Lily-of-the-valley can be forced for indoor bloom or allowed to naturalize in the spring garden. The blue flowers are lobelias.

A Hanging Garden of Bromeliads

There are a series of plants that are perfect for an indoor situation as long as you pass by once a day and give them a spritz with a mister, and once a week dunk them in a of pail of water. They are called epiphytic bromeliads and consist of plants with poor root systems that live aloft in trees, tucked in the bark or delicately perched at the fork of a limb. There are terrestrial varieties that have well-developed root systems and require some medium other than air to grow upon, but these are more tropical in their temperature demands, and I have not branched out to include them in my collection.

A friend of mine stopped by last winter after a trip to Florida and brought me a bag of the epiphytes that were gathered in her sister's backyard. I carefully washed them all in warm water—I had spied a few small beetles and one grub tucked in the network of leaves—and proceeded to staple them to branches from our woods that in turn were wired to aluminum hangers and moved out to the greenhouse.

The plants were all different species of the genus *Tillandsia* (named in honor of Elias Tillands, a Swedish botanist). Their curving or porcupine-straight leaves are covered with minute scales that hold all the water that the plant needs for a time and each morning in their natural habitat, the dew fills their needs. They all began to bloom in mid-April, bearing three-petalled flowers of yellow, lavender, and purple, according to their species. After blooming, the mother plant dies in about a year or so, but not before new offshoots are produced, which will bloom the following year.

The plants spend the summer outside, hanging from the various branches of a Japanese maple in the backyard, and are brought in just before the first frosts. During that time they are sprayed with a very dilute liquid fertilizer every three or four weeks.

Stocks and Linaria in Bloom

On February 1, I planted some 4-inch pots with annuals. The first was a new cultivar of stock, *Matthiola* 'Dwarf Stockpot' (named after Peirandrea Mattioli, an Italian botanist of the sixteenth century). These are very fragrant, double flowers of rose, purple, white, and red, that will bloom in seven to nine weeks after sowing. The seed packets come with special instructions that to insure double-flowered plants, be sure to transplant only those seedlings that display a notch in the young leaves. I followed the instructions and by the first week of April, the living room was graced not only with a pot of glorious color but the heady smell of the flower's perfume.

Purple-net toad flax

Right, the drawing shows a hanging garden of bromeliads; in this case the plants are various members of the genus *Tillandsia.*

The second pot contained the purple-net toad flax, of the genus *Linaria* (from the Latin word *Linum* or flax because of the similarity of leaf), particularly, *L. reticulata* 'Crown Jewels'. These charming flowering plants produce blossoms like small snapdragons and of easy culture. These began to bloom on April 14, falling over the edge of the pot with flowers in shades of maroon, red, orange, and golden yellow.

In both cases the seeds were started in flats over a heating cable and germinated within a week. When a few true leaves had developed, I transplanted four of each to 4-inch clay pots. The soil was potting soil and sharp sand, one-half each. I gave the plants full sun and made sure they were watered every day. After three weeks the first blossoms were over, the plants were cut back and both began to bloom again within two weeks.

The Palm Springs Daisy

Shortly after New Years, I filled a 6-inch clay pot with a soil mix of one-half potting soil and one-half sharp sand, then sowed the seeds of the Palm Springs daisy. The genus name is *Cladanthus* (from the Greek for branch and flower referring to the flowers that bloom at the branch tips) and there is only one species, *arabicus,* an annual that hails from Morocco and Spain. Germination time is about three weeks using a heating cable and the plants will begin to bloom twelve weeks later.

Palm Springs daisy

The 2-inch, pure yellow, daisylike flowers are borne on 2- to 3-foot mounds of lacy foliage and are strikingly beautiful when massed at the edge of a wall. Unfortunately, the foliage is also attractive to aphids, which explains why one day I noticed that the plants were crawling with these intruders. I used the mister that is attached to the greenhouse hose and literally blew the aphids off but in so doing, broke off a couple of stems. Immediately I put them into little propagating cases filled with moist peat moss, and they rooted within four weeks.

To have flowers all winter in the home, start seeds in late summer and early fall. These plants prefer temperatures of 50° to 55°F and all the winter sun they can get. Remove spent flowers to keep up the pace of bloom.

Flower Feature: The Orchid Cactus

The orchid cactus, *Epiphyllum* × *hybridus* (from the Greek *epi*, upon, and *phyllos*, a leaf, as it was thought the flowers were borne on leaves, which are really flattened stems) is a member of the Cactus Family that comes from the jungles, not the deserts, and produces spectacular flowers.

First described in the early 1800s, the plants come from Brazil, Mexico, Costa Rica, and Guatemala, among others. The main branches are woody, with the green stems flat or thin, with wavy margins. The typical cactus spines are usually missing on mature plants but are often present as bristles on seedlings or juvenile plants.

The older the plant, the more architectural it becomes. Then with the coming of spring, tiny buds appear between the scallops on the stems, buds that grow visibly larger every day until suddenly they open into truly breathtaking flowers with vibrant colors, the texture of the petals resembling that of glistening satin. Colors include white, yellow, red, scarlet, and red streaked with iridescent purple.

Growing Tips

Right, the satiny bloom of an orchid cactus. Flower colors in this species include white, red, yellow, and scarlet.

In nature, orchid cactuses hang from trees, rooting where the branch meets the trunk, so they are quite at home suspended in wire baskets lined with dried moss, in hanging clay or plastic pots, or merely standing on a flat surface with stems falling over a table's edge. Soil should be sandy and lean as a too-rich soil produces poor flowers.

Spray the plants with a mister during the warm days of spring and fall, withholding water from November through February (unless stems show signs of shriveling, at which time a dash of water is appreciated). During the summer months, hang the cactuses outdoors under the shade of a porch eave or a tree—mine summer under the sumac tree in the backyard. If the summer is unusually dry or the plants are sheltered from normal rains, you will have to water them, letting the soil dry out between applications. Use liquid fertilizer once a month while they are outdoors.

To propagate, take 4-inch cuttings, let them air-dry to seal the wound, then root in a mix of moist sphagnum or peat moss. They will usually root with ease.

When indoors, the orchid cactus will withstand temperatures of 45°F without ill effect, but keep it from freezing as it is not hardy.

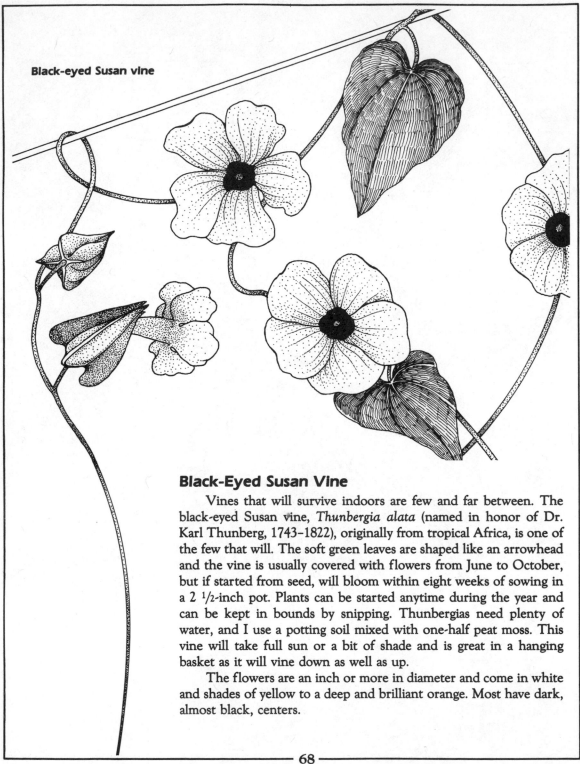

Black-eyed Susan vine

Black-Eyed Susan Vine

Vines that will survive indoors are few and far between. The black-eyed Susan vine, *Thunbergia alata* (named in honor of Dr. Karl Thunberg, 1743–1822), originally from tropical Africa, is one of the few that will. The soft green leaves are shaped like an arrowhead and the vine is usually covered with flowers from June to October, but if started from seed, will bloom within eight weeks of sowing in a 2 1/2-inch pot. Plants can be started anytime during the year and can be kept in bounds by snipping. Thunbergias need plenty of water, and I use a potting soil mixed with one-half peat moss. This vine will take full sun or a bit of shade and is great in a hanging basket as it will vine down as well as up.

The flowers are an inch or more in diameter and come in white and shades of yellow to a deep and brilliant orange. Most have dark, almost black, centers.

Outdoors: White Forsythia and Spring Bulbs

April is a high-stepping month once the rains stop. Around the first—when trout season opens—skies are often the gray color that means the weather could be up to no good and rain can quickly turn to snow and sleet. In the deep woods there is still snow but soon the mosses are greening up, the violets and the bluets (*Hedyotis caerulea*) carpet the edge of the paths, and almost overnight, the bulb bed bursts forth with spring bulbs, all in fine fettle. And finally the pond loses that murky color that presages the change in the water between winter and spring.

The White Forsythia

When we first planned on landscaping our backyard and garden, the thought of forsythia crossed our minds but was quickly dismissed when the mind's eye saw visions of acre after acre of those yellow blooms on bending branches that represents the ultimate in creative spring gardening in most of the country. No, we said, to forsythia (and to crown vetch, which threatens to overtake most of the Pennsylvania highway system).

Then I found a catalog entry devoted to *Abeliophyllum distichum* (the leaves resemble those of *Abelia*, an evergreen shrub from China and Mexico), as it is sometimes called, the white forsythia, a singular genus with one species found in Korea in 1924 and first imported to the United States in 1955. Since it was marked hardy to Zone 5, we planted one shrub in 1979.

Every year about the first week in April, this small shrub begins to bloom. At first the four petals are suffused with pink, but as they open the pink fades to a perfect white. The entire shrub—now 6 feet tall and 7 feet across—is covered with the flowers, and the corner where it grows is perfumed with a honeylike fragrance.

The buds for the following year's bloom appear by late summer, dotting the square branches with small bits of brown, and seem impervious to the worst winds of winter. If you cannot wait for spring, branches cut in late winter can easily be forced into bloom. (For more details on forcing branches, see the box in Appendix 1.) English gardeners say that the white forsythia flowers are subject to frost damage, but we've never noted it here. Average soil will suit it fine. Branches hooked to the ground will quickly root so you will be able to provide plants for friends.

By summer the blue-green leaves make a welcome background not only to pots of summering houseplants and potted dahlias that line the edge of the patio but to lilies and flowering maples that I've planted so that the flowers come up between the arching branches.

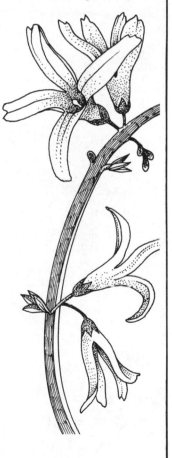

White forsythia

Daffodils of Spring

I wandered lonely as a cloud
    That floats on high o'er vales and hills,
When all at once I saw a crowd,
    A host of golden daffodils;
Beside the lake, beneath the trees,
    Fluttering and dancing in the breeze.

These words of William Wordsworth from his poem, *I Wandered Lonely as a Cloud*, are best read as you look out of your window toward the garden and spy the blossoms of the daffodils and narcissus that you planted the previous fall. These flowers are called narcissus when the central cup or eye is small and daffodils when the cup assumes the proportions of a trumpet, yet they all belong to the genus *Narcissus* (from the Greek word for torpor, referring to the poisonous qualities of the bulbs).

Daffodils and narcissus naturalize with ease and spread over almost any terrain except waterlogged soil, solid rock or clay. They need a sunny spot in early spring but do not object to shade after tree leaves unfold. Even the midst of your lawn is a good spot as long as you don't cut the grass until after the leaves have withered and browned—this allows the bulbs to store energy for next year's blossoms—which usually is over by the end of June. Don't naturalize bulbs in the center of your lawn if you can't abide the sight of unmown grass.

Many of the smaller species are at home in the rock garden and a few like *Narcissus Bulbocodium* and *N. calcicola* will do well in pots of well-drained soil if given very cool growing conditions in a greenhouse.

For instructions on naturalizing these flowers of spring, see page 157 in September's chapter.

A rock garden narcissus

A blossom of the very large daffodil 'Foresight' sits in a window vase. The petals are white and the trumpet is yellow.

Garden Plan: A Spring Flower Bed

One of the problems with today's smaller backyards is planning a spring bulb bed that will not be an affront to both gardener and visitor while all wait for what seems to be an interminable time for the foliage to ripen and disappear.

The following plan gives a layout for a small bed of spring-blooming bulbs including some of the new narcissus cultivars that are particularly attractive when used for cut flowers. The bulbs are planted in a bed with a Japanese maple to the left and a bank of hay-scented fern (*Dennstaedtia punctilobula*) to the rear—that could just as easily be a fence or a hedge—and surrounded by hostas. These will grow as the bulbs die back, eventually covering all, with the exception of some bare spots along the edge that could be seeded with annuals or bordered by a line of impatiens.

Bulbs used are the brilliant red *Tulipa eichleri*; the cobalt-blue fringed tulip, *Tulipa* 'Blue Heron'; *Puschkinia scilloides*; a lovely yellow daffodil, *Narcissus* 'Dutch Master'; a bicolored jonquil, N. 'Suzy'; a short-cupped daffodil, N. 'Barret Browning'; a small daffodil, N. 'February Gold'; *Crocus* 'Pickwick'; *Phlox subulata* 'Alexander Pink' and 'Bluets'; and *Scilla siberica*.

The hostas used are large plants and consist of the variegated *Hosta undulata*; the yellow embossed H. 'August Moon'; and the green H. *ventricosa*.

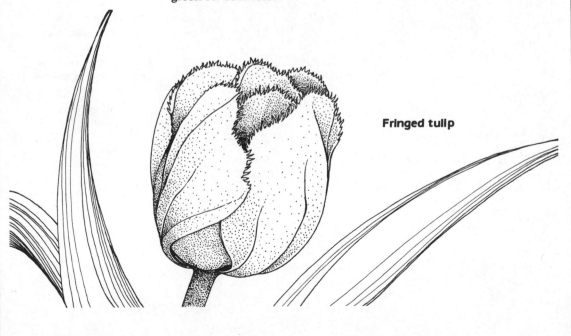

Fringed tulip

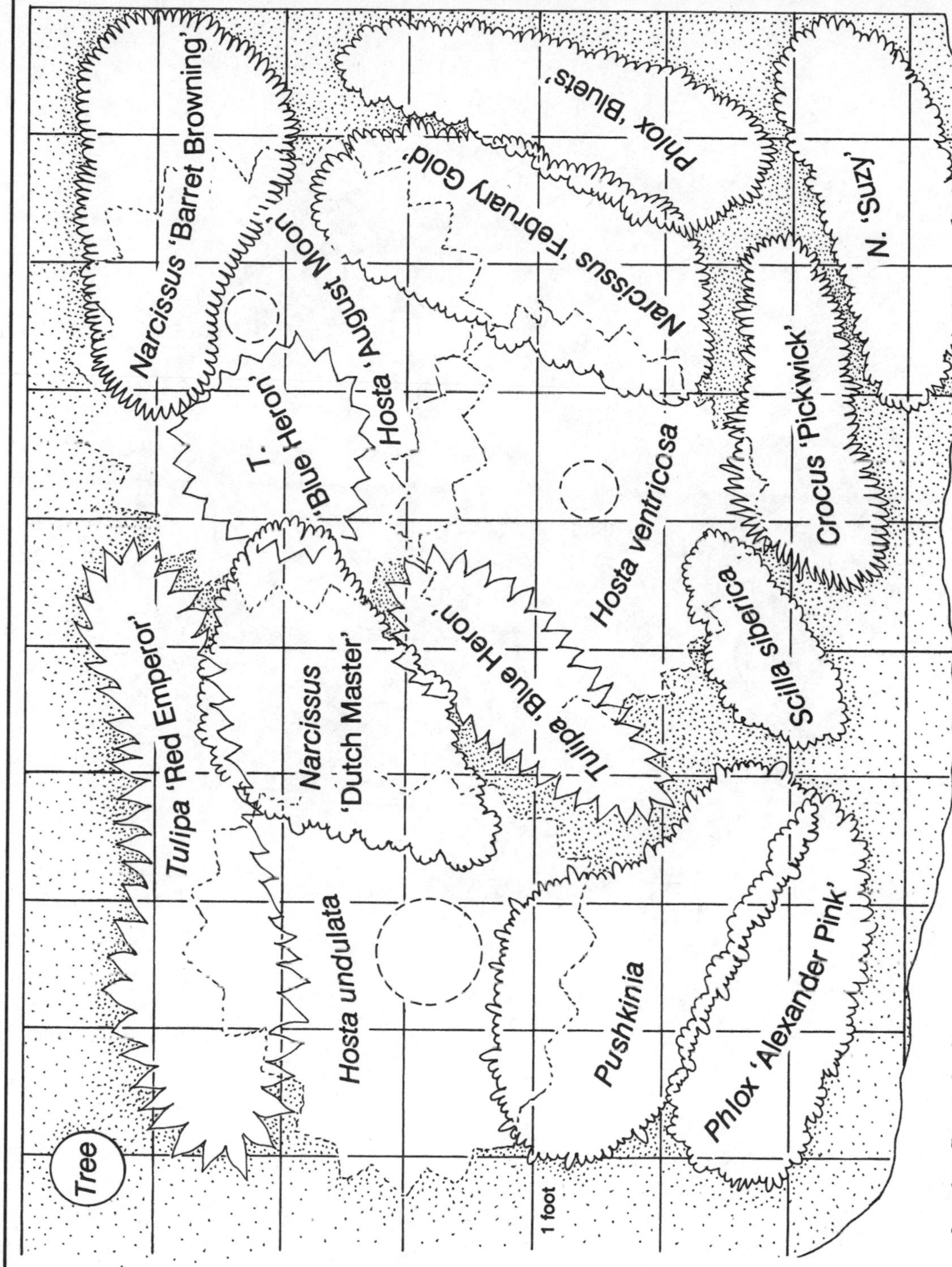

Narcissus 'Barret Browning'

Phlox 'Bluets'

N. 'Suzy'

Hosta 'August Moon'

Narcissus 'February Gold'

T. 'Blue Heron'

Crocus 'Pickwick'

Hosta ventricosa

Scilla siberica

Tulipa 'Red Emperor'

Narcissus 'Dutch Master'

Tulipa 'Blue Heron'

Hosta undulata

Pushkinia

Phlox 'Alexander Pink'

Tree

1 foot

A spring flower bed

> *I remember a bit of limestone wall dancing in the moonlight amongst the deep shadows of trees, which gave me the feeling of a folk song. Suppose a clipped hedge had been put in its place. Would that have solved the same problem so beautifully and so well? Could the moonbeams have played as pleasingly on the clipped hedge as on the stone wall? And what a joy the stone wall was in the waning evening light, when the stone turned into a beautiful rose, or when it led the way in the darkness of night. Such a delicate expression has never been produced by shears.*
>
> Jens Jensen, *Siftings, 1939*

May and June: Soft syllables and gentle names for two of the four best months in the garden year (the others being September and October), when cool and misty mornings with the fog gently burned away by a warming spring sun are followed by breezy afternoons and usually chilly nights with spring constellations shining above and fireflies flickering in the night . . .

The Window Darkens

Now that the sun is higher in the sky our greenhouse begins to heat up earlier every morning and by ten o'clock the thermometer is already up to 85°F. Most of the houseplants—including the now 8-foot high cabbage palm (*Cordyline australis*) that is getting harder for me to move every year—are out in various places in the backyard and terrace where they will spend the summer storing up energy for the coming winter. So the only flowers on view through the living room window are two late stalks of cymbidium orchids springing up from the largest of the orchid pots, some early caladiums with such pretty leaves they qualify as flowers, a white an-

Left, the flower is a salmon blood lily. This African bulb is grown for its fantastic and showy blooms—up to 100 individual flowers—that form a perfect 6- to 7-inch ball.

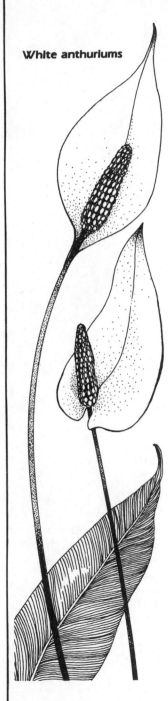

White anthuriums

thurium, an ancient beefsteak begonia (*Begonia × erythrophylla*), a blood lily, and a pot of oxalis that has been in continual bloom since last fall.

I have a set of plastic roll-up blinds that I hang over the slanted greenhouse windows to cut out the sun's heat during the summer months so eventually even the inhabitants mentioned above must to be moved. The living room window will eventually look out on a cool, green shade and thoughts of flowers will turn to the outdoors.

The Salmon Blood Lily

Blood lilies are African bulbs that are grown for their fantastic flowers. The showy blooms—with up to 100 individual flowers—are a perfect 6- to 7-inch ball, with each flower sending out 6 brilliant red stamens topped with bright yellow pollen for a total of 600 for each sphere of bloom. The botanical name is *Haemanthus multiflorus* (*haema* is the Greek word for blood, *anthos* for flower), and in pots the bulbs will bloom in May. And pots are a good idea so the flowers can be moved about to their best advantage.

The bulbs—which are up to 3 inches in diameter—should be potted in 6- to 8-inch containers in a good soil mix that includes sharp sand and composted manure. They need a winter rest with temperatures about 50° to 55°F. The flowers appear before the foliage, and once the flowering begins keep the soil moist. During active growth provide blood lilies with full sun and temperatures of 60° to 70°F. When the leaves start to yellow, gradually dry off the bulb, give it a winter rest, and restart growth the following spring. From May to August give the plants a liquid fertilizer once a month. Bulbs should be left undisturbed until they outgrow their pots.

The White Anthurium

Another tropical plant that is blooming this May in the living room window is called the white anthurium, a free-flowering hybrid of uncertain origins. Also termed the peace lily, this particular plant is correctly called *Spathiphyllum Clevelandii* (a *spathe* is a decorative leaf that surrounds a *spadix*, itself a spike with tiny flowers; *phyllum* is also a Greek word for leaf). It is one of the few foliage plants that will tolerate very low light levels. Plants will survive 20 footcandles (the light from one 100-watt bulb at a distance of 6 feet) but need 50 footcandles to bloom. Spathiphyllums also take to air conditioning, which many other plants do not.

Soil should be a mix of good potting soil and peat moss and kept evenly moist. Temperatures should always be above 60°F. Fertilize once a month while in active growth.

Lantana for the Basket

A basket plant that has been grown for years on the front porches of America is lantana (*Lantana Camera*, *Lantana* being an old word for viburnum). The plants are really shrubs that are hardy in Zones 9 and 10. The individual flowers make up a disk of bloom and are yellow when they open, turn orange and then red, with all three colors being evident at the same time. If flowers are not clipped off after bloom, small black berries may develop. Lantanas flower throughout the summer, enjoying full sun and temperatures above 50°F. The soil should be allowed to dry out between waterings and the stem tips pinched back for bushy growth.

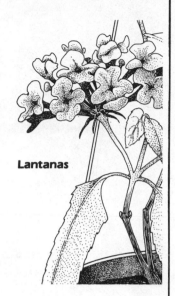

Lantanas

Probably the most exciting thing about lantanas is turning a plant into a tree. Buy a small plant, preferably with only one main shoot, and place it in a 3-inch pot. Tie the stem to a foot-long bamboo cane or stick that you have inserted in the soil at the pot's edge. Use one loop of soft cord about the stem and one loop on the stake so that the stem is never crushed. When the lantana grows to about 10 inches, move it to a 6-inch pot, adding a longer length of stake (up to 30 inches). Now is the time to remove all the side shoots, leaving just one at the tip of the stem.

As the lantana approaches 2 feet, move it to an 8-inch pot. (Remember, all the time you've been forcing the plant upward, roots have been growing, too.) Now pinch off the terminal bud and new side shoots will appear. In turn, pinch off each of their terminal buds to force the plant into bushy growth. The stem will develop a weedy look and you will have a beautiful flowering tree. The process may take up to two years, but you are creating an heirloom. Lantanas have been known to live for decades.

As the tree grows, it can be moved into successively bigger pots. Topdress the soil and fertilize during the summer months. Up north, lantanas will drop their leaves and enter a dormant period in the fall but will leaf out anew every spring.

There are a number of cultivars including: 'Alba', white; 'Flava', yellow fading to saffron; and 'Sanguiea' with red flowers.

An Everblooming Oxalis

There are many plants that are called everblooming, but few really are. At one time or another during the year, flowering ceases while the plant takes a well-deserved rest. But there is one that I know of that lives up to its reputation as a nonstop bloomer. It's one of a number of species in the genus *Oxalis* (from the Greek word for acid) that make marvelous houseplants but stands far above

its relatives in the profuseness of its flowering. O. *rubra* 'Alba' (often called O. *rosea*) is originally from Brazil so it likes good light. But my plant has been blooming steadily since a year ago last March (that's when I bought it) and has been hanging in a spot without direct sunlight all winter with nights in the greenhouse often under 50°F. And still it shows no sign of letting up.

Soil is standard potting soil mixed with one-third sand. I keep the soil on the dry side watering only when it seems absolutely necessary. And if my oxalis asks for a rest by refusing to produce new flowers, I will certainly grant it. Other members of the Oxalis Family are described in the November section, but they only bloom part of the year.

Left, the flower is the everblooming oxalis, blooming most of the year with only a short rest between shows.

Outdoors: The Lovely Month of May

Of all the months in the year, May is probably the most popular with gardeners in the United States. It's not too hot and not too cold, the rains are usually gentle and few, and the days are long enough to allow plenty of time to work in the garden.

A Small Rock Garden

Rock gardens were originally designed for English gardeners to grow alpine and high-meadow plants brought back from the mountains of Europe and Asia. They were often the result of monumental labors involved with moving tons of soil and rock, installing drains, digging ditches, and in fact, sometimes complete terra-forming. Today few people have the time or the money for such projects so a simpler course makes more sense.

Choose a site in full sun preferably off to one side of your property. If you are graced with any large stones or banks, by all means start there. The garden can be level or installed on a slight rise.

Mark the area to be used; it need be no larger than 3 by 2 feet or it could be as grand as you have the effort for. Carefully dig up the soil, placing the clumps on a plastic sheet for neatness, and remove all the weeds. This you must do as weeds win any battle against rock garden plants.

Now you need rocks, the larger the better, and they should all be of the same kind. Place the rocks to the rear of your plot, always putting the heaviest end down. If necessary, hollow out a place for the rocks to sit for they must not move about. You could also build a raised bed using a low wall of fieldstones, then filling in with soil. If your present soil is mostly clay and has poor drainage, a layer of rubble—small stones and the like—should be added prior to

Overleaf, the rock garden features (1) leopard's-bane; (2) Greek forget-me-not; (3) alpine popples; (4) aubrietas; (5) ophiopogons; (6) dwarf bloody cranesbill; (7) fringed pinks; and (8) alpine pinks.

(continued on page 82)

(5)

(6)

(7)

(8)

bringing in new dirt. Excess water will then have a place to go. The following sketches should give you some ideas.

Since rock garden plants need perfect drainage, use a soil mix of garden soil, sharp sand, small gravel, and some composted manure—although these plants do not need an excess of fertilizer.

Some Popular Rock Garden Plants

Aubrietas form mats of brilliant, starlike flowers in varying shade of blues and purples. *Aubrieta deltoidea* 'Dr. Mules' is a very attractive cultivar often available from nurseries. Plants are easily grown from cuttings or seed and if given a favorable spot in full sun will soon cover large areas of ground, being especially happy on stone walls and abutments.

The pinks are mat-forming perennials that are crowded with fragrant and spicy-scented five-petalled flowers in mid-spring. *Dianthus Noeanus* bears fringed flowers of white, while *D. alpinus* has larger blossoms of pale pink to light purple, depending on the plant. Seeds germinate with ease and plants often self-sow.

Leopard's-bane, *Doronicum cordatum*, grows in a small clump and blooms in early summer or late spring. The daisies are a bright golden yellow.

The geranium pictured is a diminutive form of the bloody cranesbill, a wildflower from Europe and England. Known botanically as *Geranium sanguineum* var. *prostratum*, these are not the same plants as the popular bedding geraniums, which are correctly termed pelargoniums. The cranesbill likes full sun and old blossoms should be cut off to encourage more buds. Propagation is by division.

The Greek forget-me-not, *Omphalodes linifolia*, is an annual plant that produces long sprays of lovely white, five-petalled flowers and more than enough seeds to keep both family and friends in supply.

Ophiopogon planiscapus 'Arabicus' is a member of the Lily Family grown not only for its lavender flowers but the striking dark purple, almost black color of the leaves. These leaves make an eye-catching accent, highlighting the other flower colors of the rock garden.

The alpine poppy, *Papaver Burseri* but usually called *P. alpinuim*, is an annual or a biennial depending on the climate where you garden. It will easily self-sow but never becomes a pest. This charmer will resist transplanting since its taproot is quite long (but it can be done by digging very deep, making a large rootball and using plenty of water at the new site). Blossoms come in orange-red, orange, yellow, and white and have a very sweet and delicate fragrance.

Among the other flowers at home in a rock garden are dwarf rhododendrons, many species of columbines, hypericums, saxifragas, sedums, sempervivums, gentians, and many kinds of the smaller ornamental grasses.

The Poppies

Those marvelous drifts of flowers that the Wicked Witch of the West used her crystal ball to charm into blooming were poppies, vast fields of poppies that released sweet vapors that sent Dorothy and her friends from Oz into slumberland. And it is the poppy that brings to mind the dark and demonic shadows of opium dens and unspeakable vice, horrors of the nether world belonging to Fu Man Chu and Doc Savage. Yet it is also the poppy that is the symbol of the First World War, the poppy of Flanders Field.

For the Poppy Family is, to say the least, a diverse clan of flowers, brilliant perennial plants and delicate annuals, each with petals like the sheerest of crepe paper and the most elegant of colors, either watercolor tints or blasts of pigment equal to the gaudiest of poster paints.

The genus *Papaver* (the ancient Latin name for poppies, said to refer to the sound made in chewing the seeds) represents some 50 species of annual or perennial plants that range from the opium poppy, *P. somniferon*, to the delicate alpine poppy, *P. Burseri*, of rock gardens.

Flanders poppy

High on the list of eminent garden perennials is the oriental poppy, *P. orientale*, for no sunny border or old-fashioned cottage garden should be without it. The flowers bloom on 3- and 4-foot stems, chalices of brilliant color with wavy filaments and a stylized ovary for centers, flowering in late May and June. Cultivars include 'Watermelon' with flowers 7 inches wide of a brilliant watermelon pink; 'Helen Elizabeth', a pure pink without any dark spots upon the petals; and 'Maiden's Blush', white but with a 2-inch-wide band of pink around the edge.

These plants want full sun and a deeply worked soil with a goodly amount of humus because once ensconced they should remain where they are; no poppy likes or often lives after moving.

The Iceland poppy, *P. nudicale*, comes from the arctic regions of North America and is a short-lived plant that works best as a biennial, bearing incredibly beautiful flowers on foot high stalks with petals like dyed silk in colors of white, orange, yellow, or scarlet. Seed is available from many seedhouses but among the finest of the new cultivars is 'Oregon Rainbows', a strain that bears single and semidouble flowers of apricot and peach, pink and lavender, shocking pink, picotees (petals of one color, edged with another) and soft white. If seeds are sown in early January, plants should bloom by the following June.

Another dashing perennial poppy that has unfortunately taken a backseat to its blue relatives from the Himalayas, is the yellow or orange Welsh poppy, *Meconopsis cambrica*, originally from Great Britain and western Europe. I tried my hand at the fabled blue meconopsis but was continually dashed to the ground by failure because of soil, or water, or climate, or whatever, so I was happy to fall back on the yellow charm of this so-called Welsh flower. The four petals close up at night in a flat fashion, even when in a vase— remember to singe the stem ends of all poppies in a flame after picking—but open up again in the morning. Plants self-sow quite readily; be on the watch for minor color variations for some are quite beautiful.

"In Flanders' fields the poppies blow between the crosses, row on row," from the poem by John McCrae, refers to the annual field poppy of Flanders. *P. Rhoeas* bears flowers often 3 inches wide on 2-foot stems with colors of pink, scarlet, crimson, salmon, and white. Sow them from seed in late fall or early spring where you want them to grace the garden.

The plume poppy, *Macleaya cordata* (sometimes called *Bocconia cordata*), is another perennial relative in the poppy clan with 6- to 8-foot stems topped with feathery, small, pinkish-white blossoms of great charm. But it is best grown for the lovely foliage, somewhat like an oak leaf that is light green on top and a felty and pale greenish-white on the bottom, leaves that twist and turn to great effect in summer winds blowing through the garden.

Oriental poppy

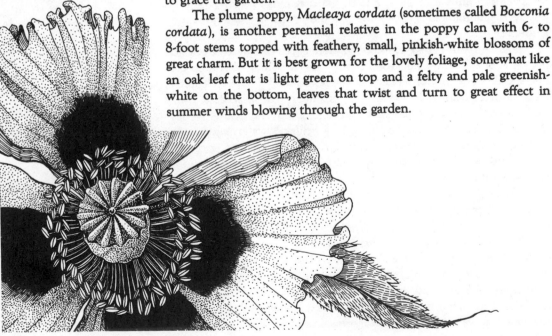

Flower Feature: Tree Peonies

There is nothing quite as spectacular in the garden as a tree peony when it bursts into bloom. The genus *Paeonia* (the name is from a Greek physician, Paeon, who first used the plant medicinally) is known for its beautiful flowers, and for centuries the root has also been used as an antispasmodic. But the tree peony, chiefly *P. suffruticosa*, *P. lutea*, and *P. Delavayi*, first cultivated in China of the sixth century, A.D., can cause a gasp from even the most hardened of garden visitors. Even though the flowers have often come and gone within a week or at best two—especially with the late springs of the past few years becoming overly warm—they are worth the effort. I know of few plants that necessitate contemplation; this is one.

The Chinese originally called tree peonies *Mow Tan* meaning male scarlet flower or *Muh Sho Yo*, for tree most beautiful. It was not until the 700s that the Japanese imported the tree peony, calling it *Botan* (probably the same word as *Mow Tan*).

The English were introduced to the tree peony in 1669, but the first flowering plant—a double pink—was not seen until 1787, when it bloomed in the gardens at Kew. After that, the English, then the French, and finally the Americans were smitten with the flower.

The tree peony is not really a tree but a bush, usually reaching a height of about 5 feet and a spread up to 6 feet. The flowers are usually between 6 to 8 inches wide, but some of the more exotic of the Japanese cultivars can be a foot across. Unlike other peonies, the branches develop a bark and should never be cut off unless when pruning an old plant.

Because of the spectacular nature of this plant, plus the fact that it blooms in late May or early June when the rest of the perennials are just getting started, it should be a focal point in any garden, placed so that you can walk up to it and hopefully see it from inside the house. Luckily the soft green foliage is also attractive. Even a small city yard should have a spot for this plant, complemented with small roses and hostas.

Tree peonies are expensive, especially when you buy grafts that are at least 3 years old, but these older plants are more established and usually succeed where younger grafts fail. They are also chancy in climates below Zone 5 and will need extra protection and care if they are to survive temperatures below −20°F. If your winter provides temperatures of −20°F for any length of time, it's a good idea to cover the tree every year with a wooden box filled with dried leaves.

Planting and General Care

The new plants want a deep, sandy, rich soil, neutral or slightly acid, with plenty of added humus and compost plus a cup of bone-meal. If your soil is too heavy, lighten it with the addition of sand. Dig a hole about 2 feet deep and 3 feet in diameter and fill it with the prepared soil well before planting time, giving the mix a chance to settle. Since these plants have been known to live for over 90 years, it's worth the effort of a proper planting.

The best time to plant is late September or early October, depending on your climate zone. Set the plants at the same depth they were at the nursery making sure that you use plenty of water and muddy-in the roots making a slurry of water and soil. Since most tree peonies are grafted onto regular peony roots, the graft junction or joining should come about 6 inches below the ground level so the graft will develop its own root system. For a time your tree peony will send up two kinds of leaves. The deeply cut leaves are the tree peony. The other shoots growing from the regular root should be cut off at the ground. If planting more than one, space them at least 4 feet apart.

Keep the plant well watered until frost. For the first winter, cover the new plant with an inverted bushel basket or some such housing to protect it from bitter winter winds.

Since the tree peony develops a strong system of feeder roots close to the soil's surface, you must use care in cultivating. I pull out any weeds rather than dig them up. Every spring I scratch in a cup or so of bonemeal.

Sometimes an old plant or one that suffers from excessive winter winds can get tall and straggly looking. In early fall the branch that offends can be cut back or the entire plant can be cut back to the ground, forcing new growth for the following spring.

Diseases and Pests

Every so often the branch of a tree peony will wilt without any obvious cause. The cause is a fungus blight called botrytis. Quickly sever the wilted branch and burn it. Pick up any leaf litter around the plant and remember to remove all the old plant debris in the fall. Botrytis usually will not bother plants that have good drainage and plenty of air circulation.

Ants are attracted to the sweet sap produced by peony buds but are not known to be harmful to the plants.

Left, a tree peony in full bloom. The blossoms are among the most beautiful in the garden.

Starting from Seed

Although it's a good idea to remove spent blossoms to conserve the plant's energy, you could let one flower go to seed and try your hand at raising your own tree peony. It requires patience since five to seven years are needed for bloom and there is no guarantee what your flower will look like.

Seeds are ready to harvest when the pods split open and the seeds are just beginning to turn brown. If the seeds are allowed to dry out completely they will take two years to germinate instead of one.

Plant the seeds immediately in individual peat pots using a mix of potting soil, peat moss, and sharp sand. They can spend the first winter either in the greenhouse or outside in a cold frame. Seeds will germinate in the spring. They should spend the first year either in the peat pots or outside in the cold frame, protected from the hot summer sun and taking care that the soil never really drys out. Transplant to their permanent spot in the spring of the following year.

Noteworthy Cultivars

Some of the cultivars of tree peonies are 'Hana-kisoi' with flowers of cherry blossom pink; 'Chinese Dragon' with semidouble blossoms of a rich crimson; 'Age of Gold' with large, double, golden blossoms; and 'Gauguin' with yellow petals inked with rose-red lines.

Garden Plan: A Wildflower Garden

The following plan is for a small flower garden that includes 17 different kinds of wildflowers. It does not require a large plot of land and can easily be changed to fit your own yard configurations. Included in the plan is a small tree—it could be a Japanese maple, a golden chain tree (*Laburnum* × *Watereri* 'Vossii'), or even a small grove of staghorn sumac (*Rhus typhina*)—to provide open shade during the hot summer. A few stepping stones could be added.

The soil should be well laced with humus or leaf litter to a depth of at least 6 inches. And if you are in a dry area of the country—which in this year includes most of us—remember to water this garden well at least once a week. Both a summer and winter mulch is helpful and if your garden is in Zone 5 or below, a blanket of evergreen branches or a carpet of leaves is welcomed by the plants, especially if you have little or no snow cover. Plants are arranged both for height and light requirements.

Favorite Wildflowers

In addition to the general growing guidelines given above, any special cultural requirements are noted here for each flower.

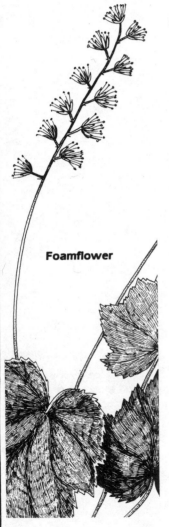

Foamflower

Wood leek, *Allium tricoccum*, is a wild onion with small white flowers on foot high stems and attractive leaves. By late spring the plants will disappear so a good idea is to overplant with wild ginger (see below) since its leaves really start to grow as the alliums decline. Wood leeks need partial shade.

Columbine, *Aquilegia canadensis*, is especially easy to grow and the charming red and yellow flowers that move about on thin and wiry stems usually less than 2 feet high, should be in every garden. After the flowers fade, the foliage remains attractive. If happy, they will soon self-sow. In the North they will take full sun but farther south, partial shade is best. (Columbines are discussed in further detail as the Flower Feature in June.)

Rue-anemone, *Anemonella thalictroides*, is another diminutive and charming white flower with delicate foliage up to 8 inches tall. With the hot summer the plants will fade away. They like filtered shade.

Wild ginger is so-called because the roots have a hot spicy taste. The southern flower is *Asarum shuttleworthi* and is evergreen; the northern, *A. canadense*, is not but is hardy into Canada. They both make superb groundcovers under shrubs. The flowers lay upon the ground and look like "little brown jugs." Both types need shade.

Stiff-leaved asters, *Aster linariifolius*, bear lavender daisies about an inch wide with bright yellow centers that appear in August and bloom well into frost. If you cut plants back in mid-summer before the buds form, they will give more compact bloom. Plants want full sun.

Golden star, *Chrysogonum virginianum*, is the only species in the genus, originally from Pennsylvania and south to Florida, so it's hardy only to Zone 6. Yellow daisies are about 2 inches wide on foot high stems. Spent blossoms should be picked to prolong bloom. They need full sun in the North but partial shade in the South.

Golden star

The dwarf blue grass daisy, *Coreopsis auriculata nana*, is a true, almost everblooming American native with bright orange flowers on 6- to 9-inch stems that likes full sun. Keep deadheading to prolong bloom.

Fringed bleeding heart, *Dicentra eximia*, is a beautiful plant that needs a cool run, especially where summers are hot, so make sure it never lacks for moisture and has some shade. Plants are up to 18 inches high.

White snakeroot, *Eupatorium rugosum*, will take dry woodsy soil and will even bloom well in rather dense shade. Plants often reach up to 4 feet high, so in the plan snakeroot is located near the tree. Flow-

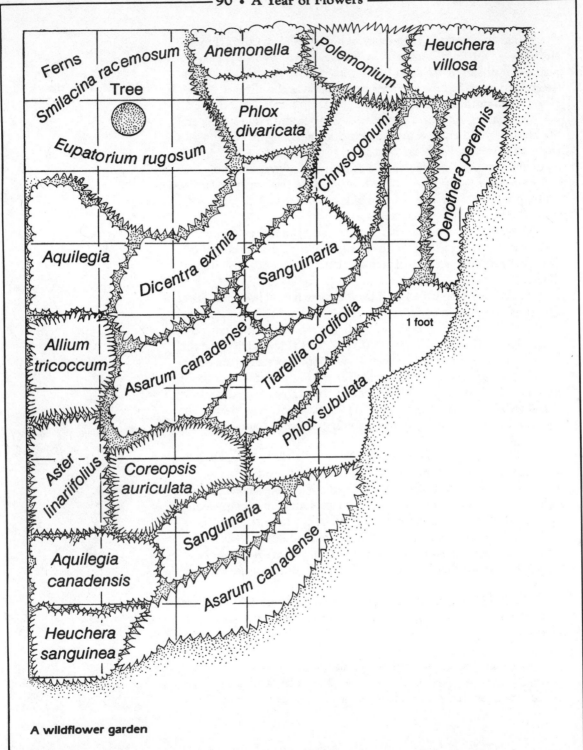

A wildflower garden

ers are white and resemble ageratums. Plants are said to be poisonous to cattle.

Coral-bells, *Heuchera sanguinea*, produce a cloudlike burst of bright red flowers on 1- to 2-foot stems that hover over attractive green leaves, needing very little fuss except full sun. They do need dividing every few years as the roots become overgrown and corky.

Jacob's-ladder, *Polemonium reptans*, produces clusters of small blue bells on 1-foot stems with attractive foliage, prefers partial shade in hot climates, and needs extra water when soil is very dry.

Bloodroot, *Sanguinaria canadensis*, should be surrounded by other plants because as summer approaches, the plants disappear. The common name refers to the red juice produced by the roots when cut. There is a double form 'Multiplex' (what an awful name for such a beautiful flower), with flowers that look like small waterlilies on 8-inch stems. Bloodroots need partial shade.

Solomon-plume, *Smilacina racemosum*, is another shade-loving plant with tiny starry white flowers that eventually become red berries, all on a 2-foot spike. It also needs extra water when summers are dry.

Foamflower, *Tiarellia cordifolia*, is a creeping plant with maple-like leaves and clusters of tiny white flowers on 10-inch stalks, which will spread by underground runners, eventually forming a large patch. It needs a moist spot and partial shade.

Sundrops, or various species of *Oenothera*, are aptly named for their clusters of yellow flowers. They really seem to be as bright as Old Sol. Appropriately enough they require full sun. *O. perennis* is a shorter than normal species, being less than 20 inches high. (Other sundrops are discussed in June.)

Woodland phlox, *Phlox divaricata*, bears blue to lavender flowers on 18-inch stems and is an outstanding woodland groundcover. Blooming in early to mid-spring, it needs shade later in the season.

Dwarf phlox, *Phlox subulata*, is also known as ground or moss pink and produces evergreen mats of needlelike foliage with flowers from white to pink and lavender. When too many of the bright pink and magenta flowers are placed too close together, the colors begin to fight each other and the result is not too attractive. This is one of the few wildflowers that asks for forbearance.

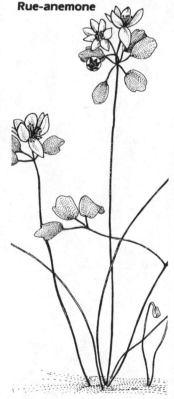

Rue-anemone

From the house, we visited the gardens; and here I am lost, not in confusion, but amidst scenes of grandeur, magnificence, and beauty. They are spacious, and include a great variety of ground. The plain, or as artists term it, the lawn, before the palace, is kept in the most perfect order: not a single spire of grass rises above another. It is mowed and swept every other day, and is as smooth as the surface of a looking glass. The gardener, who [has] lived twenty-five years upon the place, told us that he employed about sixty-three hands during the summer, in mowing, sweeping, pruning, lopping, and in ornamenting the grounds.

Abigail Adams in *a letter describing a visit to Blenheim, 1787.*

I t's June: The perennial border is so awash with color that even the hummingbirds seem to be stupefied with the flower count and the rock garden also, is outdoing itself with blossoms. But it's hot! We need rain and the daily stint with moving the sprinkler never seems to do the job that a good soaking rain will do. Even the small amount of lawn is becoming parched and brown.

We do not have a great deal of lawn with our garden because the lawn, I believe, should be used as a frame for the flower beds, not a vast sea of green to be tended to. Not that it wouldn't be nice to have a vast sea of green but in our northeastern climate coupled with the restraints on our time, it's an impossible thing to have.

And I'm reminded of the story of two American visitors to a grand English estate: "Goodness," said one, as they trod the palatial lawn, "this grass is beautiful," and turning to the head gardener asked: "How do you get a beautiful lawn like this?" "Well, sir," he answered, "first you roll it for about four hundred years."

Left, **New Zealand flax is a half-hardy evergreen that does beautifully in a pot. The striking swordlike leaves make a decorative statement both in the garden and on the patio. The inset shows the flowers. The garden boot is in homage to England's master gardener, Miss Jekyll.**

Outdoors: A World of Flowers

The greenhouse is empty and except for a pot of *Oxalis rubra* 'Alba', all the houseplants have been moved outside by now. It's time to clean the benches and sweep up the empty spider webs now that their tenants have followed the plants to their summer home. For the next few months, the indoor flowers are provided by bouquets from both the perennial border and the cutting garden.

New Zealand Flax

The plant pictured is a half-hardy evergreen, a member of the genus *Phormium* (from *phormos*, basket, referring to the use of the leaf fibers) that is only hardy to a low of 20°F. Rather than dig New Zealand flax up every fall for moving to the greenhouse, I grow them in self-watering pots—they love water—and dot them around the garden landscape for marvelous color accents.

There are only two species listed in *Hortus Third* (P. *Colensoi* and P. *tenax*), but these plants have given rise to a bewildering range of colors including: scarlet, deep maroon, orange, yellow, rose, pink, pale green, and numerous variegations and combinations of stripes. Some of the named cultivars available are 'Dazzler' with 2-inch wide magenta and chocolate-striped leaves; 'Apricot Queen' with a leaf combination of yellow and cream with green stripes and red edges; and 'Surfrider' with narrow, twisted leaves of orange and green.

Plant height varies between 2 and 5 feet so they are large enough to stand up and be counted. I have one pot of P. *Colensoi* that I grew from seed. It bears deep maroon leaves and stands next to a small concrete urn containing impatiens 'Firelake Hybrids' with predominantly pink blossoms. The other pot holds an unnamed variegation of P. *tenax*, which is now a large plant with 4-foot variegated green and white leaves. This flax stands before the armillary sphere, itself entwined with a passion flower vine (*Passiflora vitifolia*).

Flax prefers a sandy soil under full sun and lots of water. It is very tough and impervious to pests and disease. Propagation is by division of mature clumps in the spring. Mature plants will flower with tubular blossoms on long stalks.

An Old-Fashioned Flower

The carnation, or pink, is mentioned in John Parkinsons's book, *Paradisi in Sole Paradisus Terrestris*, 49 times, and that was way back in 1629. One hundred years before that first garden book in the English language was published, two carnations are to be found carefully rendered in an illuminated manuscript, *The Prayer Book of Charles*

A carnation

Summer

Tuberous begonias bear big and blatant blooms. The flowers above are called fimbriata or carnation-type begonias.

Ixias or corn bells originally came from Africa. Although the charming flowers will close at night, they are still beautiful as cut flowers and literally gleam when planted in the garden border.

Daylilies are about the most popular flower in America and with good reason. They come in a vast array of colors and are literally carefree. The cultivar pictured is 'Red Landscape Supreme'.

The cone flower is an American original, a wildflower from the nation's heartland. They belong both in the garden border and the cutting garden.

Cannas will bloom from midsummer throughout the fall and the rhizomes can then be stored over the winter for use the following year. The cultivar above is 'Wyoming'.

Foxgloves are easily grown biennials that are happy in full sun or partial shade. Pictured above is 'Foxy', a long-blooming type that will flower in just five months from seed.

Dahlias originated in Mexico as a wildflower. Today there are hundreds of cultivars available. Dahlias are found in a number of floral shapes and come in many beautiful colors. The flowers at left are called 'Eveline' while those below are 'Unwin Dwarfs'.

Achimenes will reward the gardener with flowers from early spring until well into fall, if protected from frost. The cultivar pictured is 'Blue Rose'.

Nothing makes a finer summer picture than pots full of bedding geraniums. These plants will produce flowers if planted directly in the garden or placed in pots, hanging baskets, or window boxes.

The white form of lily-of-the-Nile makes a wonderful floral show in the summer garden. Bulbs can be overwintered in the greenhouse or basement where winters are cold.

Transvaal daisies, or gerberas, provide flowers for the summer border or can be grown in the house over the winter. Flowers will last up to two weeks when cut.

the Bold of Burgundy. To call this endearing flower "old fashioned" is a bit of an understatement.

The genus is *Dianthus* (from the Greek, *dios,* divine, and *anthos,* flower) and during Elizabethan times, carnations and pinks were in every garden worth its salt. But by the early 1800s, the wealthy gardeners had begun to eschew these fragrant treasures, thinking them flowers of the common folk. Flowers, though, like most of the pursuits of man, fall into cycles of fashion, and during the reign of Queen Victoria, the carnation and pink (the first is *D. caryophyullus,* the second *D. plumarius*) rose again in popularity, so much so that in 1897 one new variety sold for $3,000.

These garden flowers are not to be confused with the perpetual-flowering carnations sold by florists; those are tender perennials and only for the greenhouse up north.

In 1902, the nursery firm of Messrs. Allwood crossed the old-fashioned pink with one of the perpetual-flowering varieties and created the Allwood Laced Pink, *Dianthus × Allwoodii.* In 1980, I purchased seeds from England, and one year later, in June, they bloomed. The flowers have that wonderful carnation scent, are brilliant pink or white, all with a pheasant-eyed center, and stand some 12 inches tall. They are short-lived plants but easily flower the first year from seed, if sown in January.

These flowers are said to resent overly acid soil—a problem always at hand in my garden—so I think they owe their health to the fact that a mortar and stone foundation once stood where they now grow. They do not need a rich soil, but it should be well drained. Add a dash of bonemeal every spring.

There is another new member of the family, *D. chinensis* 'Fire Carpet'. This is a hybrid that if sown by the middle of January will be in flaming bloom by the middle of June. The 2-inch flowers are scarlet-vermilion and will bloom all summer until hard frost. At that time, if dug up and potted, they will continue to flower well into the winter, rest a bit, and start up again for another season in the garden.

The Purple Bells Vine

Nurseries usually don't rest on their laurels but are continually looking for new plants to whet the public's appetite. One such find is the purple bells vine, *Rhodochiton atrosanguineum* (from *rhodo,* red, and *chiton,* cloak, alluding to the large, colored calyx, that part of the flower that supports the petals). This free-flowering vine, native to Mexico, will bloom in four months from seed. For most of the year, the plant will bear 2-inch long, pendant tubular flowers, literally

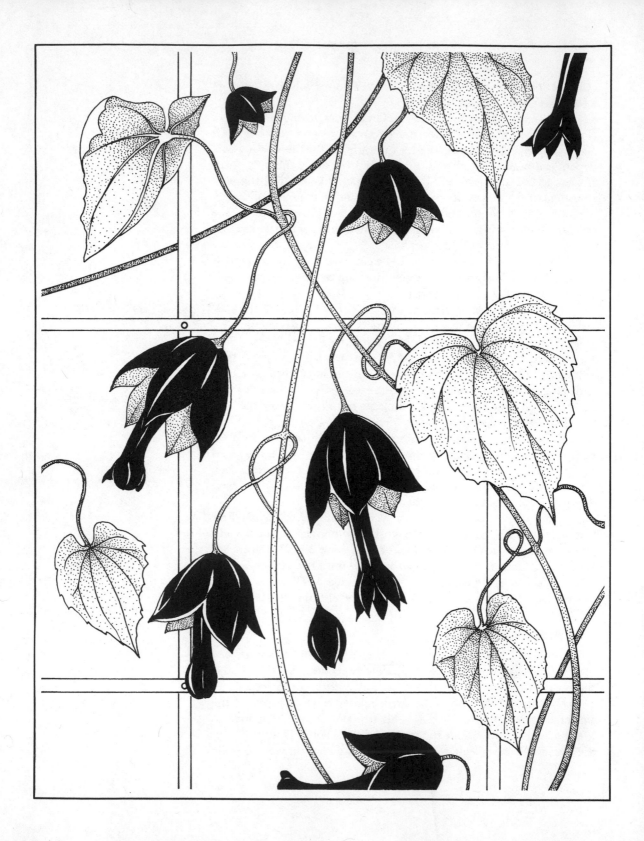

smothering the vine, itself usually reaching a height of 8 to 10 feet. It will winter over in frost-free areas and makes a desirable hanging pot plant, which requires as much sun as possible in the winter and partial shade during the summer. Use regular potting soil with some peat moss and keep it evenly moist. Watch out for spider mites as they delight in this plant.

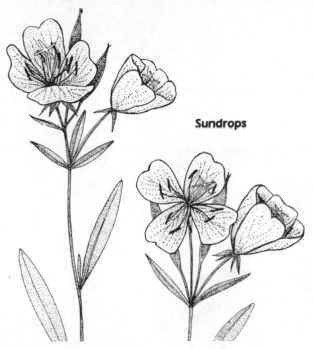

Sundrops

Sundrops In the Garden

As I look out of the window at the garden covered with the last drops of rain from the night's cooling showers, I see a vast billowy cloud of bright, bright yellow that stretches from one end to the other: The sundrops, *Oenothera* (an ancient Greek name for a like flower) are in bloom.

These plants are not idly named; the spirits of all the poetic muses stood by the first person who saw these delicate flowers of early summer and dubbed them with a name that inferred that molten drops of the sun had fallen to the earth, there to root and grow.

Sundrops are day-blooming members of the Evening Primrose family. They bear their bright yellow flowers in clusters on stems that usually grow from 1 to 2 feet high. Individual flowers are about 2

Left, the blossoms are purple bells. This free-flowering vine will bloom in four months from seed.

inches across, each having four petals of the same golden hue. Some gardeners think them common because they spread with ease, but this trait can be used to advantage if you have a bare and dry area on the side of a bank that has been unplantable up to now. Being shallow rooted, unwanted plants are easily pulled out of the ground if you feel that your garden is threatened.

Sundrops will adapt to almost any soil conditions and even tolerate a bit of shade. When gathered in late fall, the seed heads are useful in dried arrangements.

The Ozark sundrop, O. *missourensis*, has 4-inch-wide lemon-yellow flowers with a trailing habit, but it dislikes acid soil so add some lime when planting. O. *fruticosa* is the typical wildflower of the eastern states and quite invasive. O. *tetragona* 'Fireworks', 'Headlights', and 'Illumination' have especially large flowers and are not as aggressive spreaders.

The Bonnet Bell Flower

Bonnet bell flowers might not be everyone's cup of tea. The plant itself is not very interesting: a few small leaves, slight green stems, erect for a while but soon beginning to sprawl. What's the attraction? It's the flower, a nodding bell of the palest of blues, almost, but not quite white. But wait, there's more. The inside of the bell is marked with two bands of purple, bright yellow, dark brown, and pale bands or veins of blue. Bell flowers should be planted on the top of a bank or a wall so the inside of the blossom can easily be seen. Or they should be picked and put in water to really enjoy their particular beauty.

Codonopsis (from the Greek for resembling a bell) often need some protection in areas north of Zone 6. In my garden the roots are granted a haven by a low wall of fieldstone behind them. Plants germinate readily from seed and a number of different species are offered by many of the plant societies. Soil should have good drainage and be slightly on the acid side. The foliage has a slight foxy smell when bruised but not enough to be offensive.

C. clematidea is the flower in my garden. *C. pilosulla* bears flowers about 1-inch long of a light yellow-green marked with purple veining.

A Bog Garden

The hot days of July and the dog days of August will soon be upon us, and the major part of our work in the flower garden will be over until fall cleanup and planting, so thoughts might turn to a couple of projects.

Left, the blooming bonnet bell flower has been drawn to show the intricate and delicate shading on the inside of the bell.

One such project could be the establishment of a bog garden, allowing you to grow the many plants that will not thrive in the harsh and dry environment of the garden border. All have beautiful or profoundly interesting flowers, even many of the grasses and sedges that are found growing in a bog. Some of the more spectacular blossoms belong to the North American pitcher plant, *Sarracenia purpurea*, (named for Dr. Sarrazin of Quebec who sent plants from North America to Europe in the 1600s), a number of hardy sundews (*Drosera* spp.), and, of course, most of the wild orchids. All of these plants require wet feet for proper growth.

Find a spot of ground as large as you feel will remain under your control. I know a lady who buried an unwanted bathtub for a bog garden so let your imagination run rampant. If the location is close to the downspout of a roof, all the better. Remove all the soil from an arbitrarily selected irregular shape to a depth of 2 to 3 feet, leaving the hole with slightly sloping sides. Make sure these sides are free of sharp rocks, and then proceed to line the cavity with either heavy wet clay or black plastic, depending on the amount of work you wish to do and whether you are a purist when it comes to gardening or not.

Replace the soil that you have gathered with a mix of peat moss and good garden loam or humus, using one-half of each. If the soil that was removed was of good quality, use that. When the hole is full, start to wet the mix with a garden hose. Don't use water full force but let it trickle in, since the peat moss will take quite a while to become saturated. It's helpful to include a plastic container of about a gallon with no bottom openings and a wide top, about a foot under the surface to act as a water trap for the deeper-rooted bog plants.

Among the plants that will do well in bog surroundings are sweet flag (*Acorus calamus*), any number of wild water irises (*Iris fulva*), cardinal flower (*Lobelia Cardinalis*), and the marsh marigold (*Caltha palustris*). See the bibliography for a book on water and bog gardening for more details on caring for this particular sort of garden.

Sweet flag

Flower Feature: The Columbine

Few spring flowers delight the heart with the ease that columbines can. The lovely flowers of the wild American columbine, *Aquilegia canadensis*, gleam with colors of bright ruby red and golden yellow, the down-turned blossoms nodding on wiry stems and surrounded with lobed leaflets of wood's green.

> "—A woodland walk,
> A quest of river-grapes, a mocking thrush,
> A wild-rose or rock-loving columbine,
> Salve my worst wounds,"

wrote Emerson, and his thoughts perfectly express the charm of this flower.

The genus, *Aquilegia* (from the Latin, *aquila*, for eagle, for the curved form of the petals), is easy to grow compared to many other wildflowers and a number of species are marvelous plants for the rock garden. (The wild American columbine is included in the plan for A Wildflower Garden featured in May.)

Given good drainage—the wild forms are usually found in stony soil or clinging to rocky clefts—they adapt to most situations. The flowers have spurred petals on wiry stems and are beloved by hummingbirds. The compound leaves are attractive in their own right and are often evergreen in the South. If the leaves get tracings on their surface, resembling unintelligible handwriting by an elf, it is the work of leaf miners, tiny insects that tunnel their way about, inside the leaf. They do not bother the plant at all.

Although many columbines are short-lived compared to most perennials, the flowers self-sow and hybridize with ease so there is never a lack of new plants and often, new color combinations. Older plants usually develop a tuberouslike root system that does not transplant with ease, but younger plants recover quickly. Remember to remove flowers before seed is set to prolong blooming.

The common name is said to be derived from the Latin word *columbinus* or dove, again referring to either the birdlike claws or the beaklike spurs of the flowers. It's interesting to note the use of both eagle and dove when describing this unassuming flower.

In addition to the wild A. *canadensis*, look for A. *caerulea*, the Rocky Mountain or Colorado columbine with flowers of blue and white and a host of cultivars including 'Citrina', with yellow flowers and 'Alba', with white, the latter which *Hortus Third* cautions does not breed true.

A. *vulgaris* is the European columbine, responsible for a number of garden hybrids, including the 'Dragonfly Hybrids', with long-spurred flowers of many shades of pink, rose, and maroon. These are shorter plants than average and perfect for the front of the border.

A. *flabellata* is a Japanese species of great beauty with flowers on 14-inch stems. Look for 'Nana Alba' (sometimes called the variety *pumila*) with its lovely white flowers on 8- to 12-inch stems.

There are dozens of other species and an infinite number of hybrids, usually available from seed obtained from the various rock garden seed exchanges.

Wild columbine

Lilies in a Pot

There are few flowers that take to pot culture with the ease of the lily. Once in a container they can be moved around the terrace or garden with ease, bringing color to tedious corners. Then when the flowers fade, move the container to that area of the garden that every gardener needs: a spot where flowered-out plants recover to bloom again.

I have a white forsythia bush (*Abeliophyllum distichum*) that I use as a green backdrop along one edge of our terrace. In amongst the thicket I planted lilies that will rise up through the layered foliage of the bush, blooming in late July and through August. But until these particular Oriental hybrids bloom (see below), I have placed pots of other Oriental hybrid lilies on the terrace, including the cultivars 'Nancy', with lovely pink flowers on 2-foot stems and 'Mont Blanc' with a choice cluster of eight to ten white flowers on 20-inch stems.

The Oriental hybrid lilies are a cross between *L. speciosum* from Japan and *L. auratum* of Japan. They flower from late summer into autumn. I have two particular favorites of exquisite beauty: 'Magnificum' with ruby-carmine petals with white margins on strong stems up to 5 feet high and 'Album Novum' (often called the white rubrum lily) with snow-white flowers with a golden-green stripe that runs down the center of each petal disappearing over the edge of the curled ends.

Then there is the 'Yama Yuri' cultivar of *L. auratum*, a lily that blooms in September with fragrant flowers of pure white, banded with gold down each petal's center. This plant was discovered on the slopes of snow-capped Fuji-Yama, so it prefers a garden spot with well-drained soil, sheltered from strong winds, where its roots can be kept cool.

There are dozens of other lily cultivars representing an endless array of colors and forms and by growing them in pots in addition to directly in the border, you add the ease of mobility to designing your garden.

Potting Up the Bulbs

Buy or order your lily bulbs as early in the spring as possible. If they arrive and you're not prepared for them, store the bulbs in the refrigerator. If they come in a plastic bag, open it so air can circulate around them.

Anything that is over 6 inches high, can comfortably hold a lily bulb or bulbs, and has drainage holes can be used as a container. I often use commercial black plastic pots that will fit inside decorative containers like stone crocks and colorful jardinieres.

When potting up, put at least an inch of pebbles, broken pottery, or shards in the bottom of the container. Use a planting mix of good potting soil, peat moss, and sand, lacing it with a dash of lime.

Next put at least an inch of soil mix in the pot bottom, then set the bulb in place (it needs this depth for the stem roots to develop). Fill up to within a half-inch of the pot's top. Gently firm the soil. You can plant bulbs singly or in groups of three to five. For small bulbs use three to an 8-inch pot.

Finally, water the pots well and place them in a protected nursery bed in the garden, plunging the pots right in the soil. They will need at least six and preferably eight hours of sunlight. Water them well and feed with a liquid fertilizer once a month.

When the buds have developed to the point of showing color, remove the pots from the nursery bed and place them in your decorative pots and you are ready for the big show.

After blooming is finished, move them back to the nursery bed for the foliage to ripen, then either plant them out in the garden or carry the bulbs in the pots over the winter by placing them in a deep cold frame or another cold and protected place.

Garden Plan: A Perennial Border

The following plan is for a small perennial border roughly based on part of my garden. It contains flowers that will bloom from late spring well into fall. Except for the bearded iris and the penchant of its leaves to turn brown after flowering, the other plants have leaves that are interesting in the design either before or after their blossoms appear.

The garden's length is about 15 feet and its width about 10 feet. There is a narrow path of flagstones about 5 feet long that ends in an armillary-type sundial. The path can be used as a spot to place potted plants during the summer and the sundial could be entwined with an annual vine like a morning glory or a vining houseplant sitting out in an attractive pot for a summer in the sun. In addition to being an attractive garden ornament, garden visitors are continually amazed at the accuracy of the sundial, and I'm always delighted to explain a few of the minor mysteries of the solar system. For an edging in this garden I use a border of common red bricks. This enables me to run by with the lawnmower and saves a world of time.

The plants used in the garden (listed below) begin to bloom in late May with the ajuga—a stunning combination with the bright gold of the yellow barberry—and end in late fall with the last of the phlox and the silvery plumes of the zebra grass.

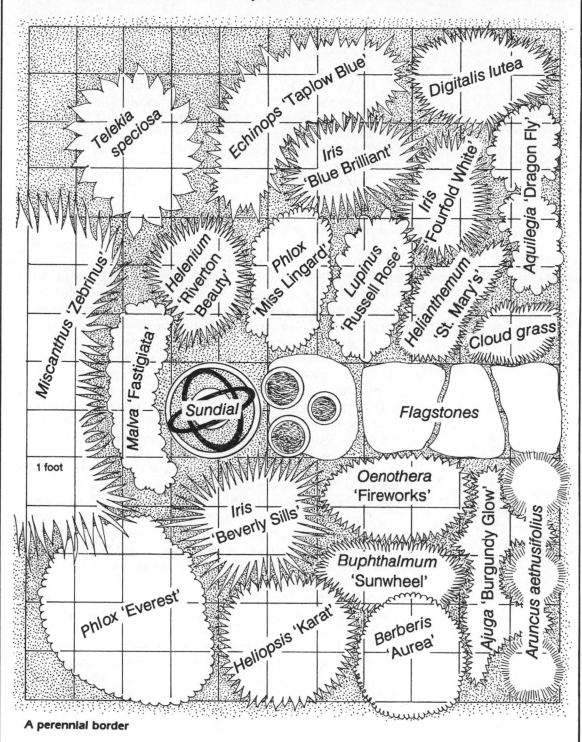

Telekia speciosa

Echinops 'Taplow Blue'

Digitalis lutea

Iris 'Blue Brilliant'

Iris 'Fourfold White'

Aquilegia 'Dragon Fly'

Miscanthus 'Zebrinus'

Helenium 'Riverton Beauty'

Phlox 'Miss Lingard'

Lupinus 'Russell Rose'

Helianthemum 'St. Mary's'

Cloud grass

Malva 'Fastigiata'

Sundial

Flagstones

1 foot

Oenothera 'Fireworks'

Iris 'Beverly Sills'

Ajuga 'Burgundy Glow'

Aruncus aethusifolius

Buphthalmum 'Sunwheel'

Phlox 'Everest'

Heliopsis 'Karat'

Berberis 'Aurea'

A perennial border

Favorite Plants for the Border

The following plants appear in the design and are arranged with the tallest in the rear.

Bugleweed is a great ground cover, usually spreading quickly throughout the garden. *Ajuga reptans* 'Burgundy Glow' is about 6 inches high and blooms in May and June. This cultivar is known for both its colorful foliage and its attractive flowers. The new leaves are a dark maroon, fading with age to pink, and are complemented by the blue flowers.

Goatsbeard is usually thought of as a tall and robust plant. But one particular species, *Aruncus aethusifolius*, which comes from Korea, bears small mounds of dark green, lacy foliage and 12-inch spikes of tiny white flowers in June.

Nurseries often call *Berberis Thunbergii* 'Aurea' the nugget shrub and should be talked out of it. I realize this nickname refers to the bright yellow color of the leaves in early spring, but it's another example of cute plant names that really don't work. A member of the barberry clan, this particular shrub remains small, never topping an average of 2 feet. The perpetual color of the leaves makes it an excellent foil for the flowering perennials in the border.

Buphthalmum salicifolium 'Sunwheel' is a member of the Daisy Family bearing lovely yellow flowers with golden centers on 2½ foot plants. They begin to bloom in June and if old flowers are removed, carry on well into July. If flea beetles attack, use a pyrethrum spray.

One of the prettiest of the columbines are the 'Dragonfly Hybrids', blooming in June on 2- to 3-foot stems. Deadhead for continued flowering.

Most gardeners are familiar with the large foxgloves but *Digitalis lutea*, with its 3- to 4-foot spikes of yellow flowers are a special treat in the early summer border, blooming from late June to July.

The globe thistle that I recommend is *Echinops ritro* 'Taplow Blue', an imposing plant reaching 4 feet in height and blooming from August to September with thistlelike but soft floral balls larger than a golf ball. They self-seed with ease, and you will soon have a number of plants to give to friends.

Next to the stone path I've planted the rock rose, a low-growing plant with small five-petalled flowers. *Helianthemum nummularium* 'St. Mary's' bears white flowers on 10-inch stems from June into July.

For fall flowers look to the sneezeweeds—so-called because of the profuse yellow pollen that has never bothered anyone I know. Their bright blossoms start to bloom in September. *Helenium autumnale* 'Riverton Beauty' grows on 4- to 5-foot stems with yellow flowers and eyes of dark brown. Though plants are tall they do not need staking.

The false sunflower, *Heliopsis helianthoides*, blooms in summer on 4-foot stems, resembling the typical sunflower but not as big and certainly not as clumsy looking. 'Karat' is a cultivar with single flowers.

Siberian iris not only have stunning flowers but the grasslike foliage is also attractive in the garden. *Iris sibirica* 'Blue Brilliant', lives up to its name, producing flowers on 3-foot stems. The cultivar 'Fourfold White' is shorter with 30-inch stems.

For more color in late spring, there are the bearded iris. I especially like *Iris* 'Beverly Sills', 35 inches high with pale coral-pink flowers and *Iris* 'Victoria Falls', bearing light-blue flowers on 42-inch plants.

The lupines have pealike flowers on stately stems. *Lupinus polyphyllus* 'Russell Rose and White' blooms in late June to July on 30-inch stems, each crowded with dozens of blossoms.

The mallows are often thought to be weedy, but *Malva alcea* 'Fastigiata' bears dozens of small pink flowers atop 3-foot stems from August into September.

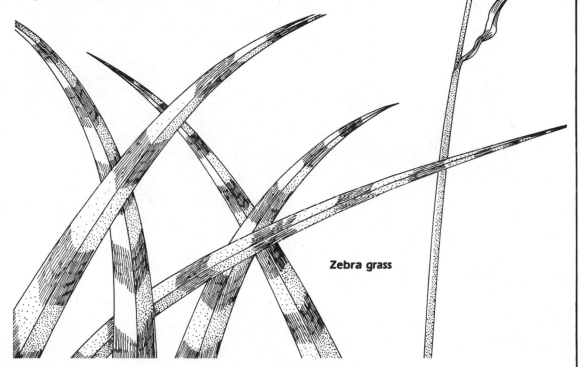

Zebra grass

Zebra grass, *Miscanthus sinensis* 'Zebrinus', is one of my favorite ornamental grasses with green leaves banded with butterscotch yellow, leaves that form large clumps, often over 6 feet high. Then in late September, the plants bloom with waving feathers that are first shimmering silver-purple but open to white plumes that last on into fall and then winter.

Sundrops are described earlier in this chapter. In this garden *Oenothera tetragona* 'Fireworks' blooms in June and July, with a mass of bright yellow flowers on 26-inch stems.

The summer phlox bloom on into September. They make attractive plants in the border even before any flowers appear. Maintenance consists of thinning out plants every few years and making sure there is adequate air moving through the garden since these plants are susceptible to fungus. *Phlox paniculata* 'Everest' is one of the Symons-Jeune strains developed by a captain in the British army. Flowers are white on 40-inch stems. They bloom in late July until well into September. *P. carolina* 'Miss Lingard' bears white flowers on 36-inch stems and flowers in July.

The final flower in the selection is *Telekia speciosa* (*Buphtalmum speciosus*), a large and almost crude perennial perfect for the back of the border. It puts on a beautiful show with dozens of yellow, daisylike flowers on 6-foot stems, blooming in late June.

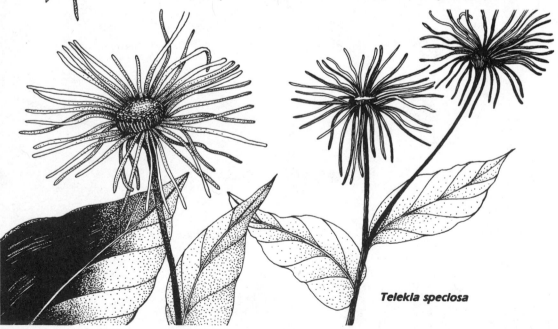

Telekia speciosa

Goatsbeard

There are very few activities in the world of gardening that I disapprove of, but one is the continuing habit of being cute when naming cultivars. The practice reminds me of a restaurant in the Manhattan of the 1960s. Called Phoebe's Whamburger, it was located on a fashionable block of Madison Avenue. Whenever I ate there I had a difficult time asking for a "Whamburger," in fact with the deportment of the staff in Phoebe's, I was downright embarrassed.

I feel the same way about the cute names of many recent cultivars. Calling a plant 'Ity Bity' (*Picea glauca*) or 'Eenie Weenie' (*Hemerocallis* spp.) or 'Spritzer' (*Hosta* spp.) or 'Fat Albert' (*Picea pungens*), while considered the height of imagination by some, is, to me, the bottom of the concept barrel. If it keeps up—and it shows no sign of letting up—as I grow older, I will become progressively more embarrassed as I lead visitors through the garden and will eventually just point at the plant in question and use flash cards.

Left, the lily-of-the-Nile is a member of the Amaryllidaceae Family and thrives with a minimum of care.

Outdoors: A Few Notes on Heat and Water

Of course there is no need to dwell on the heat of July; it is always hot—much too hot! And when the sun beats down in combination with a brisk wind, potted plants dry out with undue speed. Before you turn around, your fuchsia is drooping too far for its own good, or the verbena is done to a turn.

So take additional time to check those plants that are summering out-of-doors and make sure they have enough water to last through the hot hours of the day. Take additional care with any cuttings or transplants in peat pots since the pot fibers act as wicks, evaporating valuable soil water into the air.

One trick is to put ice cubes on the top of the soil in hanging pots. The cold will not hurt the plants, and the slow melt will provide water for quite a while. Remember, too, when watering, that soaker hoses do a better job than sprinklers—although I must admit you can't put on a bathing suit and run through a soaker hose on a hot day in July.

Lily-of-the-Nile

The Egyptian lily or lily-of-the-Nile is a member of the Amaryllidaceae Family. The genus is *Agapanthus* (from the Greek, *agape*, love, and *anthos*, flower) and the species is, of course, *africanus*. The plant does very well outside in warm regions (Zones 8 and 9), but in the rest of the country the practice is to grow the plants in tubs or pots, storing them over the winter in the greenhouse, in the basement, or a corner of the coolest room in the house.

These lilies thrive in any fertile and well-drained soil, with full sun in the summer and monthly applications of fertilizer from April to September. Water them well while in active growth for they do need plenty of water. You will be rewarded with large heads of flowers that stay in bloom almost two months.

Deep blue flowers in globular clusters bloom on 36-inch stems surrounded by glossy, straplike leaves. They are excellent as cut flowers and the dried seed heads are a fine addition to winter bouquets.

From October through late April (depending on your location), move them indoors, giving only enough water to keep the soil moist. Remove any leaves that yellow since they will rot. Use division to get more plants; seeds will germinate, but it will take up to three years for a flowering plant to develop.

These cultivars are commonly available: 'Albus' with white flowers and 'Peter Pan' with deep blue flowers on 18-inch stalks.

Some Unusual Annual Vines

Do you have a spot along your property line where a hedge is needed but the space is limited? The solution could be a trellis planted with moonflowers. Do you want to screen a front porch from the sun? A network of strings to support a scarlet runner bean might fit the bill. Do the children want a playhouse? Use cedar poles from the nursery center, set up in tepee style and plant morning glories around the bottom. Or do you just pine for the idea of a tropical vine full of tropical flowers? Then cup-and-saucer vine or Barclay's maurandya might be the answer. All of the following vines are tropical perennials in their native land, usually treated as annuals, and prefer a good, moist, well-drained soil.

Moonflowers, *Ipomoea alba*, will vine up to a length of 10 feet in a good summer but up to 40 feet along the jungle's edge. The sweet-scented flowers are 6 inches long and 6 inches wide, opening in the early evening like a slow-motion nature film on flowers from PBS. They will climb on a trellis or strings and even the seed pods are interesting because of their unusual shape.

Scarlet runner beans, *Phaseolus coccineus*, grow up to 12 feet on a trellis, on strings, or even through the branches of a small tree or bush. The flowers of today's vines—thanks to new cultivars—come in the original scarlet red, plus pink and white. The dark green leaves provide excellent shade. But above the flowers and shade, the plant produces three crops of vegetable: snap beans when pods are small, shell beans when the pods ripen, and dry beans when the pods are mature. Seeds will germinate in about five days if the soil and the days are warm.

Cup-and-saucer vine, *Cobaea scandens*, produces rosy purple, 2-inch-long flowers that sit on a saucer-shaped calyx. Flowers are at first green with an unpleasant smell but when open, the odor turns to honey. The vines can grow up to 20 feet a year and do well on a trellis or an arbor. Start seeds six weeks before the last frost using individual 3-inch peat pots. Use two seeds per pot sticking them in an upright position. After a germination period of 15 to 20 days, remove the weaker seedling.

Barclay's maurandya, *Asarina Barclaiana*, comes from Mexico and reaches a length of 10 feet in a summer. The leaves are arrow-shaped and vines bear pretty long-necked flowers about 3 inches long that are pink when newly opened but turn purple with age. Start seeds eight weeks before the last frost and plant out when all frost danger is past.

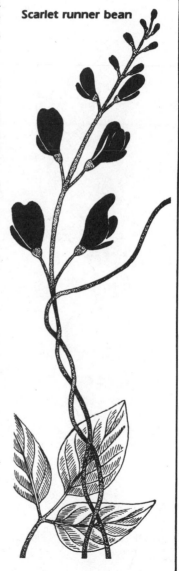

Scarlet runner bean

Cup-and-saucer vine

Fairy's Joke

I have a fancy and a passion for ornamental grasses and among the grasses that bloom in July there is one that is not only beautiful but is also amusing both in name and nature. Its full name is *Deschampsia caespitosa vivipara* 'Fairy's Joke'.

The plant itself is a self-contained clump of attractive dark green grass, between 18 to 20 inches across with nothing really spectacular about it. Then in late June the flowering spikes begin to appear and by mid-July, they are up to 4 feet tall. Now instead of flowers on the ends of this spike or culm, there are hundreds of tiny plants, hence the reference to fairies.

The clue is in the species name, *vivipara*. This refers to a type of vegetative reproduction found in the Grass Family called the viviparous habit, where the flowers are replaced by young plants. The visual effect in the garden is a plant topped by patches of lace since the delicate leaves of the tiny plantlets easily become interlocked as the culms wave in the wind. By mid-month, the culms will bend to the ground under the weight of the burgeoning but still tiny plants, but few if any will root. Some specialists claim that this is not truly a viviparous habit but instead proliferate growth.

Any garden soil will do but the better the humus content, the larger the plant. The positioning of this grass is rather important. It's best when seen against a dark background and at the same time, in a spot that allows the flowers to spread about and dance in the breeze. It is especially beautiful when covered by a film of dew.

Hollyhocks from Turkey

During the winter of 1987, when I was getting ready to plant seeds for the garden of the following summer, some friends gave me an envelope of seeds from a hollyhock they saw blooming along the Street of Curetes, a thoroughfare that runs through the ruined Turkish city of Ephesus. They had collected the seeds in 1984 on a trip to the Near East and had remembered that I love to get seeds from anywhere in the world. In fact whenever I hear of someone who is going to travel I ask them to think of me and the garden whenever they pass an unusual plant or visit a seed store.

Ephesus was one of the world's richest and most fertile cities from the beginning of the Ionian age through the end of the Roman era. Today the ruins are being continually restored by the Turkish government.

For all I knew these flowers had been in the region for centuries. I excitedly prepared a flat of sphagnum moss and scattered

'Fairy's Joke'

the seeds on the top, putting the affair on a heating cable, and was surprised to see a healthy germination some ten days later.

That summer, I set a row of the plants—now about 6 inches high—along the nursery bed in the back of the garden, an area set aside for new plants that might need special attention. Since hollyhocks are biennial, blooming in the second year of growth, and are from the lands around the Mediterranean Sea, I fully intended to dig up a few plants to spend our mountain winter in the greenhouse. But summer in the garden is a busy time and soon the hollyhocks were hidden by a burgeoning rose bush and some annual larkspurs. By the time fall came around, I had completely forgotten about the seedlings.

This spring about the middle of May, I looked past the nursery bed and saw a line of plants with large blue-green, lobed leaves, standing about 18 inches high. The hollyhocks had survived. By June the stalks were 6 feet high and covered with buds. On July 2, the plants were 9 feet high and the first flowers had opened: a lovely shell-pink with a white center. They were spectacular!

I hit the reference books. Luckily I have a copy of *Flowers of Europe*, a field guide that covers the northern part of Turkey. On page 245 I found the answer. The plants were the original hollyhock, *Alcea rosea* (an ancient name for a mallow), the forerunner of all the hollyhocks around the world.

There are enough buds on these stems to keep us in flowers well into August. And the combination of the pink petals with the blue-green leaves looks as if it were made to dwell next to a marble temple, surrounded by drifting sands, gray rocks, and blue, blue, waters.

You may not be fortunate enough to have seeds delivered from far-off places, but seeds from any nursery catalog will give you a lovely display of hollyhocks. Any well-drained soil in a sunny spot will do for these and other hollyhocks.

The Annual Foxgloves

Most foxgloves are biennials or perennials but one member of the *Digitalis* genus (the word is Latin for the finger of a glove, referring to the blossom's shape) will bloom the first year from seed started in February. This is the cultivar 'Foxy' of *D. purpurea*. Two-inch flowers of white, cream, yellow, or rose-red will cover stems up to 3 feet tall. The plants are especially beautiful at the edge of a woods, either massed or spread about. They are tolerant of slight shade, but are more demanding in their need of well-drained soil. Space the plants about 1 foot apart.

Left, the flowers are the hollyhocks from Turkey, blooming in our mountain garden.

The Vesper Iris

For years I've been interested in flowers that open late in the afternoon or after the sun has set. The idea of a night-blooming garden is to me the height of romanticism, and our own terrace is surrounded by moonflowers, evening primroses, and four o'clocks (*Mirabilis*).

But there is another flower with the name four o'clock, only it's a member of the Iris Family. Known as *Iris dichotoma* (*Iris* is the ancient name for this plant), this particular species comes from Siberia and northern China so it's hardy to Zone 5. Happy in either full sun or partial shade, the swordlike foot-long leaves are attractive on their own, but then starting in July, small orchidlike flowers of bluish white with dark purple spots and sometimes spotted with orange proceed to open. The flowers choose the hours between three and four o'clock, taking about five minutes to unfurl and staying open all night until they fade by morning. There are a number of buds on each stalk so, like daylilies, they flower over a long period.

These iris prefer a good soil with a high humus content and a dash of bone meal. Plant in either full sun or partial shade. Rhizomes should be between 2 and 3 inches deep; they will adjust themselves to the correct level. As with other iris, remove the stalks after flowering is over.

The Tiger Flower

The name of this genus, *Tigridia*, comes from the Latin *tigris* because the markings were thought to be vaguely tigerlike. It is quite beautiful, one of the most beautiful flowering bulbs that can be grown in the United States.

The colorful flowers are from 3 to 5 inches across, consisting of three outer petals holding a center cup somewhat resembling a tie-dyed circle of flamboyant reds and yellows. Three small tonguelike petals rest on the lip of the cup. Although each flower lasts only one day, the succession of buds produces weeks of color.

Originally from Mexico and Central America, tigridias, or as they are often called, shell flowers, are not hardy and cannot withstand frost. But anywhere that gladiolus will grow, they will do well. This means the bulbs should be planted outdoors in full sun—though in hot climates afternoon shade will help maintain the colors—in good, well-drained garden soil. Set the bulbs 4 inches deep and 5 to 6 inches apart. If your soil is heavy clay and/or hardpan, use deep-digging to break it up and add sharp sand to aid in drainage. Use at least a dozen bulbs per planting to take full advantage of the colors.

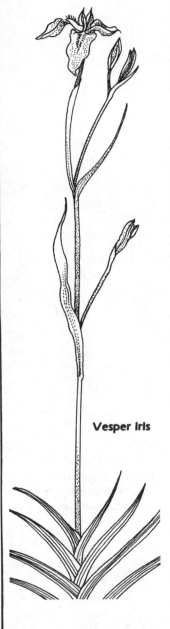

Vesper Iris

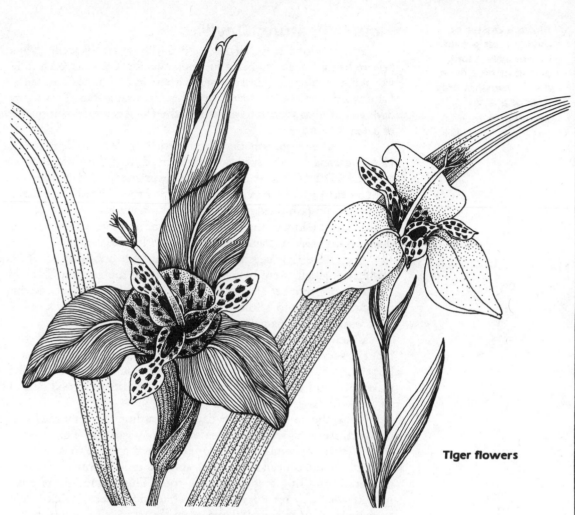

Tiger flowers

To have flowers in May and June, pot up five or six bulbs in an 8-inch pot in February using good potting soil, composted manure, and sharp sand. With night temperatures of 50°F, the roots develop. Then when top growth appears move them to 60°F. As with most potted bulbs, water sparingly until growth really begins.

Once flowering is over, let the foliage ripen and withhold water. Finally remove the foliage and store the pots with their bulbs in the basement until the following February.

Some of the cultivars available are 'Aurea' with flowers of yellow and red; 'Liliacea Immaculata' with crimson-carmine flowers with a white ring at center; and 'Watkinsonii' with deep orange-yellow centers, streaked and spotted with red.

Flower Feature: Daylilies

The scientific name of the wild daylily is *Heremocallis fulva*, *hemero* being Greek for beautiful and *callis* for day, since each individual blossom opens, matures, and withers in 24 hours. *Fulva* is the Latin word for the color tawny or a shade of orange-tan. This tawny daylily is used as food in Asia, where the flowers are fried in batter of dried for future use.

The other common daylily of yore is called the lemon lily, *H. Lilioasphodelus*, the species name derived from the name used in the year 1570. "Often its unbounded luxuriance exiled it from the front yard to the kitchen dooryard . . ." wrote Alice Morse Earle. "Its pretty old-fashioned name was Liricon-fancy, given, I am told, in England to the Lily of the Valley. I know of no more satisfying sight than a good bank of these Lemon Lilies in full flower."

They were first described in a garden text published in 1629. Daylilies originally were brought over the trade routes from China— the home of a number of Hemerocallis species—and the first description claimed them to be most comfortable growing in boggy spots of what was then Germany.

When settlers came to America from England and Europe, they brought some of their favorite flowers to brighten colonial gardens. But since a homesteader's time was at a premium, any plant that did make the trip had to be hardy and able to withstand a good deal of neglect—in essence, a beautiful weed.

Thus, the common tawny daylilies that line the rural roadsides of North America are all escapees of colonial gardens. This is especially fascinating because the European form that came to America is a self-sterile hybrid called 'Europa', and can only be introduced into new areas by using sections of the root. This means plants must have invaded new territory literally in bits and pieces. Daylilies seem to be impervious to the black macadam that stops a few short inches from their crowns and unaffected by the residues of chemicals used to melt winter ice a few short months before they begin to bloom. Flowers appear about the first of July when the summer sun is hottest.

Late in the 1800s, plant breeders saw the potential in the common daylily and began to develop new cultivars using the pollen of the lemon lily and three other species from Japan (*H. Dumortierii, H. Middendorffii,* and *H. minor*). The first hybrid daylily was registered in 1892 with the name 'Apricot'. When research was slowed in Europe as a result of the two world wars, America took up the daylily banner and from a humble beginning it is estimated that there are well over 12,000 cultivars in existence, with 1,000 new cultivars introduced every year.

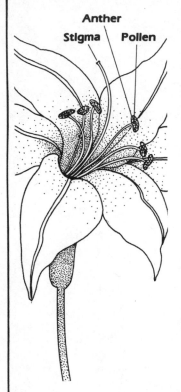

Anther
Stigma   Pollen

Daylilies are the perfect perennial (though hosta lovers might disagree). Virtually carefree, they require no special attentions—although like most living things, the more care you do provide, the better they will perform. These plants will hold dry, rocky banks together or grow with perfect ease in moist soil by the water's edge.

They prefer full sun in the North and partial shade in the Deep South. Plants may be left in one spot for many years, but once blooming starts to decline, it's time to divide. New daylilies can be planted in spring or fall. Space them about 2 feet apart except for the dwarf types. Remove the dead flowers every day and the flowering scape when blooming is over. This last action helps to keep the leaves green, as many plants have a tendency to brown after flowering.

By carefully selecting daylily varieties, you can have bloom in your garden from early spring through the heat of summer, and on into fall. The dwarf types are great in the rock garden. A few cultivars will bloom twice in one season and a few more are evergreen in the South. The only colors not available (to date) are pure white and blue.

One final note: New cultivars are often very expensive and usually meant only for those gardeners who must be continually up-to-date or desire plants for hybridizing their own plants. Within a few years, these prices do drop. The older types, no less attractive than their newer counterparts, are very inexpensive.

Hybridizing Your Own Daylilies

Daylilies with their large flowers, are fine subjects for inter-breeding experiments. You can transfer the pollen (the yellow powder that contains the male sex cells) from one blossom to the female stigma (the flattened top of the long rod that stands in the middle of the six anthers), thus starting the process of setting seed.

Be ready when the flowers open. If you are not, cover the buds with a small plastic bag to prevent other pollen from making an accidental cross. Using a cotton swab, transfer pollen from another flower, touching it to the stigma. After pollinizing, again cover the blossom with a small paper or plastic bag. The next day you can remove the bag and soon the pod will swell and mature. Remember to keep careful records of your crosses.

When fully ripe and ready to split, remove the shiny black seeds within. That seed may be germinated in a cool indoor spot (40° to 60°F) or planted outside in the fall to germinate the following spring. Most new plants require two years before flowering.

The Pineapple Lily

No one who wanders into my garden this year can resist a comment about the pot of pineapple lilies that sits upon a rock ledge overhanging the small reflecting pool. They have been in bloom for four weeks now and there are still some buds at the top of the stem that haven't opened. I planted three bulbs in an 8-inch pot on April 1, had the first flowers on June 15, and celebrated a riot of blossoms on the Fourth of July.

Eucomis bicolor (*eukomes* means beautiful headed, referring to the crown of leaves on the top of the flower spike) are bulbous plants producing 50 or more greenish-white flowers, each petal with a purple edge, in a dense cluster that surrounds a stout stem. Plants are showstoppers if potted or if the bulbs are set directly in the garden. When arranged in groups of three or four in the border these are striking plants.

Use the standard potting soil, composted manure, and sharp sand mix when growing the bulbs in a pot or good, well-drained, garden soil if putting them in the border.

Pineapple lily

Garden Plan: A Garden of Flower-Filled Containers

This summer has been one blast of torrid air. The flagstones on our terrace seem to be molten as they appear to undulate in the heat haze and the ants run about like water drops on a hot griddle. The garden must be watered every day or so and even with a good soaking, the earth quickly evaporates its moisture thanks to the continual winds that blow across the fields every afternoon. By four o'clock the sky clouds up in anticipation of a rain storm that never arrives. At midnight the heavens are once again clear and star-spangled; dawn arrives continually, dry and warm.

Thank heaven for containers. The plants growing in pots on the terrace can be watered even twice a day if need be. Some are misted when their leaves start to droop and if one or two are in really bad shape from the heat, they can be quickly moved to a shady spot for a short period of R & R.

My first experience with container growing came from a wonderful book entitled: *Pots and Pot Gardens* by Mary Grant White. It was an English book published in 1969 and although the pictures were only (horrors!) black and white, it fired my imagination.

According to Miss White's book, tomb paintings of ancient Egypt depict the use of earthenware pots for growing plants. Flowerpots from classical Greece—looking amazingly like the present day

designs—held decorative plants and were also used to root tree cut-tings for eventual installation around the temple borders.

". . . Greeks," wrote Miss White, "do not seem to have made gardens as we understand them, being hampered, no doubt, by the rocky nature of their soil. Such ornamental gardening as did exist had great religious significance, often taking the form of sacred groves dedicated to some god or goddess. Among their religious practices, none makes more delightful reading than the cult of Adonis which was thought to have originated in Phoenicia, and spread to Greece by way of Cyprus. In these particular rites, Adonis, a beautiful youth beloved by Aphrodite, was worshipped as the spirit of Nature and plant life. In the autumn he was believed to die and disappear into the underworld, to be rescued by Aphrodite and brought back to earth again in the spring. The Greeks made great play of this myth and each midsummer held festivals during which they would place a number of earthenware pots around a figure of the god. These were sown with quick-growing seeds such as fennel, lettuce, and barley, and when they sprouted, the people rejoiced to think that Adonis had come back to them . . ."

Soon the pots planted for the Adonis festivals were in every home and became such a popular item of outdoor decoration that although Adonis faded, pot gardening remained. Today all over southern Europe and the Mediterranean, earthenware pots are in continual use.

Growing Plants In Pots

The following plan shows a grouping of pots on our terrace. The backdrop is a piece of 4- by 8-foot lattice work from the local lumber yard, fitted to a 1- by 3-foot frame, then attached to the wall of the house. Pots of geraniums are clipped to the lattice.

At the foot of the lattice are pots of hostas (dig them up from the garden in spring, put them in pots, and then plant them back in the garden proper when fall rolls around); calla lilies; cannas; asparagus fern for foliage; various lilies including the pineapple lily; other assorted flowers; and a large pot of geraniums, lobelias, and petunias.

All the pots I use are earthenware, being washed every fall and used again and again. If you must use plastic pots, hide them in more decorative housing. Use a soil mix with at least a third of sharp sand and fertilize every three weeks. Make sure drainage holes are present and open.

On particularly hot days you will find you might be forced to water twice a day. If you are unable to follow such a regimen, use the self-watering pots found at local garden centers. But remember that even these often remain wet for only a few days at a time in severe heat.

Another beauty of a container garden is that when the first frosts come in autumn, you can cover the pots with Reemay cloth for protection at night. Then on those warm days of Indian summer, your garden will continue to delight until well into November.

Campanula Isophylla

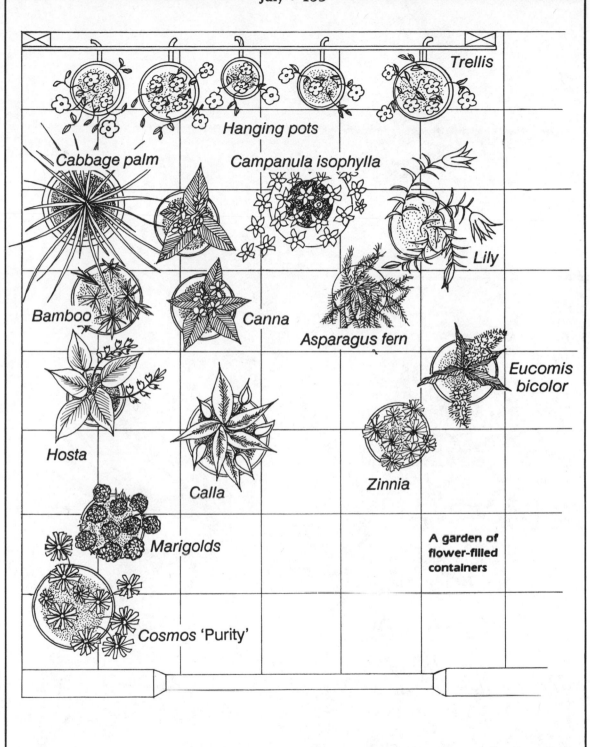

Trellis

Hanging pots

Cabbage palm

Campanula isophylla

Lily

Bamboo

Canna

Asparagus fern

Eucomis bicolor

Hosta

Calla

Zinnia

Marigolds

A garden of flower-filled containers

Cosmos 'Purity'

Untold motives and ideas are revealed to me in the out-of-doors, not to be copied, because man cannot copy nature, but from which to develop a folk song or a poem. The art of landscaping, like all other arts, is that of a fleeting thought that must be caught on the wing.

Jens Jensen, *Siftings*, 1935

The world is in great danger of looking too much alike everywhere, because the home grounds of every beginner are planted with gaudy and abnormal varieties, like golden elder, purple-leaved barberry, and shredded foliage plants. The right way to get variety in this world is to restore and intensify the native beauty upon which nature has set a peculiar stamp.

Wilhelm Miller, *Country Life in America*, 1915

August is a fine month to take stock of the garden: The blaze of early summer bloom is past—even the potent annuals have started to slow their flowering—yet it's too early to divide and transplant for the fall or set out bulbs for next year. So pick up paper and pen and make notes of what plants to move next spring or any special items slated for next season that require advance preparation. How about building a reflecting pool or starting a new perennial border? Or consider perhaps a garden devoted entirely to white flowers? Or maybe a small area devoted entirely to flowers produced by bulbs? For as William Morris said: ". . . a garden should look like a thing never to be seen except near a house. It should, in fact, look like a part of the house."

Left, the blossoms are California poppies. The structure at the base of the flower is called a torus.

Outdoors: Fertilizing Potted Plants

Whenever you water a potted plant, the nutrients present in the soil are soon flushed out of the drainage hole and the soil loses so many nutrients that many plants begin to starve. This is especially common during the month of August when summer heat begins to build and water evaporates with ease. So remember when watering your potted plants to add measured amounts of fertilizer to the watering can in order to keep your flowering plants healthy.

Ixia from Africa

The genus *Ixia* (from a Greek word for birdlime that refers to the viscid or clammy sap found in some species) is pronounced, ik'-si-a. The common names are corn lily or corn bells, and those grown in the house or garden do not have unpleasant sap. There are a number of species and I am never quite sure which one I am getting from the various suppliers.

The leaves are slender and grasslike with a myriad of small, funnel-shaped flowers of red, fuchsia, pink, orange, yellow, or white. The corms can be grown in pots for winter or summer bloom or set in the border where they make a fantastic show of vibrant color. In Europe they are raised as a cut flower, even though the blossoms will close at night.

For growing in the greenhouse or living room, start in October by placing six to eight corms an inch deep in a 5-inch pot. Use potting soil, composted manure, and sharp sand, one-third of each. Place the pots in a cold room or a cold frame until growth starts, usually late in December. If given 50 to 55°F they will bloom about April. They need plenty of water while growing. After flowering, let the foliage mature, wither, and die, then save the bulbs for the following year.

But it is in the garden border that ixias truly shine. Plant the corms in late spring after frost dangers are past. If your soil is truly acid, add some lime to the soil since these flowers are lime lovers, and make sure the drainage is good. If you plant the corms at intervals of two weeks, you can have flowers all summer long.

The California Poppy

In the late sixteenth century, Spanish sailors journeying along the coast of California looked out upon the hillsides, hillsides so awash with a golden hue that they seemed to be covered with beaten gold. Some called out: "Oro! Oro!" while others shouted "Tierra del Fuego!" believing they had found the true land of El Dorado;

and one Father Junipero Serra would spy the golden splendor of the hills and cry: "At last I have found the Holy Grail!" They had all seen the blooms of the California poppy, a flower as close to the color of gold as you're liable to find in the vegetable kingdom.

The first person to collect and return specimens to England was Archibald Menziwa, a naval surgeon and botanist who sailed on a voyage of discovery in 1791 that ended up on the shores of California, but the plants never survived the trip back and the collected seeds never grew.

Then in 1815, Adelbert von Chamisso (a poet whose work Schumann set to music in a composition called *Frauenliebe und Leben*) went with a Russian scientific expedition to search for the northern passage between the Atlantic and Pacific oceans and was joined on the trip by a young Russian naturalist of German extraction, one Johann Friedrich Eschscholtz. They never found the shortcut but von Chamisso rediscovered the poppy and honored Johann by naming the flower *Eschscholtzia californica*.

Miniature roses

In 1890 it became the state flower of California and many think that choice was partly responsible for the poppy boom that shortly occurred all over the civilized world: In art, cooking, and culture, the flower was used for everything from butter-pat designs to architectural trim. (The other reason was the romantic attachment to drugs produced by the other poppy, enjoyed by the French and English romantic poets and artists who were quite popular at the century's turn.)

The four-petalled blossoms, each lasting three or four days and closing at night, are about an inch across. In addition to the common gold, there are now many additional shades of scarlet, terracotta, yellows, oranges, and white, in single and double blooms (the doubles are sterile). The disk at the base of the flower is called a torus. The blue-green leaves are finely cut, resembling a fern.

Although sold and usually listed as an annual, the roots are often biennial or even perennial in warm areas. The plants thrive in window boxes, planters, and pots, needing only well-drained soil and as much sun as you can provide. The plants are about a foot high and should be spaced 6 inches apart where they will continue to bloom well into fall.

Miniature Roses

Back in the eighteenth century the first miniature roses appeared in the gardens of the more astute rose lovers, but these flowers were far larger than the majority of miniatures cultivated today. They were called 'Pompon de Bourgogne', or the Burgundian rose, and are still available from heritage rose suppliers. But the search was on and in the first half of the nineteenth century, a miniature was brought from China. It was called the Bengal rose (only because the ship that carried the plants stopped at the Calcutta Botanical Gardens to rest the plants) and given the name *Rosa pusilla*. (It later was proved to be a descendent of *R. chinensis*.) This rose gave rise to a number of miniatures, among them 'Pompon de Paris' and 'Caprice des Dames' (also note the sophistication of the cultivar names).

Then in 1917, Colonel Roulet, a Swiss army medical officer, was passing by a small chalet, and saw tiny pots of small roses blooming on the windowsill. The Colonel was aware of what he had found and passed a plant to the botanist, Henri Correvon, who named it *Rosa Roulettii* in the colonel's honor. But when the new miniatures were compared to 'Pompon de Paris', they were thought to be the same plant, and today the plant is called *R. chinensis* 'Minima'.

Needless to say, miniatures are now a big hit. These small beauties have the same cultural requirements as their larger relatives, with one exception: It's not easy to dig up a hybrid tea rose and bring it indoors for the winter, but with the miniatures there's no problem at all.

Outside, these roses need good garden soil, good drainage, a lot of sun, and in areas with mild winters, require no protection at all. But in areas like our Zone 5, they must be carefully mulched.

Inside, these roses need plenty of light. If you don't have a window facing south or a greenhouse, you will need artificial light to produce flowers. For pruning, clear away any deadwood and spindly canes. Cuttings will root with ease. And beware of spidermites!

Gloriosa Daisies

Right, gloriosa daisies provide color in the garden from summer to fall and are very drought resistant.

August would seem to be the month to pay homage to one of the leading flower families of the garden, the Compositae. This is the largest family of flowering plants in the world and includes 20,000 species in over 950 genera. They are usually small flowering plants, some shrubs, and a few tropical trees, often with milky or colored sap and small flowers in a disc surrounded by petallike bracts. Dahlias, cosmos, dandelions, asters, and rudbeckias are all members of this group.

Originally classified by the father of modern botanical nomenclature, Linnaeus, the genus *Rudbeckia* is named after Olaf Rudbeck (1660–1740) and his son, both professors of botany at Upsala University in Sweden.

The *Rudbeckias* include the orange coneflower, *R. fulgida*, a reverse carpetbagger that journeyed up from the South. It's usually found in garden centers in the form of the cultivar 'Goldsturm', bearing larger flowers than the species. The family also features the prairie coneflower, *Ratibida columnifera* (until recently called a *Rudbeckia*), with yellow flowers that look like Mexican hats from a 30s musical with Judy Canova.

But the biggest and best of them all for the garden is the cultivar, the gloriosa daisy, a flower produced by plant breeders from the black-eyed Susan, *Rudbeckia hirta*. The gloriosa is a glowing yellow daisy with great charm that hitchhiked out from the West to take up residence in dry fields and along roadsides across the country and makes a beautiful subject for a meadow garden.

Gloriosa daisies have an amazing resistance to drought, and even badly wilted plants will almost perk up before your eyes if given a minimum of water. They can, in fact, be moved in full bloom, with hardly a whimper. In areas where summers are dry or if your garden has the poorest soil imaginable, these flowers will bloom the first year from seed.

Dr. A. F. Blankeslee is credited with their development. He took the original 2-inch-wide flower and turned it into blossoms often up to 7 inches in diameter with varying colors of orange, yellow, gold, tan, brown, and red.

The plants begin to bloom in July and will continue well into the fall. They are easy to grow from seed, flowering the first year. Many new types are now available on the market, including the new 'Irish Eyes' that boasts a green center instead of the typical brown.

The Magic Lycoris

Every year in mid-August there is a sudden show of flowers in the garden that always elicits a sigh from visitors. Amid the summer-worn foliage of lilies that flowered in July and columbines that have long passed their prime, there appear the showy blooms of the magic lily, an amaryllislike flower of great beauty and subtle coloring. The genus is *Lycoris* (named after a beautiful Roman actress who was the mistress of Marc Antony), and the species has the unattractive title of *squamigera*.

The common name refers to the habit of flowering. In spring inch-wide strap-shaped leaves appear and continue to be seen until the middle of June. They quickly yellow and disappear. In fact there is no sign that a plant ever occupied that spot in the garden. Then suddenly in mid-August, the buds push through the ground and within a day or two, the stalks are 2 feet high and 3-inch long flowers of a sparkling rose-lilac begin to open. Each stalk is topped with up to seven sweet-smelling blossoms and a group of these in full bloom is beautiful to see. Surprisingly these bulbs are hardy to Zone 5.

Plant the bulbs in a sunny spot because lycoris like to be baked in summer sunshine. They need a well-drained soil with a good percentage of organic matter. Set the bulbs 1-foot apart and cover them with 5 inches of soil. Once they are in the ground they can be left alone for years.

Lycoris

Lycoris make excellent pot plants. Plant one bulb to a 5-inch pot. Use a mix of potting soil, composted manure, and sharp sand, one-third each. Set the bulb so that the tip is above the soil surface. Water once thoroughly, then do not water again until after the flower stalks appear. Keep the soil moist for about a month after the blossoms fade, then hold back water until the leaves appear. Feed every month with fertilizer. After the foliage fades, keep the soil dry until the flowers reappear.

Gerbera

Sun-Loving Gerberas

The Transvaal daisy belongs to the genus *Gerbera* (named for Trang Gerber, a German naturalist), which includes 70 some species from Africa, Madagascar, and Indonesia. Usually the flowers found on the market are G. *Jamesonii*, a true perennial plant but only hardy in Zone 8 and above. The flowers come in orange, pink, yellow, and carmine and are carried on 12- to 18-inch stems with dark green leaves, undercoated with white woolly hairs.

Plants will begin to bloom four months after germination from fresh seed (remember that the seeds need light to germinate). Mature plants need plenty of water during the summer and should be fertilized every three weeks. Give them a spot in full sun.

Gerberas make great cut flowers but unlike most other blossoms should be cut when they are fully open and a slit should be made at the bottom of the stalk. They will last at least a week.

If you pot them up in fall before the frost, they will continue to bloom indoors at least until January. They need a cool spot (50 to 55°F) with plenty of light and should be kept on the dry side throughout the winter.

Flowers for a Miniature Water Garden

It was a big surprise for me to find every nursery and garden center in New York and Pennsylvania carrying wooden wine barrels that had been cut in half and advertised as being perfect for patio plantings. I couldn't figure out who was drinking all that wine—I had always thought that Americans were beer and whiskey drinkers. When asked, none of the nurserymen knew the source of the barrels but obviously there was a great deal of wine produced (and consumed) in this area.

Not only are these barrels perfect for planting a small fruit tree like 'Garden Gold' peaches or stuffing with a rousing collection of annuals, they make a perfect pool for the back terrace. They certainly looked clean enough to hold water for a tub planting of waterlilies or lotus—though I'm not quite sure of the deportment of any fish that would choose to live within the confines of these tubs. But if you are worried about the eventual health of the water and ease of planting, there are brown plastic tubs available from most of the water garden nurseries that measure 19 inches across by 9 inches deep, which would easily fit within these 24-by-17-inch wooden barrels.

Now as to what to plant in that tub, I nominate either of two cultivars of the sacred or East Indian lotus, *Nelumbo nucifera*

(*Nelumbo* is the Singhalese word for lotus): 'Momo Botan' with red petals or 'Shirokunshi' with white petals. These have spectacular blossoms with a sweet fragrance redolent of the mysterious East and marvelous leaves, often 2 feet across, that repel water like a Scotchguarded couch. Finally as the petals fall they reveal a fascinating and distinctive seed pod.

Gardening under Water

After frost danger is past, fill a 10-quart (13 by 15¼ by 5 inches) plastic container with a 2-inch layer of garden soil and composted manure. Wet the soil. Then make a slight impression in it so that the long, narrow tuber—the thick end—is under 2 inches of soil and the growing tip is ½-inch above the soil. Treat the tuber with care because the growing points are brittle. Place a flat rock across the planted end of the tuber for an anchor, to prevent it from rising out of the soil.

Now cover the soil with a ½-inch layer of pea gravel—not sand—keeping the growing tip free. Next lower the container into the tub of water, setting it on bricks or stones so that the tuber is under 4 to 6 inches of water. Do not let the tuber dry out at any time. Lotus need at least 6 hours of sunlight to bloom with any constancy so place the tub where it will receive this kind of light.

Lotus

Every three weeks during the summer, put a handful of dehydrated cow manure into a small brown paper bag, fold over the top and place it carefully under that flat rock that you used to anchor the tuber. The bags will quickly disintergrate and won't harm the lotus or cloud the water. These plants are heavy feeders and need that extra nutrient boost to continue to bloom. Remember to check the water level of the tub and refill when necessary.

In the fall before frost is imminent, remove the container holding the tuber and store it in a cool but not freezing basement, keeping the soil moist until the following summer.

Tuberous-rooted begonia

Achimenes

Tuberous-Rooted Begonias

The tuberous-rooted begonia is not like other begonias. Those of you who think in terms of the flower found on bedding begonias or on the common begonia houseplant, should think again, because tuberous-rooted begonias produce blossoms of startling beauty, reminiscent of camellias and roses. Their botanical name is *Begonia × tuberhybrida,* and they are the result of hybridizing species originally from the Andes Mountains.

There are cultivars perfect for hanging baskets and others that are best grown as pot plants. You can start them from tubers purchased in the spring or begin with seed.

They do not like hot weather but instead prefer cool, moist air in a partly shaded location. Here in our mountain climate they perform with gusto, but I would not suggest them for the desert or extremely warm areas of the country.

These tubers are shallow-rooted plants and do best in a mix of two parts of potting soil, two parts of peat moss, and one part of well-rotted or composted manure. Soil should be kept evenly moist, not wet, and plants will appreciate monthly feedings.

Start seeds in January to enjoy flowers that will begin in June. Start tubers in March to have flowers for July and August, and on until frost. In November gradually stop watering to bring on dormancy. Dig the tubers up with a ball of earth around them and let them sit in a cool, dry place. After the foliage drops off, clean tubers of all the soil. Store them in an open flat in a dry place at about 50°F.

Achimenes: A Glorious Potplant

These charming flowers are relatives of the African violet and the gloxinia. The genus is *Achimenes* (in Latin, a magic plant; in Greek, a plant that suffers from the cold) and there are a number of different species and various hybrids available today. Over 100 years ago, they were very popular plants and hundreds of different cultivars were produced, most of which have since passed from view. The common names include monkey-faced pansy and Cupid's-bower.

Their culture is simple and the tiny roots—they resemble miniature pine cones—should be potted in the same soil used for the tuberous begonia. Just remember they do not like cold and at temperatures below 50°F the leaves begin to turn brown and the plants ready themselves for a rest period.

Put three to five of the tiny "bulbs" in a 10-inch hanging pot under an inch of soil. Keep the soil on the dry side until growth begins, and then never let the soil become dry until it's time for the fall and winter rest period.

Although achimenes like warmth, they do not take to full sun but prefer as much bright light as possible. They are excellent plants for the patio.

An Odd Ligularia

Ligularias are a passion of mine. Most bloom in late August to September (see the Flower Feature in September) but one, *Ligularia stenocephala* 'The Rocket', starts to bloom in late July and into August.

A well-grown plant is a delight to see. The healthy clump of triangular-shaped and deeply incised dark green leaves seem to balance tall spires of bright yellow flowers, each individual blossom only 3 inches wide, but in unison, a glory of yellowish gold. The column often tops 6 feet.

Ligularias need fertile and well-drained soil; the only trick is water. Even when the plants are growing with abundant moisture, on those very hot days in midsummer the large leaves will quickly wilt, recovering with the evening hours. So the best place for these plants is streamside or bogside, or at least in a spot where water is available. Beware of the four-lined plant bug (*Poecilocapsus lineatus*), for this leaf sucker can quickly damage a ligularia—or for that matter many other plants in the garden—in a very short time. Keep it under control with a pyrethrum-based spray.

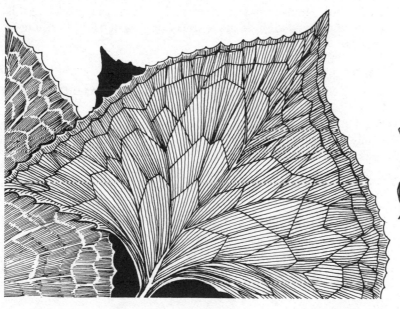

'The Rocket'

Flower Feature: Dahlias

Remember *The Blue Dahlia*, where Alan Ladd was accused of murdering his unfaithful wife and with the help of Veronica Lake and William Bendix, solved the mystery? Well an interesting thing about blue dahlias is that there just aren't any. The flowers come in white, yellow, red, lilac, maroon, and dark purple, but the one color that so far has eluded plant breeders is blue.

Dahlias grew wild in Mexico and Central America and were 5-foot tall plants that produced blood-red flowers. In 1519, the Cortez expedition discovered the plants and gave them an Aztec name, *cocoxochitl*. Soon the flowers grew in Spanish monastery gardens.

The rivalry over exotic flowers was so intense that when the Empress Josephine obtained stolen dahlia seed from her Spanish rival, she refused to share them with anyone. When a member of her own court stole tubers, Josephine was so incensed she banned the flowers from her garden.

Meanwhile seeds were sent to Anders Dahl, a Swedish botanist, who began selective breeding and started a whole new line of plants. In 1789, the King of Spain decided to celebrate the flower's history and renamed it dahlia in honor of Dr. Dahl because *cocoxchitl* was extremely hard to pronounce.

During the 1800s, fortunes were made and lost in dahlia dealing because everyone wanted them for their gardens, and there were just not enough seeds or tubers to go around. In the mid-1860s, Peter Henderson, a nurseryman in New York City, began producing his own dahlia seeds and this marked the beginning of dahlia breeding in America.

Starting Your Own Dahlias

Right, a selection of four flower types found in the dahlia clan.

To determine when you should start dahlia seeds indoors, find the last frost date for your area and count back six weeks. Begin with a sterilized soil or soilless mix using fiber flats or any handy container with drainage holes in the bottom. Make a half-inch trench in the soil, add seed, and cover. Water with a fine spray, cover the containers with plastic or glass, and place the containers on a heating cable since the seed requires 65° to 70°F for germination. The seed will germinate within two weeks. Once the sprouts are up remove the covers and as the seedlings grow move them into full sunlight. Feed the plants every three weeks with a diluted liquid fertilizer.

After frost is over, plant the dahlias outside in a good garden soil with plenty of humus. And remember that dahlias need sunlight, at

Decorative

Single-flowered

Collerette

Ball

least eight to ten hours of direct sun. Dwarf plants may be spaced a foot apart while the taller plants like the cactus or pompoms need 18 to 24 inches between plants. When watering, keep in mind that dahlias resent wet feet but do need water. If rainfall is inadequate, water the plants every seven to ten days.

Dwarf dahlias are perfect for pots on the terrace or in a border. Dahlias of intermediate height (2 to 3 feet) make perfect temporary hedges or are excellent for massed plantings. The large-flowered dahlia (5 to 6 feet) should go to the back of the border.

All dahlias, large and small, make glorious cut flowers and will last seven to ten days if they're treated right. Cut when they are fully open and store in a bucket of cold water overnight before arranging.

The National Garden Bureau recommends growing dwarf or semi-dwarf dahlia cultivars indoors, sowing seed in February in 2 to 3-inch pots, and maintaining temperatures of 70°F. These plants will bloom for you by summer. Seeds sown in December or January will bloom for Mother's Day. They need as much sunlight as possible or should be placed under growing lights.

Garden Plan: A Cutting Garden

A well-tended cutting garden should be in an out-of-the-way spot, perhaps towards the rear of the vegetable patch, or behind a row of shrubbery, or at the back of a large perennial border. In any case, a place that you come upon and with a cry of surprise, like Shazam!, the flowers are revealed to you in all their glory and ready to cut. I, myself, hate to cut flowers in the garden proper: Whatever I take I soon will miss, as though a favorite picture was removed from the living room wall.

If you have the room for a large cutting garden, all the better. You will soon find that any overflow of flowers can be sold to the local florist or general store. In fact, quite marvelous small businesses have been started with cut flowers as the jumping-off point. But even a small spot of only 5 by 5 feet will produce a host of cosmos or gloriosa daisies to eventually grace your dining room table.

Our cutting garden varies from year to year as the spirit moves us but usually winds up to be about 20 by 20 feet. It's located behind a stand of ornamental grasses, a hearty clump of *Telekia speciosa*, and a stand of biennial hollyhocks.

The soil was once part of the vegetable garden so over the years has had a great deal of compost and manure added to it. It's also not far from the back water faucet, so on those really hot dog days of summer, there is ready access to plenty of water for the drooping

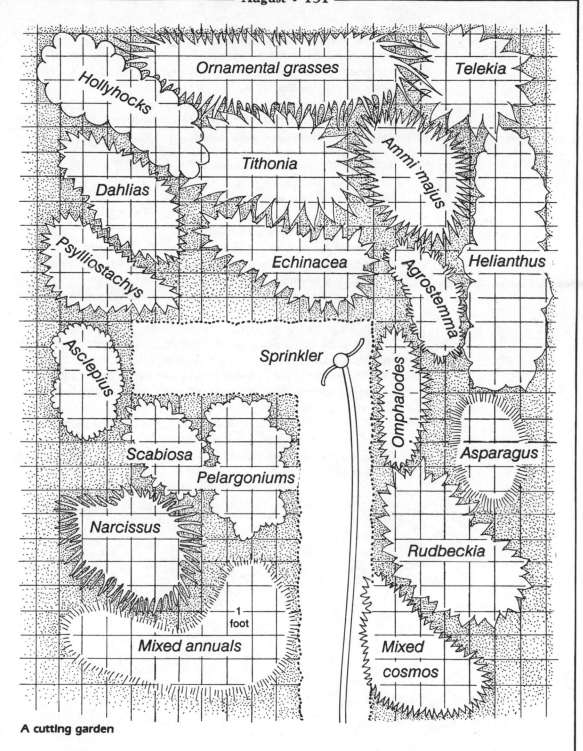

A cutting garden

flowers. Remember that all those petals on all those flowers unfurl and expand because of the pressures of water moving through the plant stems and internal plumbing. When there's too little water, the flower display suffers. But when you do water, do it with a splash! Be sure to soak the soil thoroughly, not just lightly wet the surface. A mulch will help if you live in an area of the country exposed to hot sun and daily winds.

Some Exceptional Annuals for Cutting

Agrostemma Githago (corn cockle) has magenta rose flowers on 2-to 3-foot stems that bloom profusely.

Ammi majus (Bishop's weed) is similar to Queen Anne's lace but is a true annual, not a biennial.

Asclepius curassavica (bloodflower) is a perennial in South America but grows as an annual with scarlet and orange flowers.

Helianthus annuus (sunflower) can't be mistaken for anything else, but the larger plants are often too horsy for the garden proper. So we keep a row in the cutting garden for arrangements reminiscent of Van Gogh and later in the year, for the delight of the birds.

Omphalodes linifolia (navelworts) resemble large baby's breath and are elegant when used in floral arrangements.

Pelargonium species (geraniums) make excellent cut flowers.

Psylliostachys Suworowii (statice), often called *Statice* in seed catalogues, is a flower arranger's delight.

Tithonia rotundifolia (Mexican sunflowers) have large 3-inch-wide flowers of brilliant orange and yellow. When using for cut flowers, seal the hollow stem ends with a match or gas flame as you do with poppies.

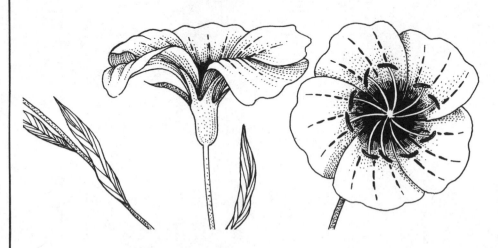

Corn cockles

Some Exceptional Perennials for Cutting

Asparagus officinalis var. *pseudoscaber* (dwarf asparagus) is from Romania and so graceful in habit that it belongs both in the flower garden for texture and in the cutting garden where it assumes the same role for future bouquets.

Dahlia × *hybridia* (garden dahlia) is such an effective cut flower that it seems a pity not to have armloads of them ready for the center of the dining room table.

Echinacea purpurea (cone flower) has daisylike flowers with spiny centers that are true American wildflower perennials. They are so beautiful in the border that it's absolutely necessary to have plenty more in the cutting garden.

Narcissus species (daffodils and narcissus) not only belong on every hillside and in every border but should be a part of every cutting garden.

Rudbeckia species in the guise of gloriosa daisies are wonderful cut flowers that will last for ages in water.

Scabiosa ochroleuca are pale yellow scabiosas that provide just that touch of color to an all blue bouquet.

Mexican sunflowers

Show me your garden, provided it be your own, and I will tell you what you are like. It is in middle life that the finishing touches should be put to it; and then, after that, it should remain more or less in the same condition, like one-self, growing more deep of shade, and more protected from the winds . . .

Alfred Austin, *The Garden That I Love,* 1885.

My father still goes out every spring and he's now eighty and plants an apple tree. Next year he plans on starting oaks . . . now that's really faith!

Anonymous

W e just came back from a short vacation where one afternoon we stopped at a roadside restaurant that was serving an "Ike and Tuna Turner Sandwich." I was glad to get back to our neck of the woods, to home ground, where life is a bit calmer and more ordered, even if it was September and the days were getting measurably shorter and some of the leaves already were showing telltale hints of color.

Left, for cut flowers of unsurpassed beauty coupled with a clean, brisk charm, choose the annual cosmos. The cultivar pictured is 'Early Wonder White'.

Bringing in the Plants

Always be careful when you bring plants in from the outside after their summer vacation in the open air. Pests abound and it's unfair to infect other houseplants when it can easily be avoided. Don't bring pots directly into general contact; keep them isolated for about two weeks so you can spot insects or diseases before they start to run rampant.

Although aphid hitchhikers can be a problem special honors must go to the spider mite for damage that multiplies at an alarming rate. Mites are extremely tiny but can be seen by a normal pair of eyes as small specks marching up and down the undersurface of a leaf. Once they become established, the female lays about a hundred eggs during a two-week cycle, and each of these will hatch—there are no mite enemies in the confines of the home—and produce another hundred, and so on and so on and so on.

The first signs of damage are small, dried out areas that appear on the top of the leaf. Soon the entire leaf browns and dies, but not before the undersurface is covered by tiny, crisscrossed webs. These webs make control difficult since they protect many eggs and mites from being dislodged by a strong force of water, the cure usually suggested.

Mites like it warm and dry, so cool and damp surroundings will slow them down. Daily mistings help, too. But the only effective and safe method that I've found is a soap and water spritz or one of the new insecticides that uses a safe chemical soap as a base.

Outdoors: Autumn around the Bend

Around our garden fall creeps in on little cat feet. As the nights slowly become colder and the stars seem to get brighter we are suddenly aware that all of the leaves have lost the vibrant green of youth. The crickets chirp continually now, never stopping their chorus until the frosts of October. Sometimes after an especially chilly evening we will find an early woollybear caterpillar curled up in a corner of the garage. But out in the garden, color is still the king.

The Beautiful Cosmos

For cut flowers of unsurpassed beauty coupled with a clean, brisk charm, choose the annual cosmos, *Cosmos bipinnatus* (from the Greek word for order and harmony). Four cultivars are especially attractive both in bouquets and in the border: 'Sensation Mixed', showing colors of white through the pinks and reds to carmine; 'Picotee', which bears white flowers with a thin crimson edge; 'Purity' a pure white; and 'Sea Shells', whose petals form fluted sea shells as they fold over on themselves like Italian pasta, in colors of white, satin pink, and shell pink.

If plants are grown in a reasonable soil you will get flowers up to 5 inches across on plants that could top 6 feet in height. The seeds are tender so don't start them outdoors until after the last frost in your area. Plants tolerate poor and dry soil but need excellent drainage. Too much nitrogen in the soil produces rank foliage and holds flowering back. If they get too tall they may need staking.

Cosmos sulphureus is the yellow cosmos and is also available in many cultivars including both single and double flowers. These yellow-flowering relatives don't grow as high as C. *bipinnatus*.

Naturalizing Narcissus and Daffodils

Back in the spring we talked about naturalizing bulbs and now is the time to act. Plant the bulbs as soon as you receive them—never let them lie about in paper bags and be forgotten; before you know it they will start to sprout and be almost a complete loss.

Go outside and scatter the bulbs at random, planting them where they fall in order to achieve a completely natural look. In ground that has never been planted before, put a pinch or two of bonemeal at the bottom of the hole before setting in the bulb. For a major planting effort use a special bulb planter, a nifty tool that will take out a plug of soil and leave the right-sized hole.

It may seem like a lot of work now but next spring when the bulbs all bloom, you will be glad you planned ahead.

The Silver-Lace Vine

If you have a wall, fence, or trellis that begs to be covered with a fast growth of leaves and flowers, the silver-lace vine may be just the vine for you. The genus *Polygonum* (from the Greek for many knees, referring to the joints on the stems) contains a number of pests including the infamous Mexican bamboo (P. *cuspidatum*) and some attractive members like kiss-me-over-the-garden-gate (P. *orientale*), an annual with arching tresses of red flowers. But the indomitable P. *Aubertii* from Western China and Tibet—often billed as the fastest growing vine in existence—will reach a length of 15 to 20 feet in the first season. The small flowers that cover twining stems with great abundance become a white haze from a distance, sometimes completely hiding the leaves from view.

The vines are harmless to foundations, walls, and brick mortar—unlike ivies—because they cling by twining about and not with suckers. They like a warm and sunny spot.

Buy container-grown plants for faster growth; bare root vines will take a few weeks to settle in before they snap out of their self-imposed lethargy. Give the plant good soil to start out with since once this vine is established, you will never get it out of that spot again.

Overleaf, the plant pictured is the silver-lace vine, one of the fastest growing climbers around. The small flowers are white.

Obedient plant

The Obedient Plant

One of the flowers that refuses to give up the ghost as autumn rolls around is the obedient plant or *Physostegia* (the name refers to the swollen calyx of the flower). *P. virginiana* is a native perennial plant with flowering stalks often reaching 4 feet in height. The common name comes from the peculiar habit of the individual flowers: Move them around as you will. They remain in the last position you gave them, until another tap with a finger rearranges them.

The native plant is somewhat invasive in the garden because as it has creeping roots. The cultivar 'Alba' is less inclined to wander and is usually only 3 feet tall. Both these plants prefer a damp soil in full sun.

Count Sternberg's Flower

Sternbergia are a genus of five species of crocuslike flowers (crocus have three stamens, sternbergias have six) named for Count Sternberg, a German botanist. All (except one) bloom in September.

Some authorities think that *Sternbergia lutea* (the species usually available from dealers) is the original lily mentioned in the Bible: "Consider the lilies of the field, how they grow; they toil not, neither do they spin," a reference to the autumnal appearance of the golden flowers carpeting the grassy hillsides of many Middle Eastern and Mediterranean countries.

The bulbs are easily identified since they are covered with a black tunic, and the straplike leaves are evergreen fading away the spring after flowering. Marginally hardy in Zone 5 (although they do well from Zones 6 to 10), they need a spot with well-drained soil with added lime and in full sun where they can bake in the summer heat. Sternbergias will survive with a minimum of moisture. Space the bulbs 3 inches apart and cover them with 6 inches of soil. Every spring add some bonemeal to the site. The bulbs should be left undisturbed for up to eight years until they form large clumps; then they can be divided.

Sternbergias can be potted up in the spring. Nestle four or five bulbs in a 6-inch pot. Prepare a mix of good potting soil, peat moss, and sharp sand, one-third each, and cover the bulbs with 2 inches of soil. Let the roots develop in a dark, 50°F room for six weeks. Then take to a sunny spot in the garden and water lightly. When the bulbs bloom bring them indoors for the display, and then put them out again to let the foliage ripen. Once the leaves have dried, withhold water and store the pot until the following spring.

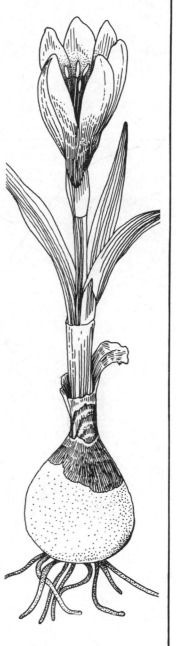

Sternbergia

The Autumn Snowflake

Remember the snowdrops of spring? The following flower is a similar species called *Leucojum* (from the Greek for white violet). The full name is *L. autumnale*, a member of the Amaryllis Family that blooms in late September with two to three white flowering bells that are tinted pink and nod atop 4- to 5-inch stems. The leaves are long and threadlike and appear after the flowers have bloomed.

The autumn snowflake should be planted in March and, since it is a native of Spain and Portugal, should be given a sunny but sheltered spot. Space the bulbs 4 inches apart and plant 3 inches deep. They need a well-drained soil that has incorporated some leaf litter or peat moss.

There are two other species, *Leucojum nicaeense* and *L. vernum*, that can be potted up in September with 5 to 6 bulbs to a 6-inch pot. Place them 2 inches deep in a soil mix that is half potting soil and half sharp sand, and set in a cool, dark spot of 50°F for rooting to take place. When the first shoots appear, water well and bring into a sunny but cool window. After they bloom, keep the plants growing and in early spring take the pots outside to a sheltered spot and bring indoors again the following fall.

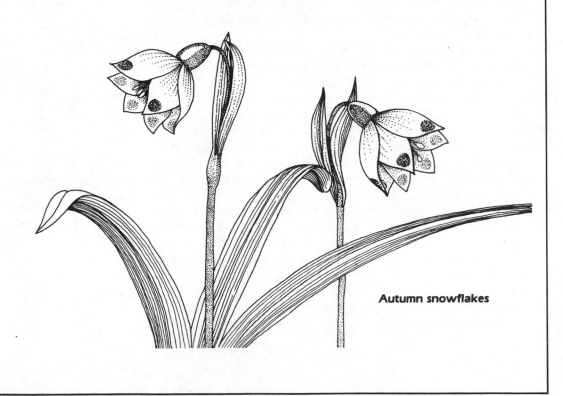

Autumn snowflakes

The Bottle Gentian

One of the most unusual flowers of the autumn season is called the closed or blind gentian, sometimes the bottle gentian or *Gentiana Andrewsii* (the genus is in honor of Gentius, a King of Illyrica who, in ancient days, is said to have been the discoverer of the medicinal value of gentian root).

The blossoms appear in late September and October, usually in slightly acid, somewhat moist soil, and in a place that offers partial shade. There are always plants that refuse to follow the rules, though, and you just might find a clump of these flowers in the midst of a sunny field, where they are protected by tall grasses.

The deep and intense blue of this flower is reason enough to grow it—a colony of them is a thrill to the eye. But the fact that an unopened flower is pollinated by bees makes them a fitting subject of a short lesson in natural history. I quote the following description from the 1904 edition of Neltje Blanchan's *Nature's Garden:*

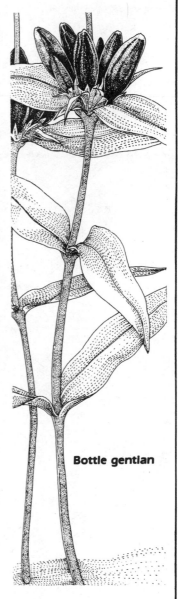

Bottle gentian

> "How can a bumblebee enter this inhospitable-looking flower? If he did but know it, it keeps closed for his special benefit, having no fringes or hairs to entangle the feet of crawling pilferers, and no better way of protecting its nectar from rain and marauding butterflies that are not adapted to its needs. But he is a powerful fellow. Watch him alight on a cluster of blossoms, select the younger, nectar-bearing ones, that are distinctly marked white against a light-blue background at the mouth of the [blossom] for his special guidance. Old flowers from which the nectar has been removed turn deep reddish-purple, and the white pathfinders become indistinct. With some difficulty, it is true, the bumblebee thrusts his tongue through the valve of the chosen flowers where the five lobes overlap one another; then he pushes with all his might until his head having passed the entrance most of his body follows, leaving only his hind legs and the tip of his abdomen sticking out as he makes the circuit. He has much sense as well as muscle, and does not risk imprisonment in what must prove a tomb by a total and unnecessary disappearance within the bottle. Presently he backs out, brushes the pollen from his head . . . into his [pollen] baskets, and is off to fertilize an older flower with the few grains of dust that must remain on his velvety head."

Every once in a while, the spirit of Nature indulges in a bit of carelessness and a white-flowered form, called Forma *albiflora*, is produced.

The Crinodonna Lily

This flower is the result of two independent plant crosses, one by an unknown experimenter near Florence, Italy, and the other by a Mr. F. Howard in California. The result is now known as x *Crinodonna* (*krinon* is the Greek for lily). The full name is C. *corsii* and these bulbs will—in late summer and early fall—produce two flower stalks, usually about 3 feet tall, that will bear long-lasting clusters of 4-inch pink blossoms. The leaves are straplike, often 2 feet long.

Although they are said to be hardy in Zone 6, I would suggest a heavy mulch north of Zone 7 (where they are evergreen), and in Zone 5, dig them up and bring them in before the first frosts. Or grow the lilies in pots, because these plants do best with crowded roots.

Blend a mix of potting soil, sharp sand, and peat moss, one-third each, and add a dash of limestone for each bulb. Use one bulb per 8-inch pot, leaving the top third of the bulb above the soil surface. Feed with a liquid fertilizer once a month while they are in growth. Remember to keep the soil moist during growth.

Crinodonnas need at least four hours of sun a day and temperatures not below 50°F at night. After flowering is finished, cut off the stalk. Then in late fall hold back on watering and keep the bulb dry and cool until new growth shows up in the spring.

Crocosmia

Crocosmias are relatives of the gladiolus but I find them immensely more attractive. If you see the bulbs offered, I suggest you snap them up. *Crocosmia* (*crocus* meaning saffron, and *osme*, smell, because the dried flowers when immersed in warm water smell like saffron) produces double rows of flame-colored flowers set amid sword-shaped leaves. C. *aurea* has golden yellow flowers, C. x *crocosmiiflora's* shades range from yellow to scarlet, and C. *Masonorum* carries blossoms of orange-yellow.

They occasionally bloom in late August but usually in September and are hardy to Zone 6. In our area, after the first hard frosts, we lift the corms from their border position of full sun and store them in a dry spot for the winter.

Space the corms 3 inches apart under 2 inches of soil, and make sure there is sufficient compost.

One word of caution: Grasshoppers chew these plants unmercifully and can quickly eat all the buds and chew most of the leaves past recognition. Don't be fooled by these insects. They can wreak havoc in the garden.

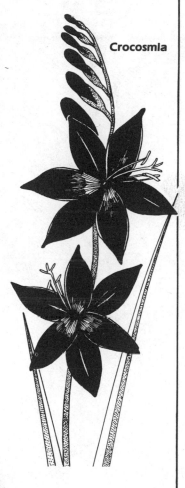

Left, the lovely blossoms of the crinodonna lily are among the most beautiful of the fall flowers.

Crocosmia

Sneezeweed and Goldenrod

Never have two more beautiful groups of plants been burdened with more unfortunate names or reputations. Both have golden pollen, both bloom in the early fall when many people suffer from hay fever, and neither cause the problem. The hay fever culprit is, of course, ragweed, with its insignificant green flowers.

Sneezeweed or *Helenium* (named for Helen of Troy) is a much underused plant for adding color to the fall garden. The wild species, *H. autumnale*, is usually about 5 feet tall but three new cultivars of varying heights are now available: 'Bruno' bears mahogany flowers on 2-foot stems; 'Butterpat' has golden yellow flowers on 3-foot stems; and 'Riverton Beauty' delights with yellow flowers with bronze eyes, on 4-foot stems. Give any of these plants a spot in full sun in ordinary garden soil and divide them in the spring. Sneezeweed will tolerate wet soil.

Goldenrods glorify the autumn fields and many varieties of the wild plants can be moved to the garden border. There are over 140 species of *Solidago* (from the Latin *solidare*, meaning to unite and referring to healing properties), and they all interbreed so identification of individual species is difficult.

The English have been breeding these plants for years and occasionally a few cultivars are available on the American market. In order to make up a plant collection try the seed exchanges. Usually *Solidago* 'Peter Pan', bearing the typical goldenrod plumes on 2-foot stems, is available.

These plants will do well in full sun or light shade and in moist, moderately fertile soil.

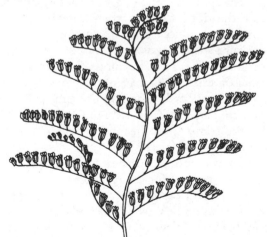

Solidago odora

The Autumn-Flowering Nerines

These beautiful flowers open from late summer on into fall bearing petals that are truly iridescent. The sparkling highlights are produced by the particular shape of the petal's epidermal cells that concentrate the light on drops of pink sap found at the base of each cell. Nerines belong to the Amaryllis Family.

The genus *Nerine* (named for the water nymph, Nerine) contains 20 some species and a number of them are available from flower merchants. Nerines are truly fantastic—they are excellent cut flowers—appearing in clusters of long-lasting blossoms on 12- to 24-inch stems from September to November. The leaves appear about the same time as the flowers.

Bulbs can only be planted outside in Zones 9 and 10 since they are extremely frost sensitive. Everywhere else the rule calls for growing nerines in pots, starting in midsummer when they are dormant. Use three bulbs to a 6-inch pot. The mix should be potting soil, sharp sand, and peat moss, one-third each. Make a depression for each bulb with a pinch of bonemeal at the bottom and set the bulbs so that only one-half is below the soil. Do not water until the flower stalks appear, then keep the soil moist until the leaves die back early the following summer. The bulbs prefer light shade. Feed monthly when in active growth with a liquid fertilizer. Keep the plants in a cool (60°F) spot with good light during the winter. Start the cycle over again the following fall, repotting every three or four years.

Nerine Bowdenii bears 3-inch long magenta flowers; *N. filifolia* and *N. undulata* have pink flowers; and *N. sarniensis* (often called the Guernsey lily) has flowers of red, pink, rose, or white.

Nerines

Flower Feature: Ligularias

Hearing the word ligularia for the first time, I thought it might be a rare bird from the mountains of Borneo or perhaps the title of one of Shakespeare's minor plays, somewhere between *Cymbeline* and *The Rape of Lucrece*. On learning that two important cultivars in this genus of plants were called 'Desdemona' and 'Othello', I was sure of it.

But no. The word ligularia refers to some 150 species of one handsome genus of the Daisy Family and was unknown in Shakespeare's time. It was not until the late nineteenth century that the first specimen of a ligularia (*Ligularia dentata*) arrived in Europe. Carl Maximowicz, a Russian plant explorer, had collected these plants in Japan.

The plant's name comes from the Latin word *ligula*, which means "little tongue" and refers to the tonguelike shape of the large petal on each of the ray flowers surrounding the central "eye" of simpler disc flowers. When we, as children, played "She loves me, she loves me not," we tossed away one ray-flower petal of the typical field daisy for each pronouncement and finally were left holding the button of disc flowers. Originally, ligularias were included in the genus *Senecio*, and some older books list them as such.

These plants are desirable perennials for a number of reasons: Their leaves are large and well shaped; the plants can be grown with ease in wet, almost boggy conditions; they thrive in nearly all soils, including those packed with clay; they are, for the most part, tall and stately yet have stems that are strong enough to withstand heavy rains and winds without staking; the flowers are bold and beautiful and some of them have an attractive scent (*Ligularia dentata* smells of chocolate); and in my garden they bloom from middle to late summer until the killing frosts of autumn cut them to the ground.

These plants also have what may at first be an alarming habit; on hot days the large leaves of these plants will wilt, even when the plants are growing with plenty of moisture. With the approach of evening, they recover their former state.

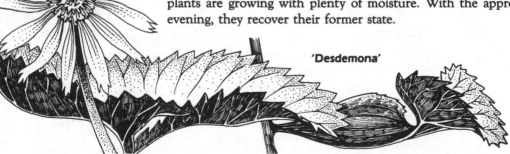

'Desdemona'

Fall

Colchicums are flowers that resemble crocuses but bloom in the fall. They are especially suited for naturalizing in grass and are marvelous when circling a tree trunk.

The plumes on ornamental grasses are made of hundreds of tiny flowers that have gone to seed. The plant above is zebra grass after a heavy frost has bleached the leaves.

The yellow heads of strawflowers appear in the fall. They are everlasting and are perfect for dried bouquets. The blue flowers are annual scabiosas.

Long after the first frosts of fall, the best of the sedums, 'Autumn Joy', continues to bloom. The dead heads are attractive all winter. The grass is cord grass.

In late October the blossoms of the American witch hazel appear in the woods, resembling furled shreds of yellow crepe paper.

The colorful heads of ornamental cabbage and kale are at their best when nights are cold with temperatures in the mid 20s. Plants do well in pots.

Looking down on the blossoms of the best fall sedum, 'Autumn Joy'. The flowers will last over the winter and are fine in dried bouquets.

An American wildflower called the saw-toothed sunflower blooms in early to late October with blossoms that top 10-foot stems.

Golden crownbeards are annual flowers native to the western United States and Mexico and produce their lovely blossoms until well into fall.

The blossoms of the 'Desdemona' strain of the garden ligularia appear in early fall and will continue to bloom well past frost. The flowers bear the scent of chocolate.

Heleniums were named after Helen of Troy but are commonly known as sneezeweeds because of their abundant pollen. The flower is 'Riverton Beauty'.

Shrimp plants are aptly named. In full bloom the plants resemble an explosion of prawns. They are attractive outdoors in the border and indoors as a house plant.

Cinerarias (Senecio × hybridus) are perennial plants usually grown as annuals and bearing abundant flowers in all colors except yellow. Seeds sown in May will provide blooming plants for autumn and early winter bloom.

The orange-yellow of *Ligularia dentata* 'Desdemona' first brought the genus to my attention. I chose a 2-foot square area in my perennial border—near the bog garden—that was lightly shaded in early morning by a Japanese maple. Within a month of transplanting, the plant began to produce new leaves—leaves dark green with a decided purple cast and purple veinings on top and mostly suffused with purple underneath. By late August it was ready to bloom. With colder nights, as the red of the maple leaves deepened, the leaves of the ligularia also became darker, and the bright orange flowers continued to glow under a heavy coat of dew each morning.

Slugs are a problem due to the moist conditions in which the plants grow, and sap-sucking beetles and bugs also enjoy the great expanse of leaf surface that is probably visible to them across vast distances. So far a pyrethrum spray keeps them under control.

In late November, I break up the soil around each plant and cut off the leaf-stalks at ground level, just before the ground freezes, spreading them around as a mulch.

All the species are easily grown from seed. Sown indoors in early spring, seeds will germinate in less than a month with bottom heat of 60°F. Plants can be moved to a sheltered spot in the garden by early fall and will produce flowers the following year.

Some Ligularias

Ligularia dentata (also known as *Senecio clivorum*) grows about 4 feet high and often that wide. Its somewhat kidney-shaped leaves are about a foot wide and coarsely toothed. The flower heads have 12 to 14 bright orange ray-flower petals, measuring 2 inches long. 'Desdemona' and 'Othello' both have the purple cast to the leaves, but 'Othello' is a shorter plant.

Ligularia dentata × *L. Veitchiana* has produced a hybrid called *L.* × *Hessei* 'Gregynog Gold', described by Graham Stuart Thomas as having "grand, handsome, heart-shaped leaves and the vivid orange flowers of *L. dentata* in a grand conical spike." This plant prefers a better soil than the rest.

Ligularia Hodgsonii resembles *L. dentata* but only grows between 2 and 3 feet high making it better for the smaller garden.

Ligularia stenocephala is listed in the August section.

Ligularia Veitchiana needs more room than the rest; as a mature and healthy plant, it can reach 6 feet in height and spread out to 4 feet. Its leaves are almost round, lightly serrated, and nearly a foot wide. The flower heads are bright yellow and cluster on a stalk some 2 feet high.

Gregynog Gold'

Garden Plan: A Garden of Everlastings

Just because most of us in the United States will soon face winter, that's no reason to be without vases full of flowers. By establishing a special cutting garden of plants that are especially suited to being dried for winter bouquets and then preparing our harvest of blossoms or leaves, this winter need not be one of discontent—at least when it comes to the floral arts.

A bountiful garden of everlastings includes the following plants:

False indigo, *Babtisia australis*, suited to Zones 3 to 9, is a perennial with pealike flowers and marvelous seed pods, which start out blue then darken to brown when ripe.

Even though most people think that ornamental grasses do not blossom, they really do. It's merely that the blossoms are meant to shower pollen to the wind rather than to rely on bees, so colorful petals are not present. Quaking grass, *Brizia maxima*, *B. media*, or *B. minor*, all have flowers that in turn become lovely seedpods. *B. maxima* and *B. minor* are annuals and *B. media* is a perennial. Common wheat, *Triticum vulgare*, is an annual that produces beautiful seedheads with spiky awns. Broomcorn, *Sorghum vulgare* var. *technicum*, is an annual grass that is used to produce the nation's brooms. But if the seeds are not removed as broom-makers do, it's quite beautiful.

Annual grasses

Teasel, *Dipsacus sylvestris*, is a biennial with a seed head used by the Indians to brush wool fabric to raise the nap.

Globe thistle, species of *Echinops*, grow in Zones 3 to 10. These are perennials with round prickly globes of steel blue. Pick them before the florets open.

Strawflowers, *Helichrysum bracteatum*, are annuals from Australia with daisylike flower heads of red, pink, yellow, orange, and white, that have the texture of straw.

Hydrangeas, various species of *Hydrangea*, suited to Zones 3 to 9, are perennial shrubs with marvelous flower heads of brown, cream, or pink.

Honesty, *Lunaria annua*, is a biennial grown for both the flowers and the second-year seed pods that look like silver dollars. Pick honesty when the pods turn brown and remove the husks by hand.

Bells of Ireland, *Moluccella laevis*, are annuals from the Mediterranean that produce tall columns of tan bells.

Love-in-a-mist, *Nigella damascena*, is another annual with charming flowers that turn into seed pods resembling inflated jester hats.

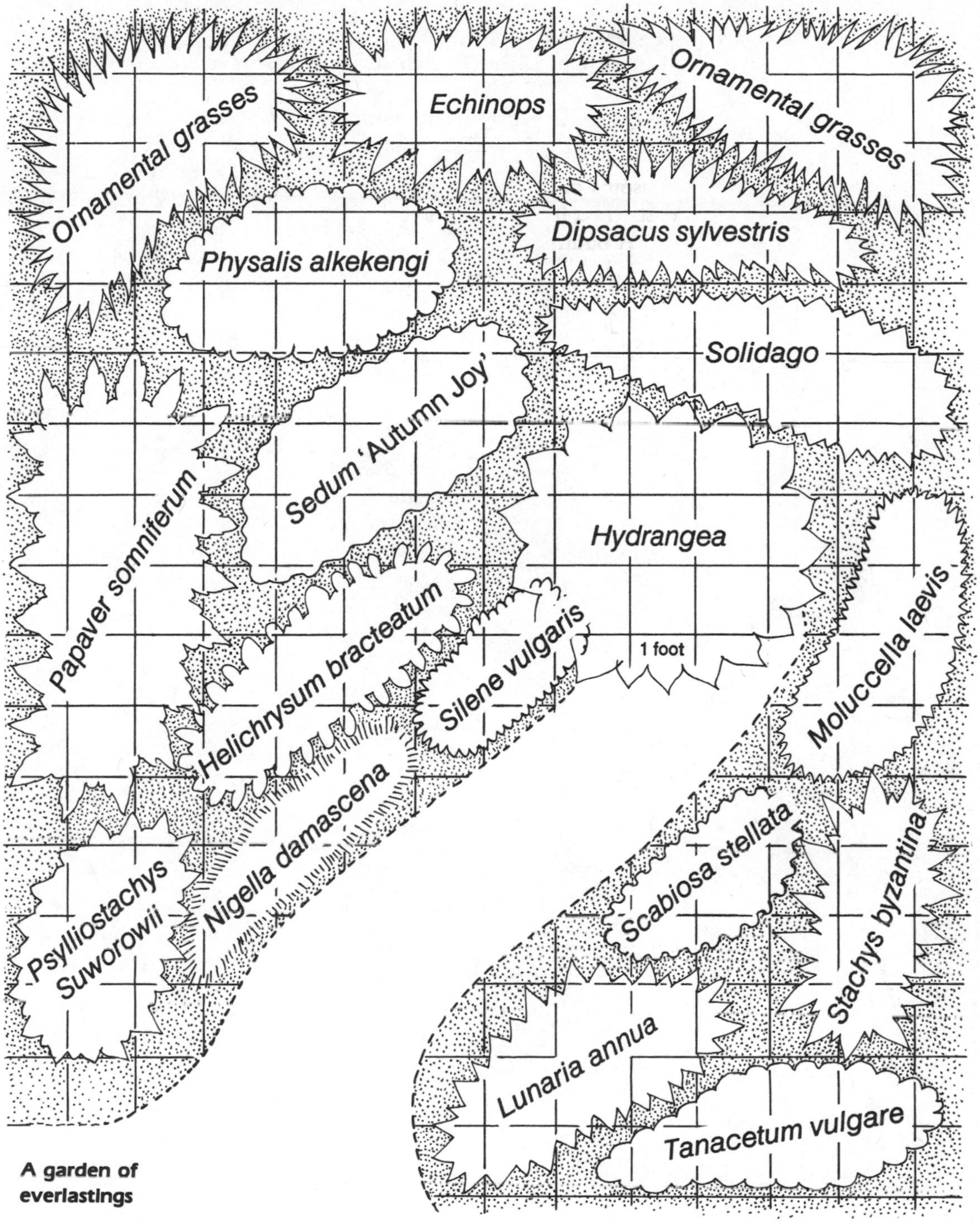

Ornamental grasses

Echinops

Ornamental grasses

Physalis alkekengi

Dipsacus sylvestris

Solidago

Sedum 'Autumn Joy'

Papaver somniferum

Hydrangea

Moluccella laevis

Helichrysum bracteatum

Silene vulgaris

1 foot

Psylliostachys Suworowii

Nigella damascena

Scabiosa stellata

Stachys byzantina

Lunaria annua

Tanacetum vulgare

A garden of everlastings

Psylliostachys Suworowii is an annual lumped in the statice group that produces 18-inch spikes of bright rose flowers on curving stems.

Poppy, in particular *Papaver somniferum,* is an annual that produces the largest and most attractive pod of all.

Chinese lanterns, *Physalis alkekengi,* for Zones 3 to 10, are rampant perennials that produce heart-shaped balloons of orange. Since growth must be contained they are best in a cutting garden.

Starflower, *Scabiosa stellata,* is an annual scabiosa with nondescript flowers that form beautiful globes of star-shaped florets.

Sedum 'Autumn Joy', good in Zones 3 to 10, is a particularly fine perennial cultivar of *S. Telephium,* with clusters of tiny flowers that should be picked in September for drying.

Chinese lanterns

Bladder campions, *Silene vulgaris*, Zones 3 to 8, are perennial weeds in the fields of America that produce balloon-shaped calyxes that dry to a pale green.

Goldenrod, species of *Solidago*, grows well in Zones 3 to 10. These are native American perennial wildflowers with yellow plumes of flowers that keep much of the color if dried when some have yet to open.

Lamb's-ear, *Stachys byzantina*, suited to Zones 3 to 10, is a perennial herb with silvery white woolly stems and tiny purple flowers.

Tansy, *Tanacetum vulgare*, for Zones 4 to 9, is supposed to keep ants from the door but is better for dried arrangements where its masses of yellow buttons are very attractive.

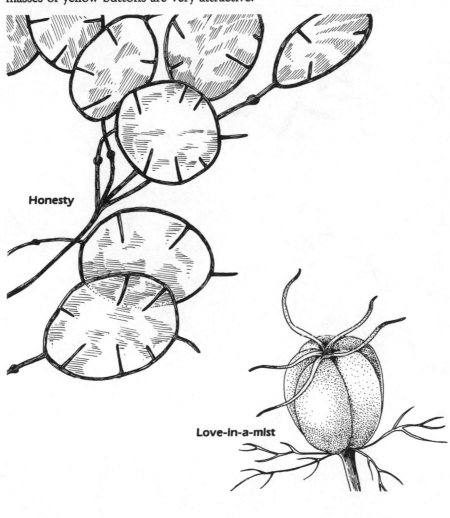

Honesty

Love-in-a-mist

Walked for half an hour in the garden. A fine rain was falling, and the landscape was that of autumn. The sky was hung with various shades of gray, and mists hovered about the distant mountains—a melancholy nature. The leaves were falling on all sides like the last illusions of youth under the tears of irremediable grief. A brood of chattering birds were chasing each other through the shrubberies, and playing games among the branches, like a knot of hiding schoolboys. Every landscape is, as it were, a state of the soul, and whoever penetrates into both is astonished to find how much likeness there is in each detail.

Henri Frederic Amiel, *Journal Intime*, 1852

October is often a melancholy time of the year since it bridges the gap between the sunny late summer days of September and the first sticking snow and dark afternoons of November. But in those years when the jet stream is favorable and Canadian highs settle over the mountains of the Northeast, we get an Indian summer, a time of crystal blue skies and a friendly sun that warms the frost-burned leaves of fall. And the garden is a beautiful place to be.

The Window Blooms Again

Both the greenhouse and my window of flowers are once again full of plants. Many of them are in bud and many more in bloom. Summer geraniums are still covered with blossoms and just before the killing frosts, I moved in a few pots of garden marigolds and ageratum from the garden border. No matter what lies ahead, at least we'll have flowers for another winter.

Left, one of the most beautiful flowers of autumn is the Japanese anemone. The plants prefer partial shade.

The African Hemp

Three years ago I bought seed for the African hemp or the indoor linden tree. Today it's 6 feet high and a beautiful specimen plant for the greenhouse or sunporch. The genus is *Sparmannia* (the plant is named in honor Dr. Anders Sparrman, who discovered it in 1790) and originally came from South Africa. Hardy only to Zone 9, the leaves are evergreen, lime-green of color, hairy and heart-shaped, usually 6 inches long and 4 inches wide. Their shape is reminiscent of the linden, hence one of the common names.

Soil should be a mix of potting soil, peat moss, and sharp sand, one-third each. I also use a self-watering pot because sparmannias need evenly moist soil while the shrubs are in active growth.

The flowers are borne in umbels, with four white petals and a center disc of anthers tipped with purple. My plant blooms for me in October after I've brought it in from a summer on the terrace. Partial shade is needed except in the dead of winter, where a sunny window is best with temperatures of about 60°F. Seedlings will grow rapidly, but if they get out of bounds they can be pruned back in February.

Amazon Lilies

These flowers are serenely beautiful. The genus is *Eucharis*, from the Latin for agreeable, which is quite an understatement where this plant is concerned. The fragrant 2-inch wide nodding blossoms of pure white are often used by florists in bridal bouquets and make excellent cut flowers. *Eucharis grandiflora* is the species usually offered by bulb dealers. The leaves are broadly ovate on long stalks and evergreen.

Plant three to six bulbs in a 6-inch self-watering pot using the same soil as for sparmannias. The bulbs can remain in the same pot until they become rootbound. Temperatures should be warm (65°F) accompanied by filtered sun in the summer and full sun in the winter. Feed with a liquid fertilizer every three weeks while in active growth.

Since the Amazon lilies are evergreen they can be started into blooming at any time of the year. After each flowering period is over, withhold watering for about a month to give the bulbs a short rest, but don't let the leaves wilt. Then resume watering and new flowers will appear. By alternating two pots of bulbs you will always have these flowers at hand.

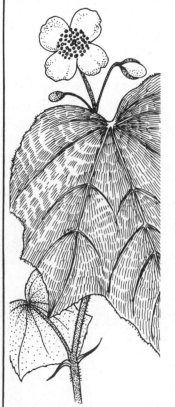

African hemp

Outdoors: Flowers Still Bloom

Even though there are now some days that force gardeners to tie scarves around their necks and brace their backs against the rising winds, the garden is full of flowers. Chrysanthemums, sedums, flowering cabbages, and autumn crocus are often coated with frost early in the morning, but their colors soon warm in the autumn sun.

The Japanese Anemone

The only problem with Japanese anemones is you never have quite enough of them. The genus is *Anemone* (*anemos* is the Greek word for wind), and the common name for many members is the windflower.

Most Japanese anemones are sold under the name *Anemone* × *hybrida*, *A. hupehensis*, or *A. japonica*. But by any name, remember this to be a treasured flower in your autumn garden. These anemones prefer partial shade (one look at the flower will tell you this is a delicate creature) and dislike drought of any kind, preferring instead soil that is somewhat moist during the summer's heat. Strangely enough, they seem to resent any appreciable wind.

For our garden I built up the typical clay soil with woodland leaves and compost, giving them a spot shaded by our sumac grove and some adjacent ligularias. They bloom for us in late September and if the frosts are not too hard, will persist into October. In Zone 5 they need a winter mulch when snow cover is slight or nonexistent.

Most cultivars are between 2 and 3 feet in height. 'Kriemhilde' has salmon-colored flowers on 2-foot stems; 'Prince Henry' is a double flower of deep rose on 3-foot stems; and 'Alba' is a pure white on 2-foot stems. Any of these make marvelous cut flowers.

Kirengeshoma

It is unfortunate this plant has no common name. The botanical *Kirengeshoma* (*ki* is Japanese for yellow and *rengeshoma* is a name for a similar plant) seems to be a bitter pill to swallow for such a lovely addition to the autumn garden. Originally from the wooded mountains of Japan, *K. palmata* grows to a height of between 3 and 4 feet bearing maple-shaped leaves on arching stems and in late September and October, nodding, creamy-yellow, bell-shaped flowers.

The English gardener, Christopher Lloyd, has hostas planted in front of his *Kirengeshoma* and warns that in the cold of Scotland, winter often overtakes the flowers before they have opened. Unfortunately, the same can happen here in the northern reaches of Zone 5,

Kirengeshoma

but for such a lovely plant any effort to keep it going seems to be justified. For good healthy growth, the soil should be richly laced with peat moss.

New England asters

Garden Sedums

Along the roadsides and on steep banks and hills, the goldenrod continues to bloom and farther north than my garden, it's already on the wane. The sweep of yellow dominates the view unless shared with the purple of the wild asters.

In many area gardens, however, it's a different story as a dozen or so varieties of *Sedum* are now in full flower. Sedums, members of the same family as the common jade plant of indoor garden lore, have been cultivated in gardens for centuries. The name (from the Latin *sedo*, to calm or allay) dates back to the Roman era when the smaller members of the clan were grown on house roofs because folks believed that these plants would keep lightning away.

Sedum leaves are fleshy and able to withstand long periods of drought. Indeed they demand well-drained soil, and although tolerant of poor fertility, the richer the soil, the better they will grow.

Flower heads start to form in the middle of summer and remain one of the best features of the plants, glowing with greenish-white patterns until most begin their long period of bloom in early fall.

They are all perfectly hardy in Zone 4 and will even grow well in pots. They make admirable cut flowers, most beautiful when left to themselves in a vase.

The winner in the sedum category and surely one of the most attractive and useful perennials to appear on the market over the past few decades is a hybrid between *Sedum spectabile* and *S. telephium* known as 'Autumn Joy' or sometimes 'Indian Chief'.

The color of the flowers in late summer is pale pink. As the days shorten, the flowers age and darken, until they are a deep mahogany or rust color. The flowers persist over the winter as a russet brown.

Sedum Sieboldii is a Japanese import that is called October Daphne because the pink flowers that begin in September will continue on into October. The plant is decumbent, trailing along the edge of a border or in the rock garden. Since it hugs the ground, early frosts in our garden pass it by but early in October, I cover it when hard freezes threaten.

Flowering Cabbage and Kale

If you've never seen or grown an ornamental cabbage or kale, a treat is in store for you. Not really a flower at all, the rippled and colorful "blossom" is in reality a type of cabbage with leaves masquerading as petals, their ends often filigreed and painted in colors of white, red, and shades in-between. These plants are biennials grown as annuals. The kales have leaves with frilly edges, and the cabbages have flatter leaves and a broader head. They both belong to the genus *Brassica* (from the Latin name for cabbage) and are now so popular that Manhattan hotels use them for fall decorations interplanted with mums.

Start seeds indoors four weeks before the last frost, setting the seedlings out in the garden when frost danger is past. Or you can start seeds directly outdoors in early spring. These plants want full sun in average garden soil. Space them 12 to 14 inches apart.

The colors start to gleam when nights become cold. 'Cherry Sundae' blends colors of carmine and cream while 'Color Up' hybrids have bright centers of red, pink, cream, and mixed green and white surrounded on the outside edges with green leaves and colored veins.

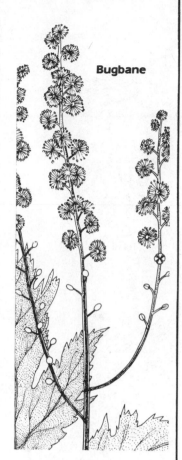

Bugbane

One Bugbane for Fall

The *Cimicifuga* genus (*cimex* is Latin for bug and *fugare* to drive away) contains beautiful and stately flowers usually found in the wild garden or at the back of the border, blooming in midsummer. But one species, *C. simplex* or the Kamchatka bugbane, blooms in October with 3-foot spires of tiny white flowers in long racemes. These plants need good, moist soil and in the southern parts of the country, partial shade.

The New England Asters

Michaelmas daisies are members of the genus *Aster* (from the Latin and Greek for star). They are beautiful and fetching flowers from around the world and are often called starwort or frost flowers in America. If you would closely examine some of the asters blooming in the fields or along the rural roadside, you would see many individual variations in the colors presented. What at first seems to be lavender, turns out to be shades of rose, light and dark blues, almost white, and pink—all quite beautiful. Unlike stars, the blossoms close up at night.

Most of the garden cultivars of the late blooming asters are the result of hybrids usually derived from the New England aster, *Aster novae-angliae*; the New York aster, *A. novi-belgii* (regardless of the common names, both are found from Canada to New Mexico); and *A. Amellus*, the Italian aster. They are usually hardy from Zones 4 to 8.

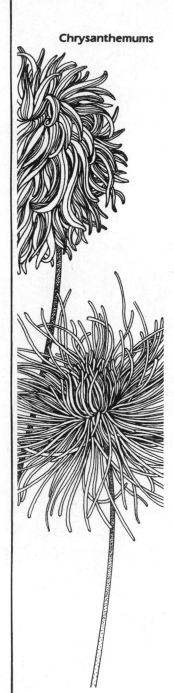

Chrysanthemums

These plants, needing only full sun and plenty of water, are tolerant of most soils. If you move wild sorts into the garden, they will usually get bigger and unless staked, eventually flop over. I don't stake, since the reclining plants proceed with flowering with all the verve of their upright neighbors, but are now more in scale for a spot in the front of the garden.

The following cultivars all begin to bloom in September and continue on well into October. *Aster* 'Alma Potschke' bears salmon-tinged rose flowers on 3-foot stems; *A.* 'Harrington's Pink' has pure pink flowers on 3 to 4 foot stems; and *A.* 'September Ruby' has flowers of deep crimson on 40-inch stems.

Chrysanthemums

There are many levels of cold. I've found in my garden that one year flowers will often survive a nip of frost that comes along in September or October and the next year suffer dreadfully. Then I started to pay attention to accurate temperatures. As a result I know that 30°F is not too deadly but anything below 27°F usually means the plant is nonrecoverable, at least until the following year.

Chrysanthemums will put on a great floral show across the country from August to November, and most of the cultivars will continue to open their buds until that 27°F temperature is reached.

Now I've loved to garden for years but I must confess that when it comes to autumn mums, I buy mine every year from the garden centers rather than grow my own. Since they come potted up, I can move the plants about the garden until the color matches up with my perceptions of what the fall garden should be.

If you do wish to grow your own, remember they should be dug up every year and divided. Pinch the tips until mid-July to encourage a nice bushy shape with lots of blossoms, then let them grow. Watering is also important and in times of drought, it is doubly important.

Since many of the plants have shallow root systems, they are easily heaved into the open air by the alternate freezing and thawing of the ground and in Zone 5 and Zone 4 need protection with salt hay or a similar mulch. The garden soil should be laced with compost since these plants are heavy feeders.

Two Chrysanthemums of Note

I'm sad when I write about Nippon daisies. They are perfectly beautiful plants that bear elegantly beautiful flowers and belong in every American garden, but unfortunately are not hardy north of

Zone 6. I first saw them growing in beachfront gardens on the New Jersey coast, where they take to salt air and stiff breezes with nary a qualm.

Chrysanthemum (from Latin and Greek for gold flower) *nipponicum* has woody stems and shiny, spear-shaped leaves that form little bushes. The flowers resemble shasta daisies and continue to bloom until killed by the frosts. Since they are shrubs it's difficult to dig them up and divide, but the plants can be reproduced with cuttings.

There is one other late-blooming chrysanthemum species called *Chrysanthemum Weyrichii*. The White Flower Farm brought back the first seeds of this plant from Japan's northern island, Hokkaido. There are two cultivars available. The first is 'White Bomb', a plant about 1-foot high and covered with single, white flowers nearly 2 inches in diameter with yellow eyes blooming in late September to October in Zone 5. The flowers are decidedly frost-resistant and the petals turn pink with age. The second is 'Pink Bomb', which resembles the first but with pink petals.

Nippon daisy

Toad Lilies

From Japan comes a strange and valued garden dweller with the unfortunate common name of the toad lily. Toads in my estimation suffer from bad press: they are not the warty and detestable creatures that the public perceives. And I'm afraid that until the plant's name is changed, most gardeners will give it wide berth.

The genus *Tricyrtis* (from *treis*, three, and *kyrtos*, convex because the three outer petals have little bags at their base) has creeping rhizomes and requires a semi-hardy spot with moist soil. The pointed leaves on arching stems are attractive in the garden from spring to fall but the unusual happens in October; at that time mauve and purple flowers bloom within the leaf axils and stem tops, each with a split pistil that closely resembles the texture of chenille.

Most nurseries offer *Tricyrtis hirta*, growing to a height of 3 feet with flowers about an inch long.

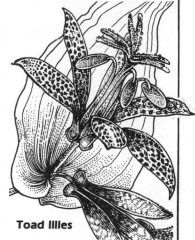

Toad lilies

Flower Feature: The Autumn Crocuses

Colchicum! What an intriguing genus of flowers and what a fascinating history they have. The name comes from the ancient city of Colchis, a port on the Black Sea, nestled on the edge of the Caucasus Mountains at the mouth of the River Phasis, and the infamous port of the poison dealers of the Dark and Middle Ages.

For there in the back alleyways of Colchis, in buildings made of thick blocks of quarried stone and possessing tiny, barred windows, dealers in perfidious potions would reach for small glass bottles, each sealed with an elegant stopper, that stood arrayed on open shelves covering the wall behind the marble counter. With all the surety of a modern pharmacist, the dealers would dispense poisons made to order: Something quick and deadly to stop a healthy young Duke in his tracks or perhaps just a debilitating brew of colchicine, enough to force a tired King to take a vacation and leave the forces of government to the man whose henchman now takes a bag of gold from his cape, and, with his face in shadow, trades it for the proffered toxin.

Colchicine is a fascinating drug. Not only has it had applications for medicine, both ancient and modern, but many of the flowers now blooming in your garden are there only because the parent plants were treated with this drug. *The Columbia Encyclopedia* writes of colchicine:

> "An alkaloid obtained from the meadow saffron or autumn crocus, *Colchicum,* used in plant and animal experimentation. When sprayed on the surface of plant tissues or injected into them, the drug interferes with the separation of daughter nuclei at cell division, resulting in cells with chromosome numbers which are multiples of those present in untreated tissue. Sometimes colchicine is used in medicine, chiefly for relieving pain in gout and rheumatism."

Yet for all their splendid history there are reasons of beauty to include them in your autumn garden. It's hard to believe how cheering a sight these plants can be when they bloom in late September, October, November, and in the warmer parts of the country, into December. The bumblebees and honeybees from neighboring hives love the pollen and gorge themselves to such an extent that many late afternoon visitors remain within the folded petals until the following morning. And human visitors to the garden, never having seen such flowers before, will usually express surprise.

Colchicums may be planted outdoors with abandon. No rodent will bother these corms because of the poison content—a poison

Crocus 'Fontenayl'

that has been featured in a number of mystery stories. Edmund Crispin in his novel, *Frequent Hearses*, confounds his detective until the last demise by having the murderer distill the poison from a number of the corms of *Colchicum autumnale*, the species with the highest content of the drug.

Although called crocus, the colchicums, like the sternbergias, are slightly different: They have six stamens to the crocuses three. (In fact the colchicums belong to the Lily Family, the crocus to the Iris Family, and the sternbergias to the Amaryllis.) But to the untutored eye, they look like the same kind of flower. These chalice-shaped blossoms appear on white stemlike funnels that are divided into six petallike segments. They shoot up directly from the soil without any leaves. The leaves, in turn, usually show up the following spring and then die back like those of other spring bulbs. The long-lasting foliage varies in height between 6 to 18 inches depending on the species, so be sure to keep this in mind when choosing a spot. The leaves are rather untidy as they die so be prepared to supply some camouflage like a few bedding annuals from April through June.

Plant all colchicums 3 to 4 inches deep (measuring from the top of the corm) and space them 6 inches apart on center. They should be left alone until the flowers start to diminish due to overcrowding; then dig them up, divide, and replant. They are especially suited for naturalizing in grass and are marvelous circling a tree trunk.

Choosing a Colchicum

Colchicum agrippinum is checkered with purple squares on a pink background. Flower height is 4 inches and the plants are hardy from Zone 5 south. They bloom at the end of August into September.

C. autumnale is known as meadow saffron, mysteria, naked ladies, and the wonder bulb. Blooming in late September and October, the flowers are between 3 and 4 inches high with leaves up to a foot long. They are hardy from Zone 4 south. 'Album' has white flowers, and 'Plenum' has double flowers of a lilac hue.

C. byzantium bears rosy-lilac flowers, often up to 4 inches across, blooming in September. This species is hardy from Zone 6 south.

C. cilicicum has flowers of a deeper shade of rosy-lilac than *C. byzantium*, on 5-inch stems. They are hardy from Zone 5 south.

C. speciosum has rose to purple flowers 5 inches high and often 4 inches across. They are hardy from Zone 4 south. 'Album' is white and 'Atrorubens' is dark red.

C. 'Waterlily' is a hybrid with mauve-colored, double blossoms that look like the cultivar name, blooming in October. If you only have room for one colchicum, choose this flower. It is hardy from Zone 4 south.

The Fall-Flowering Crocus

The fall-flowering crocus, closely resembling their spring relatives and the colchicums, bloom from early September on into November. The leaves, however, appear either with the blossoms or shortly thereafter.

Plant the corms 4 inches deep and 3 inches apart. After three or four years you will note that the corms have come close to—if not reached—the top of the ground. This is because the new corms form on top of the old, just like bricks added to a wall, eventually reaching the surface. When this happens just dry them off and re-plant the plump corms in July. Remember that just as with other bulbs, the leaves must die naturally in order for the corms to store enough energy for next year's flowering.

Finding a Fall Crocus

Crocus asturicus bears violet-purple flowers about 4 inches long in mid-October. The stamens are orange. 12-inch leaves appear during and following blooming. Louise Beebe Wilder, writing in *Hardy Bulbs*, calls this the Spanish crocus and reports that in its native mountains, it's called *Espanto Pastores*, or "Terror of the Shepherds" since it appears just after the autumn rains and presages the coming of winter. It is hardy from Zone 6 south.

C. goulimyi has 4-inch-high globular flowers of pale to deep purple blooming in late September. It was found growing wild in southern Greece in 1954 and only succeeds in Zone 9, where soils never freeze.

C. orhroleucus starts to bloom in mid-October and if temperatures are a bit above normal, will continue to November. The flower is a delicate cream color with the throat stained with orange. Although it needs a sheltered spot, it is hardy from Zone 5 south.

C. laevigatus 'Fontenayi' is the latest blooming autumn crocus, choosing to flower in December and bearing lavender blossoms feathered with purple. In addition the flowers have the perfume of freesias. The height is 2½ inches, and corms are hardy from Zone 6 south.

C. speciosus is the earliest of the fall bloomers, usually appearing in mid-September. The flowers are clear blue at a height of 4 inches. 'Albus' has white flowers and 'Globosus' has blue, globular flowers.

Right, the pale lavender blossoms of *Colchicum* 'Waterlily' are a wonder to behold when they appear during the cold days of autumn.

Garden Plan: A Garden for Fall Flowers

It's now the middle of October, most of the leaves have been blown from the trees, and snow flurries are predicted for tomorrow. Nights are cold and the thickening skin of ice on the birdbath water every morning forces the fox sparrows to wait for the warmth of the midmorning sun before performing their morning ablutions. Most of the geese have long since flown south, and all the summer insects have been stilled—except one cricket that found its way to our hearth. So how does the garden grow?

Surprisingly well considering the previous winter's record colds, the torrential rains of spring, summer's drought in symphony with record heat, and the early arrival of autumn frosts. The American sunflower, *Helianthus giganteus*, is still a mass of yellow blooms on its 9-foot stalks, bright against the cloudy sky and when close to your nose, exuding a wonderful smell of chocolate. The New England asters, *Aster novae-angliae*, dot the perennial border with a number of shades of blue and deep purple, since I've let them self-seed throughout the garden. And though I confess to moving the geraniums inside every night, they are outside again on reasonably warm mornings to brighten up their corner of the world.

Farther along the border, blue ladybells, *Adenophora Farreri*, are now producing their third crop of flowers atop 2-foot stems—except those that my dear friends the deer have chosen to nibble off. And the dwarf goldenrod, *Solidago spathulata* var. *nana*, dot the ground with tiny yellow stars.

Up in the rock garden, the cinquefoil, *Potentilla parvifolia* 'Gold Drop', sports ten to fifteen new flowers every day, and a few of the dwarf sedums still bear little bunches of rosy-red blossoms.

Next to the waving plumes of the zebra grass, the blazing star, *Liatris scariosa*, is covered with its white and fluffy disklike flowers. It's an odd plant since the blooming begins at the top and proceeds down the stem as opposed to the reverse procedure of most other plants.

Obviously the garden is far from over . . .

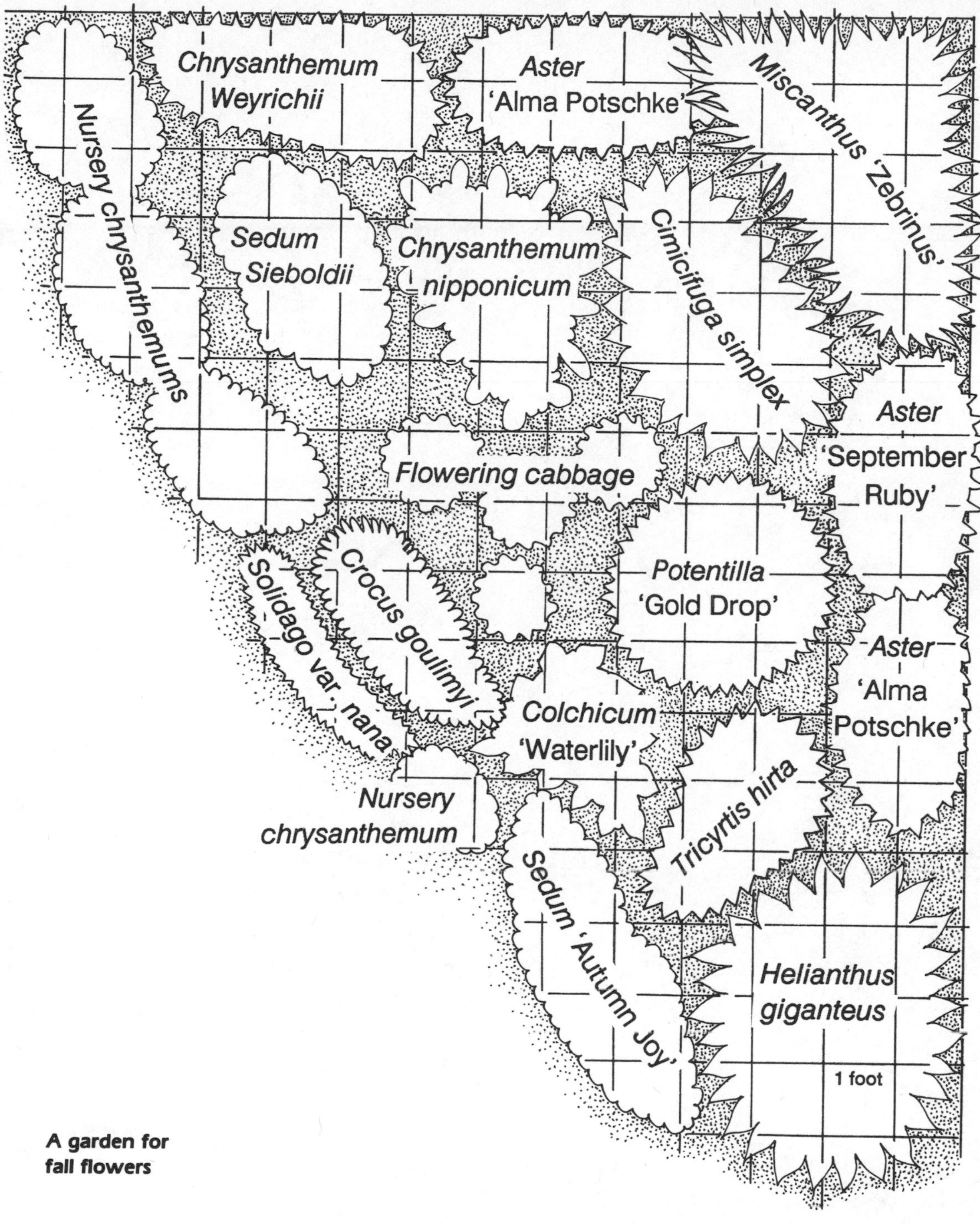

Nursery chrysanthemums

Chrysanthemum Weyrichii

Aster 'Alma Potschke'

Miscanthus 'Zebrinus'

Sedum Sieboldii

Chrysanthemum nipponicum

Cimicifuga simplex

Aster 'September Ruby'

Flowering cabbage

Potentilla 'Gold Drop'

Solidago var. nana

Crocus goulimyi

Aster 'Alma Potschke'

Colchicum 'Waterlily'

Nursery chrysanthemum

Tricyrtis hirta

Sedum 'Autumn Joy'

Helianthus giganteus

1 foot

A garden for fall flowers

A Garden is a lovesome thing, God wot;
  Rose plot,
Fringed pool,
  Ferned grot,
The veriest school of Peace;
And yet the fool
  Contends that God is not in gardens.
Not in gardens! When the eve is cool!
  Nay, but I have a sign.
'Tis very sure God walks in mine.
                Thomas Edward Brown, My Garden, 1830–97

From the gardener's point of view, November can be the worst month of all. Nature is winding down for the winter ahead. The air is cold, skies are gray, but usually the final mark of punctuation to the year has yet to arrive—the snow; snow that covers all in the garden and marks a mind-set for the end of a year's activity. There is little to do outside except to wait for longer days in the new year and the joys of the coming holidays.

Flowers in the Greenhouse

Many of the flowers blooming in the greenhouse are plants that other gardeners either had no room for or didn't want to be bothered with—yet they hated to see the plants wasted. The shrimp plant, for example, came from the local garden club president and the budding Thanksgiving cactus was the gift of an old gardening friend who claimed her own greenhouse was so crowded there wasn't even room for any pests. But as the days get shorter and the nights get colder, the sparkling color of these flowers, whether they have been grown from seed by my own hand or are orphans from the world outside, are welcome.

Left, pearly everlastings shed their feathery seeds in a November wind. The flowers are excellent in winter bouquets.

The Swamp Lilies

The genus is *Crinum* (from the Greek *krinon*, a lily) and the flowers are large and beautiful on 2- to 3-foot stems. They continue to bloom over several weeks.

A number of the crinums can be grown outdoors in a frost-free climate where they bloom in late spring or more usually in late summer and fall, but luckily most of us can enjoy these plants indoors when the outdoors is too inhospitable. Only one swamp lily will dependably bloom in November and that is *C. amabile* (sometimes called *C. superbum*). A native of Sumatra, the bulb is about 3 inches in diameter and the straplike dark green leaves reach 3 feet in length and about 4 inches wide. It bears between 20 and 30 very fragrant flowers, each between 3 and 4 inches long, bright red outside and lighter within.

To enjoy flowers in November, begin preparing the bulbs in March. As with an amaryllis, use a pot that is 1-inch larger than the diameter of the bulb. Once it's been planted, leave the bulb alone for up to five years. Use a mix of potting soil, sharp sand, peat moss, and composted or dehydrated cow manure, one-quarter each. Set the bulb in place with its neck above the soil level and give this jungle plant the heat it craves by putting the pot on a heating cable or in a warm spot while growth starts. As growth continues keep up with the watering and fertilize once a month. Crinums want partial shade in the summer but all the sun they can get in the late fall and winter. Temperatures of 65° to 70°F are perfect.

Keep the soil evenly moist while flowers are present. After blooming is finished, cut back on the water but not completely since this plant is evergreen and if allowed to dry out will go into complete dormancy taking more than a year to flower again.

If you have a spot for a plant that takes a great deal of room, try *Crinum asiaticum*, the grand crinum or the Asiatic poison bulb. The rather ominous name refers to the poison lycorine, a chemical present both in the leaf and the bulb that can cause nausea and persistent stomach upset. I've only seen one plant in an upstate New York collection where it summered outside and wintered in a warm conservatory and bloomed almost continuously. The problem is that a mature plant is big: leaves are 4 feet long and 5 inches wide and the bulb itself is up to a foot in length. The flowers are very fragrant, white with red stamens, and bloom in clusters of 20 or more on a 2-foot stalk. If you decide to share space with this crinum, cultural directions are the same as with *C. amabile*.

Swamp lily

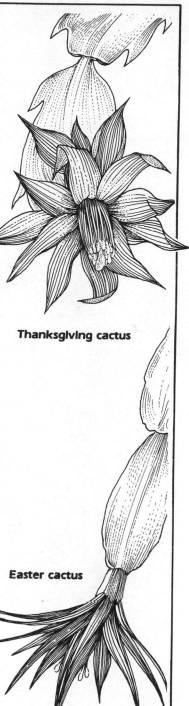

Heliotrope from the Garden

After the heliotrope blooms in the garden all summer, bring it indoors to continue the display in a sunny window. Inside the flowers will beguile you with the same scent that is favored by the perfume industry. *Heliotropium* (from the Latin to turn towards the sun) is the genus usually found in cultivation and it originally came from Peru.

Pot up the outdoor plant about two weeks before the last frost, keep it outdoors in partial shade for ten days or so, then bring it indoors to a sunny window. Use potting soil, peat moss, and sand, one-third each. Keep the soil evenly moist. Pinch the plant back and by late October it will begin to bloom again. To grow a heliotrope into a standard or tree form, see the instructions for lantana on page 77.

The Shrimp Plant

The shrimp plant is aptly named. In full bloom it resembles an explosion of prawns. The genus is *Justica* (named for James Justice, a Scottish botanist), but most books still call it *Beloperone*. If given full sun both in the winter window and the summer garden, the plant will bloom almost continuously.

The true flowers are scarcely visible as they are hidden by overlapping bracts of a rosy-brown edged with yellow, which resemble the shell of a prawn or shrimp.

Soil should be a mix of equal parts potting soil and peat moss and allowed to dry between waterings. Eventually the mother plant will become too big, especially if left outdoors for the summer, so taking cuttings is a good way to keep the mother in shape and add more plants to your collection. When about 8 inches high pinch these young plants started from cuttings at the tips to encourage branching.

Thanksgiving cactus

Thanksgiving and Other Holiday Cactuses

There are three cactuses noted for holidays: the Thanksgiving cactus, the Christmas cactus, and the Easter cactus. *Schlumbergera* (in honor of Frederick Schlumberger, an amateur student of plants) is the genus for the Thanksgiving and Christmas cactus with *S. truncata* blooming to accompany turkey and *S. Bridgesii* bursting forth for the yuletide. *Rhipsalidopsis* (resembling the plant *Rhipsalis*) *Gaertneri* is the Easter cactus.

Easter cactus

In nature these cactuses all grow in the crevices of tree branches, up in the air like many orchids and bromeliads, enjoying very little soil or natural fertilizer, just the detritus washed down the bark by the rain. In your home they need roughly the same conditions: a pot

Christmas cactus

large enough to hold the shallow root systems, and a mix of potting soil liberally laced with peat moss or shredded sphagnum moss plus some sharp sand. Even osmunda fibers, the growing medium for orchids, will work well with these plants.

Hang the cactuses outdoors in the spring, in the shade of a porch or tree, and bring them inside before the first frost. During the summer, give them plant food every two weeks or so and water well if rains are sparse.

Once back indoors, keep the plants in a sunny window. For the Thanksgiving and Christmas cactuses, withhold water until buds form, keeping close to a temperature between 55° and 60°F. After blooming withhold water again for two months. The Christmas cactus is a short-day plant (meaning buds form when daylight is less than 11 hours). Given temperatures of 55° to 60°F from mid-September on, buds should appear in four to five weeks. For the Easter cactus keep watering until December and then stop until spring. At the same time give plants a cool period of 50°F for the winter months to get the best crop of flowers.

Cineraria for Blatant Bloom

Cinerarias are quite beautiful pot plants with brightly colored blossoms that are often found flowering at nursery centers and florist shops, especially around Mother's Day. The genus is *Senecio* (from the Latin word *senex*, an old man, and used by Pliny to describe the white hairs often attached to the seeds), and the species is usually termed x *hybridus* because of the many hybrid forms of this flower. Some catalogs list this plant as S. *cruentus*.

These are cool house plants happy only with temperatures between 45° and 55°F, so if you keep your house up in the 70s and have no cool windows, don't bother with cinerarias. But if you do meet their needs for cool temperatures, you'll be rewarded by spectacular bloom. According to the cultivar you start with, plants reach heights between 1 and 3 feet with tightly packed flowerheads of 2-inch-wide flowers, white to reddish pink, blue, or purple, never yellow, and some with contrasting rings.

Start seeds in May, August, and September in order to have a succession of bloom. Use sphagnum moss or a sterile growing mix, do not cover the seeds (they need light to germinate), and maintain a temperature of 70°F during germination, which takes 10 to 15 days. After the seedlings show their true leaves, transplant them to individual 3-inch peat pots and keep them out of direct sun. As the plants outgrow the pots move them to larger containers but stop at 6-inch pots; plants that are potbound bloom with more vigor.

If you have a shaded cold frame move the plants outside for the summer months. Before frost threatens bring them back to a greenhouse or a cool window with temperatures of 50°F. Be careful not to overwater the plants. Cineraria will bloom six months after sowing. Once the flower show is done discard the plants; they never do as well in subsequent bloomings.

Bouvardias

Bountiful Bouvardias

Bouvardias are woody plants from Central America that bear showy terminal clusters of tubular, four-lobed flowers that bloom throughout the year but concentrate the heaviest flowering in fall and winter. The genus *Bouvardia* (in honor of Dr. Charles Bouvard, 1572–1658) is known for two species: B. *longflora,* or the sweet bouvardia because the flowers are intensely fragrant in the evening and B. *ternifolia,* the scarlet trompetilla. The flower colors available are white (these were once very popular for wedding bouquets), scarlet-red, and rose-pink.

In the latitude of New York State, both species flower almost continuously but produce the maximum bloom in November. The minimum temperature for bouvardias when grown indoors is 60°F. That temperature works in conjunction with the short days of fall to initiate budding. Later in the winter, cut back the plants and give them a rest until spring. Then let them spend the summer outdoors where they need maximum sun. Soil should be a good potting soil and peat moss, half and half. Water well when the plants are in growth and bloom. To propagate take cuttings in February when you cut back the plants.

Flower Feature: The Beautiful Oxalis

I've had a soft spot in my heart for oxalis every since I began growing my first houseplants. Their soil demands are relatively minor; potting soil, peat moss, and sharp sand, one-third each, are perfect for all the oxalis. They prefer temperatures around 60°F, regular watering while in bloom (but let the soil dry in between), and reduced watering when flowering is over. Then as the leaves wither, let the plants dry completely and store them in a cool place for about three months until you're ready for another period of bloom. This routine is hardly demanding and the reward, measured in cheery flowers, is certainly great. The plants also have an interesting habit: both the flowers and the leaves close up in dull weather and at night.

There are a number of species in the *Oxalis* genus (from the Greek for sharp and pungent referring to the sap) particularly suited for growing in the house and providing flowers for the winter.

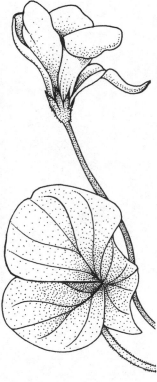

Oxalis adenophylla is hardy outdoors in Zone 6 south and often grown for the rock garden, where it blooms from May to July. But since it's from Chile, it can be adapted to producing flowers indoors during our winter months. *O. adenophylla* grows about 5 inches high with pink to purple flowers. When flowering is over, lift the bulbs and store them in a cool, dry place, then pot them up in September and start watering for winter bloom.

Oxalis Bowiei is a native of Cape Province and willing to bloom in our indoor gardens during the fall and on into winter, if dormant bulbs are watered in September. The flowers are large and pink and the leaves are downy.

Oxalis braziliensis has flowers of rose-purple, hails from Brazil, and needs the same care described for *O. Bowiei*.

Oxalis Deppei, the good-luck leaf, hails from Mexico, bearing large leaves like giant shamrocks and rosy-red flowers. There is also a white-flowered form.

Oxalis flava, from South Africa, is a slow-growing plant bearing large trumpet-shaped flowers of white, yellow, or sometimes violet and unusual five-fingered leaves, both unfurling in winter.

Oxalis hedysaroides 'Rubra', or fire fern, is a tree-type oxalis that produces a "trunk" rather than a low mound of foliage. The flowers are yellow and the leaves are a brilliant red color.

Oxalis hirta has a large bulb with branching and trailing stems up to a foot long. The flowers are a glowing purple, sometimes white, or rarely yellow. It blooms in November and December.

Oxalis incarnata, from southwest Africa, blooms in winter with white flowers ½-inch long that are tinged with lavender-pink.

The heart-shaped leaves are deeply notched.

Oxalis melanostricta is another South African plant, low and bushy, with dense foliage, each leaf covered with soft gray hairs that glisten in the sun. The flowers are yellow. The dormant period for this plant is two months in the summer, but the foliage should be kept going as long as possible to promote new buds for the most luxuriant bloom.

Oxalis Ortgiesii is another tree oxalis reaching 1½ feet in height. The flowers are yellow with darker veins. It needs the same care as *O. adenophylla*.

Oxalis peduncularis is an evergreen tree-type up to 2 feet high. From Ecuador and Peru, the plants produce dense clusters of orange-yellow flowers on long stalks, almost continuously.

Oxalis Pes-caprae, or the Bermuda buttercup, is termed a weed in Florida but produces winter bloom with nodding bell-shaped, bright yellow flowers up to 1½ inches across.

Oxalis purpurea, or the Grand Duchess oxalis, bears bright green, cloverlike leaves and showy pink flowers with yellow throats that are often 2 inches across. Flowers first appear in November but it will bloom well into winter.

Oxalis Regnellii comes from Peru and Brazil and bears white flowers almost continuously. Unlike the other members of the oxalis clan, keep this plant evenly moist. If you let up on the watering, this plant will go into dormancy. This plant is often offered by mail-order nurseries as the "Lucky Giant Shamrock, Everblooming!"

Oxalis rubra 'Alba' is discussed in May.

Oxalis valdiviensis is a perennial often grown as an annual since it will flower the first year from seed. The blossoms, appearing in long stalked clusters, bear bright yellow petals striped with brown on the inside.

Oxalis vulcanicola, or the red velvet shamrock, is an excellent basket plant with red stems and leaves topped by yellow blossoms all year-round. This plant needs plenty of sun to keep its colors bright.

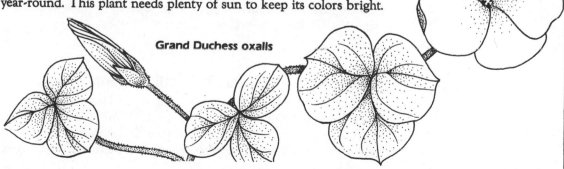

Grand Duchess oxalis

Right, the flowers in the drawing are freesias. Even a few open blossoms will perfume an entire room.

The Fragrant Freesia

I was introduced to freesias (named in honor of Elias Magnus Fries, a Swedish botanist) by the grower in one of our local greenhouses on a day when sleet was pummeling the glass roof with the sound of gravel falling from heaven. We marched past hundreds of pots of Easter lilies, just starting into bud for the approaching holiday, when I noticed a rich, sweet aroma. We walked over to pots of very tall leaves held up by corsets of string and a number of sprays of nodding waxy yellow flowers. Most had already been cut for floral bouquets, but the few that were left perfumed the entire greenhouse.

Freesias (*Freesia × hybrida*) are very easy to grow for winter bloom. The only requirements are a place where temperatures of 50° to 55°F can be maintained as the roots develop and bright light when the leaves and flowers emerge.

In August plant 10 to 12 corms (a root that resembles a bulb but isn't) in an 8-inch pot, using a light potting mix made of soil, sharp sand, and peat moss in equal amounts. Cover them with 2 inches of soil. Water well and leave them alone in that cool and dim place for about ten days. Then as the leaves develop, move the pots to a sunny but cool window (60°F) and stake the plants with canes and string (see illustration). They grow so tall that they will flop over if not supported.

Normal corms will bloom about four months after growth is initiated. Precooled corms take about 12 weeks to bloom. After blooming is over, let the leaves mature and dry down naturally. Then store the pots in a greenhouse or an outdoor cold frame so the corms ripen over the summer to reuse the following fall.

Besides the usual corms, you can also start freesias from seed. Flowers will bloom within six months of sowing seed. For winter bloom start the seeds in early May using 30 seeds for each square foot of soil mix and cover the seeds with a sprinkling of sand.

No matter whether you're using corms or seeds, look for the following cultivars: 'Florida', pure pink; 'Ballerina', pure white; and 'Safari', with buttercup-yellow flowers.

Outdoors: The Garden Still Blooms

There is often a touch of snow in the air on Election Day, but the flakes usually melt before they hit the ground. Even though every day seems to be darker and the ground sparkles with hoarfrost each morning, there are still flowers in the garden, blooming in defiance of the season.

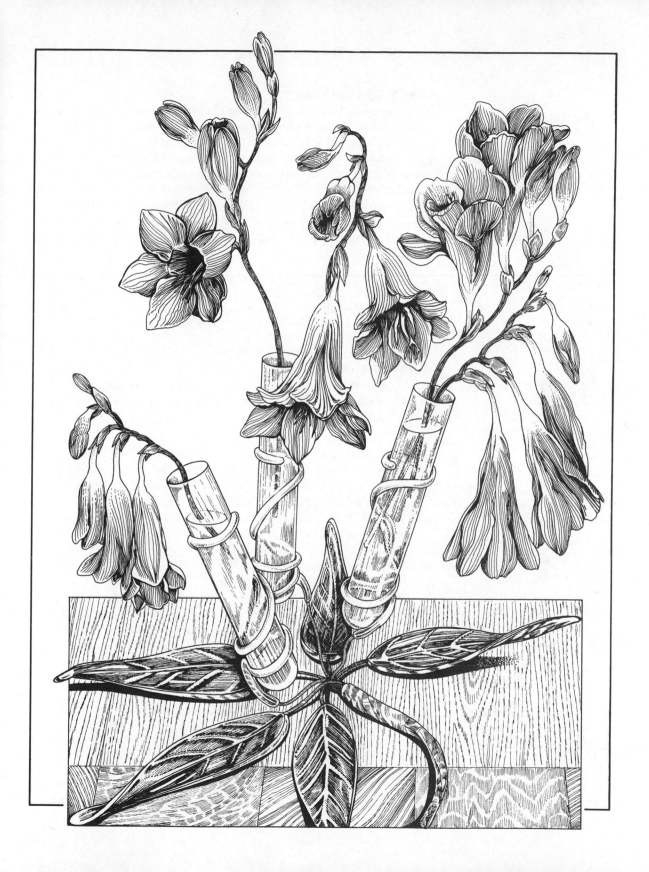

Pearly Everlasting

If you had been fortunate enough to plant a clump of this attractive wildflower last summer, it would now be evident as a white bouquet shining in the midst of your garden, unharmed by rains or frost, and waiting for the coming mantle of snow. For the petals of pearly everlasting have the ability to dry like tough paper and remain forever pure and durable.

There are two schools of thought on this everlasting quality. Neltje Blanchan (whom we have met before with the closed gentian) obviously was not very enamored of the flower:

> "An imaginary blossom that never fades has been the dream of poets from Milton's day; but seeing one, who loves it? Our [flower] has the aspect of an artificial [bloom]—stiff, dry, soul-less, quite in keeping with the decorations on the average farmhouse mantelpiece—a wreath about flowers made from the lifeless hair of some dear departed."

James Edward Smith in his book of English botany held quite a different opinion:

> "This flower, from its purity and durability, is an elegant emblem of immortality and is a common favorite in cottage gardens . . . where it is most beautiful."

So, as with most things in this world, there are two ways of looking at the longevity of the pearly everlasting.

I like the flower, not only in the garden but in those dried arrangements for the winter table. The petals are really modified leaves. The true flowers are the tiny yellow or brown florets in the center of each blossom. The stems are covered with a cottony substance meant to keep wandering ants from stealing the nectar intended only for small bees and flies. Flower heads were once used as the ingredients of expectorants in treating colds, but this seems to have been out of favor for the last 80 years.

Winter heath

This wildflower belongs to the genus *Anaphalis* (a Greek name for another everlasting flower). The familiar flower of American fields is A. *margaritacea*. A more genteel type from the Himalayas is shorter in stature and called A. *triplinervis*. Clumps are easily divided and moved but it's best to do so in early spring. The attractive gray-green leaf color of both species adds a nice touch to the summer garden long before the blossoms appear.

Both A. *margaritacea* and A. *triplinervis* will do well in full sun and average garden soil. They are very drought resistant and hardy from Zone 3 and up. Once planted they can be left alone for years.

A Winter Heath

Outside the shorter days and gray skies of late autumn cast a pall on the landscape, and something cheerful is needed to liven up the garden. The genus *Erica* (from the Greek for heath) provides a number of plants that will bloom from early winter on into late spring. But the only plant that I've found successful in our Zone 5 climate is the cultivar *Erica carnea* 'King George'. Most of the heaths like a well-drained and acid soil, and this plant is no exception. If you want winter flowers, find it a sheltered spot away from the worst winds.

The buds of rose magenta begin to form in early autumn and color up with the first frosts. The flowers remain through the winter, happy here under the snow. If the weather forecasters predict sleet, I try to cover this plant to keep the ice from ruining the flowers.

Witch Hazel

Hamamelis is the name and winter-blooming is the game. The botanical name is from the Greek for a pear-shaped fruit and it seems a shame there is no reference to the yellow flowers that decorate the winter landscape like furled shreds of crepe paper.

My problem with this plant involves the deer: They have never allowed a fancy witch hazel to survive, so the only such specimens in our garden are the native American species, *Hamamelis virginiana*, situated at the edge of the woods where the other trees get in the animals' way. These plants are really large shrubs instead of small trees—they rarely top 15 feet in height—and consistently bloom in the early part of November, their yellow blossoms looking as though they were pinned to the branches. The leaves turn a fine yellow-tan before falling. This species is not as attractive as the others in the clan but welcome to us because of the spots of color it adds to bleak November. There are many such groves of these shrubs in our area because the early farmers would distill the bark to make the witch hazel used for its medicinal properties. Another native is *Hamamelis vernalis*, a large shrub found from Oklahoma south to Louisiana. The plants are 5 to 6 feet tall, and bear orange and fragrant flowers around January in Zone 6.

Hamamelis japonica, which comes from Japan, can reach a height of 30 feet and blooms in late winter to early spring. *Hamamelis mollis* comes from Western China and blooms about the same time. There are a number of cultivars developed from *H. japonica* and *H. mollis* called *H. × intermedia* that usually bloom in January and February in the Northeast.

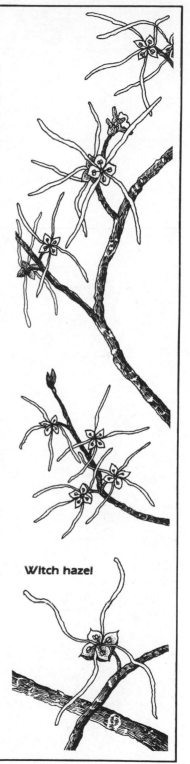

Witch hazel

All the witch hazels are easy to grow. They will do well in any average garden soil in full sun but prefer a moist spot.

Winter-Flowering Camellias

My camellias do not bloom outside; the amazing plant breeders have yet to develop one of these magnificent flowers that will take a Zone 5 climate though research horticulturists are working on it. According to Milton H. Brown writing for *Organic Gardening*, trials going on at Longwood Gardens in Pennsylvania, have produced fall-flowering cultivars: 'Snow Flurry' that is hardy to -12°F and 'Pink Icicle' that withstands −5°F. Unfortunately, these plants are still in the development phase and not yet available on the market. Until northern gardeners can buy these hardier camellias, there's really little point to growing these plants outdoors; even when some shrubs survive, the frosts of the Northeast generally blast the flowers before they can open.

But just because some of us are denied these blossoms there is no reason for those gardeners from Zone 7 and south not to partake of their beauty. Camellias need an acid soil that contains peat moss and sand to provide the evenly moist but not wet conditions that these plants require. Where humidity is low, they need a lightly shaded spot. Use a mulch to provide the steady moisture that they relish. (Camellias grown indoors are the Flower Feature in February.)

Garden Plan: Outside in the Winter Garden

The only time that imagination tinges my garden descriptions is the season when snow falls and winter storms rage. During the growing season it's easy to ignore geographic differences when writing about roses, hostas, and daylilies from the point of view of a gardener in North Carolina or in Illinois (and the same holds true for describing the flowers of spring). Easy comparisons can be made of flowers blooming in the heat of July whether it's in Manhattan, Fort Lauderdale, or Reno: What's the difference between 92° and 98°F? They're both terribly uncomfortable.

But degrees of cold are something else again. The geographic variations of winter's cold can make a significant difference in what grows where. Many plants that will survive 10°F will quickly fail with just a fall of five degrees, not to mention the additional stress associated with wind chills. These factors combine to make it tricky to describe a winter garden that does well in my part of the country while also being suited to other locales.

So unlike the other plans in this book, I cannot guarantee that my winter garden will succeed in an area with temperatures that fall below −25°F or that it will produce the same colors in another part of the country that it displays here in November.

A Stroll Through the Garden

We enter the winter garden in late November. Although it's still autumn by the calendar, for all practical purposes, it's winter in the mind.

First I pass a large multiflora rose bush, *Rosa multiflora*, that has been growing in the same spot for over 20 years. Although the blooming period in late spring is brief, we keep the bush because of the orange hips that literally cover the bare branches well into January when they are finally consumed by the birds.

Behind the rose is a mass of American bittersweet, *Celastrus scandens*, chided by some gardeners as being overly rampant but kept in bounds here by cutting it back. But how beautiful are the berries, bright orange with scarlet wrappings, that cover the twining vines.

Next on my right, as we walk down the browned grass path that extends between the borders, there is a giant clump of eulalia grass, *Miscanthus sinensis*, its 12-foot high stems now sporting waving brown leaves and topped by silver plumes of the seed heads, blooms that will persist until the following spring.

Falling over the edge of the stone scree bed are the clambering branches of the rock cotoneaster, *Cotoneaster horizontalis*, covered from base to tip with glowing red berries, a color almost ready to clash with the pink-magenta blossoms of the heath, *Erica carnea* 'King George'. Above them both are the spirally twisted branches of Harry Lauder's walking stick, *Corylus avellana* 'Contorta', bare now but in early spring festooned with yellow catkins that will look like ornaments hung upon the stems.

Opposite the scree bed is a low stone wall that in summer marks the edge of a bed full of lamb's-ear, *Stachys byzantina* (even now their woolly leaves are still in evidence). Along the bottom edge of the wall is a line of ebony spleenwort, *Asplenium platyneuron*, green and glossy still and remaining so well into winter. A Christmas rose, *Helleborus niger*, that will never bloom but still produce marvelous foliage, shares space with the spleenwort.

Nearby is a mound of *Sedum* 'Autumn Joy', its flowerheads now the color of burned mahogany but remaining until the following spring. Behind it is a clump of the eye-catching, red-stemmed

American bittersweet

Right, a garden in winter begins in most areas by mid-November. The backyard pictured contains (1) teasels; (2) gloriosa daisy heads; (3) rose hips; (4) red-stemmed dogwood; (5) eulalia grass; (6) a rhododendron; (7) Harry Lauder's walking stick; (8) a dwarf Alberta spruce; (9) a weeping birch; (10) *Sedum* 'Autumn Joy'; (11) maiden grass; (12) a gray birch.

Siberian dogwood, *Cornus alba* 'Siberica', generally nondescript in the spring and summer but making up for it when the leaves fall.

At the edge of the woods, clumps of pearly everlasting, *Anaphalis margaritacea*, its papery-white blossoms waving in a quickening wind, stand out against the darkness of the gathering night. That same wind also rustles the yellow blossoms of the witch hazel, *Hammamelis virginiana*, and the papery seed pods of the golden-rain tree, *Koelreuteria paniculata*, pods that look fragile, but will last into early spring.

It's getting colder now and the weakening rays of the setting sun have made a band of orange along the horizon. It's time to go back inside to the fire and think about the long winter to come.

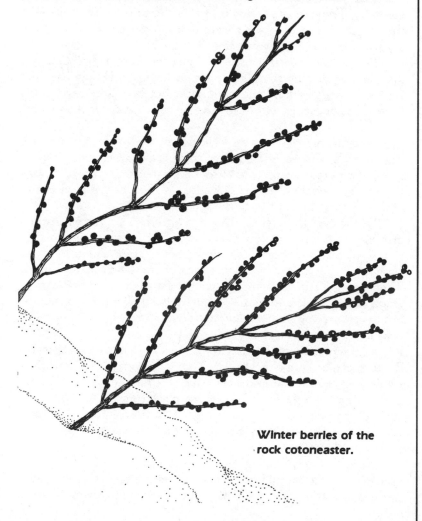

Winter berries of the rock cotoneaster.

Between the time the garden is finally blanketed for Winter and that fateful day in January when the first catalogs arrive, comes a lull. Some people get as far away from their gardens as they possibly can. The rest of us, destined to take life as it comes, either fiddle around with house plants . . . or retreat into the past. Personally I prefer to retreat. I draw a date for deadline and swear that I'll not read any gardening books written after that particular date. These dates serve the same purpose that strings dividing the lawn into blocks serve when She and I have a dandelion slaughter —they keep us from straying.
Richardson Wright, *Another Gardener's Bed-Book*, 1933

I too, retreat; when mid-December rolls around and the crush of Christmas and the holidays are upon us, I forget about the garden for awhile. Unfortunately many of the nursery catalogs now arrive in December, attempting to speed up the season so that Richardson Wright's January postal appearances are a thing of the past. But I persevere, and aside from watering houseplants, forget about all things green except the Christmas tree—at least until the 27th of the month.

Winter's Light

Plants that flower indoors in winter must contend with the lower light levels of the season. The position of the sun in the sky accounts for this lower light intensity but a number of things contribute to dull winter light in homes as well. If wood is burned for heat, a thin film of smoke builds up on windows; shades drawn to conserve heat cut the light; a continual layer of dust sticks to windows with static electricity; smoking creates a toxic haze that films the glass; storm windows filter light; and finally, cloudy days further diminish the available light.

Left, **Christmas roses bloom in the early winter. Their delicate blossoms are hardier than they appear but unfortunately not hardy in my garden.**

You can get an idea of the light intensity your plants are receiving by using the exposure meter on a regular camera to measure footcandles (FC, the amount of light cast on a white surface by one candle, one foot away, in anotherwise dark room). Set the film speed to ASA 200, the shutter speed to 1/500th of a second, and adjust the f-stop until the meter is correctly set for picture taking. The following list gives footcandles that correspond with f-stop readings:

f22 = 5,000 FC	f8 = 550 FC
f16 = 2,500 FC	f6.3 = 300 FC
f11 = 1,200 FC	f4.5 = 150 FC

Plants that need full sun, such as most cactuses and flowering annuals, generally require 6,000 to 8,000 FC. Ferns, most begonias, and many jungle-born houseplants prefer partial shade or an average of 2,000 FC. Deep jungle dwellers like 250 to 500 FC. Many plants will survive 20 FC for a few weeks, but 100 FC seems to be the minimum needed for growth and sustaining life.

In addition to the other reasons for diminished light, windows also lose light through outside refraction of the glass and the fact that some light is actually absorbed by the glass itself. Architectural details like eaves and cornices mean the loss of more light. A west window in midmorning may read 400 FC at the inside sill, but only 10 FC when measured 6 feet into the room, while outdoors the light will be 10,000 FC. A thin layer of dust on the tops of houseplant leaves further cuts down on the light received, so remember to dust your plants right along with books and tabletops. While 50 FC is enough light for reading a newspaper, it's hardly enough to keep a plant alive, much less healthy.

Care of Blooming Christmas Plants

Receiving a blooming plant for Christmas and the holidays is always a special treat. But often the florist forgets to include a tag on proper care, so I've included the following hints for your information.

Amaryllis:
See page 3.

Azaleas
These plants, a species of *Rhododendron*, are evergreen hybrids that have been forced to bloom for winter and spring holidays by the florist. When you receive the plant, put it in a cool spot with good, indirect light; if all you have is a sunny window then use it but be forewarned that winter sun will shorten flower life (it won't hurt the

plant). Azaleas will endure heated rooms but should be moved every night to an area where temperatures do not exceed 60°F. Keep the soil evenly watered since these plants have very fine and wiry roots that crave moisture. Remove faded blossoms. Later in the spring, when all chance of frost is over, summer these plants outside in a sheltered spot and fertilize once a month continuing into the fall, with an acid-type plant food. Then cut back on water—but don't allow the soil to dry out—and place the azalea in a cool spot of about 50°F. When buds have set, move the azalea into a warmer place. When a plant outgrows its original pot, repot using a mix of potting soil and peat moss, one-half each.

Cyclamen:
See page 8.

Christmas pepper:
See page 220.

Jerusalem cherry

Jerusalem cherry

This gift plant (*Solanum Pseudocapsicum*), if given proper care, will go on for years, eventually forming a small bush about 4 feet high. One word of warning: The cherries—really a variety of tomato—contain solanine, a chemical with little toxicity in adults but one that causes serious, sometimes fatal, digestive difficulties with children.

These plants prefer bright windows with filtered sun and temperatures no higher than 70°F during the day and 50° to 60°F at night. Keep the soil evenly moist and used a mix of potting soil and sand, one-half each. Put the plants outside in summer with some light shade at noon. Fertilize every two or three weeks and prune branches to half their length in early spring. When brought back indoors, plants need cool temperatures of 50°F for about two weeks to aid in forming buds.

African Violets

For years I thought of African violets as fussy plants more at home with little, elderly ladies who crocheted antimacassars (Macassar was a proprietary name of a brand of hair oil) and drank the weakest of herb teas while comparing floral notes, then my living room. Well, I was wrong.

Last year I tried two pots of these florific members of the genus *Saintpaulia* (in honor of Baron Walter von Saint Paul-Illaire, 1860–1910, who discovered *S. ionantha*) and was amazed at the results.

My pots of *Saintpaulia ionantha* began blooming in late November and continued for seven months until they stopped between June and July (due, I think, to the weak light they received in our living room). These stalwart bloomers began again last week after I moved them back to a window in the outside wall of the house. African violets will even bloom in a north window if they're moved to a brighter spot for occasional R and R, as long as the temperature doesn't fall below 60°F. In fact the only thing to watch out for is very bright sun, except in midwinter, when plants will need that light to provoke bloom.

For a soil mix I used potting soil, peat moss, and sharp sand, one-third each, and planted them in self-watering pots. African violets need evenly moist soil but not one that's wet. Feed plants once a month while they are active using a dilute fertilizer solution. Always use warm water since cold will damage the leaves.

For especially beautiful blossoms look for 'Dolly', a cultivar with ruffled white flowers accented by a pink edge; 'Alabama Improved', a striking white flower with blue edges; and 'Barbados', single dark blue flowers with a silvery-white edge.

The Sea Onion

Right, the plant in the drawing is a sea onion. Note the tiny flowers.

Some years ago, I received a gift from a houseplant aficionado; a green ball, 4 inches in diameter, with a slight depression that marked the top and a few dried roots that signified the bottom. The accompanying letter called the green aggie a climbing sea onion or *Bowiea volubilis* (in honor of J. Bowie, a plant collector for Kew gardens). "Plant it in a 5-inch pot," the gentleman said, "with a soil mix of good potting soil, humus, and sand, one-third each, placing the top half of the bulb above the soil line. Water after growth begins, and let the soil dry out between waterings. Growth will die back in late spring or fall depending on when you have started the plant. Keep temperatures above 50°F."

I did as directed and was soon rewarded by twining stems, tiny green flowers, and minuscule leaves represented by triangular flaps of green where a branchlet grows from the branch. In order to give the rampant vine a holdfast, I put its pot inside a woven basket from Japan. When the foliage starts to yellow and dry, I withhold water and give the bulb a rest for a few months.

Propagation is by seeds or offsets. A healthy bulb should eventually reach a diameter of 8 to 9 inches, with a corresponding increase in stem production.

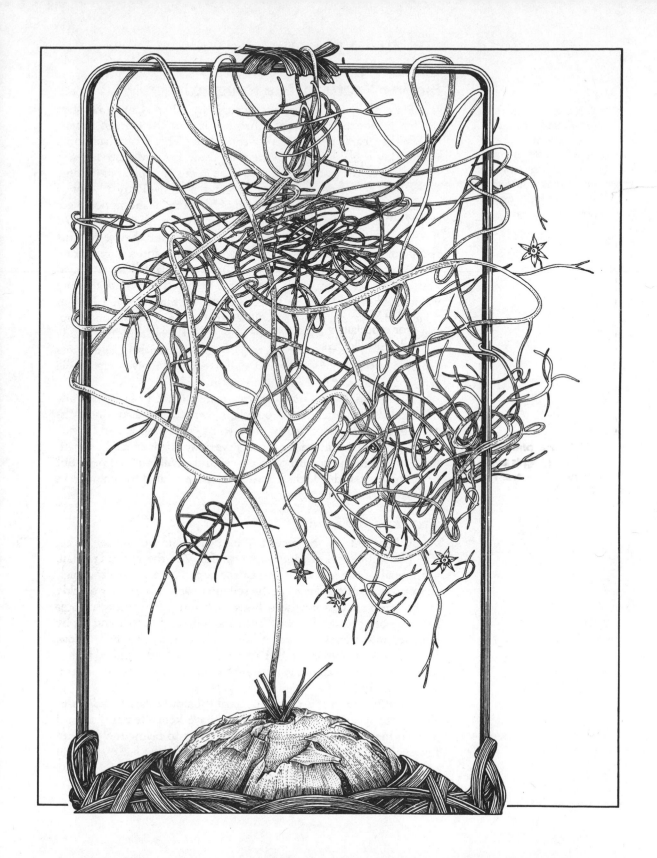

Flower Feature: The Poinsettia

Poinsettias, or as they are sometimes called, Christmas stars or Flor de Noche Buena, spell Christmas and the holidays to Americans more than any other year-end plant. That's not bad for a winter-flowering shrub that originally came from Mexico and was introduced to the trade about 1830. The genus is *Euphorbia* (a name given by Dioscorides to this plant and said by Pliny to honor Euphorbus, a physician to King Juba of Mauritania) and not only are they grown as potted plants for sale up North, they're also sold during early July in the Southern Hemisphere. And they're not just red anymore but come in various shades of pink and a pure white.

What we think of as petals are really specialized leaves called bracts that only masquerade as petals. The true flowers are the tiny yellow balls that cluster in the center of the bracts. If you look at them under a hand lens you will see that some are pistillate, or female, and others are staminate, or male. The flower tips often exude small beads of crystal-clear nectar. In tropical climates these plants assume the stature of shrubs and small trees, and if given reasonable care, they can grow to a large size even in the home.

Poinsettias, *Euphorbia pulcherrima,* are members of a large family of succulents that include the popular crown of thorns and snow-on-the-mountain, all identified by their white, milky sap, called "latex." The sap has been blamed for causing everything from a mild dermatitis in susceptible people to outright death for children and pets. But in recent years, many medical authorities have refuted the poinsettia's reputation as a dangerous plant.

Care and Flowering

When you buy or receive your plant, remove the foil wrap. The pot will be full of roots so be careful with the watering detail, wetting all of the soil and not just the top. There is usually a high concentration of peat moss in the soil mixes and this can dry quickly in the warm air of a northern house in winter. If you forget water for a day or two and the plant begins to wilt, soak it, pot and all, by plunging into a bucket of water. Keep the plant in a sunny window, rotating it to maintain its full shape. Every month feed it with a liquid fertilizer. Keep temperatures around 65°F, and try to keep it away from cold drafts.

Continue with this treatment until the bracts start to fade, usually in late spring (I've had plants that have kept their bracts until July). When they finally go, prune the stems to below the point of flowering. Don't worry about the wounds dripping latex; they will

soon dry and heal. Repot the plant in a mix of potting soil, peat moss, and sharp sand, one-third each. Move the poinsettia outside as soon as all danger of frost is past. Water well, follow the fertilizer routine, and protect it from the searing midday sun in July and August—simply done by throwing a piece of Reemay (a spun-polyester material available in garden centers or catalogs) over the top. Bring the plants back indoors before the first frost.

With autumn's arrival the days will be getting shorter. This suits the poinsettias, which are short-day plants. They will not set buds or go into flowering unless they are exposed to days no longer than 12 hours and temperatures below 65°F. Cutting back on light is not a problem in the jungles where the plants originally were found, but it does present some difficulty in civilization: even as little as 1½ FC of light will impede bud formation. Commercial growers cover plants with black cloth to shut out the light (and a greenhouse full of poin-settias all covered with black shrouds is a strange sight indeed). In the home, use boxes or bags, or move the plant into a dark closet at day's end. Begin the dark treatment October 1. Once the buds are in evidence you can forget the blackouts.

The Winter-Blooming Kalanchoe

Bablana

There are a number of species in the genus *Kalanchoe* (the name comes from a favorite plant in China). But *K. Blossfeldiana*, originally from Madagascar, is known for its winter bloom and for being a short-day plant, which means it can be cajoled into blooming for Christmas. You can have flowers by visiting your local florist or by growing your own plants and giving them a very simple dark treatment in September.

Kalanchoe Blossfeldiana is a branching plant up to a foot high but usually sold in the guise of the cultivars 'Tom Thumb' and 'Compacta', both under 8 inches in height. These are favorite holiday plants because of the scarlet-red flowers that smother the plants in bloom, flowers that remain fresh for up to two months.

Daylength governs both the vegetative growth and the flowering periods with the normal time of flower-bud initiation stretching from September's end to the first week of October. Rooted cuttings will bloom after short-day conditions even if they only possess two leaves. If plants are limited to nine hours of light per day for the month of September flower buds will be set. To do this, drape the plant with black cloth, cover it with a paper bag, or tuck it in a closet for a few hours a day. Once buds are in evidence, the special treatments can cease.

Both seedlings and plants do best at temperatures of 60°F, making little or no growth at lower temperatures. Soil should be a blend of potting soil, peat moss, and sharp sand, one-third each. Water when the surface of the soil is dry.

Kalanchoe Manginii is a hanging basket plant with shiny leaves that bears orange-red flowers resembling little balloons, which cover the plants in the winter. *K. pumila* is another winter-blooming basket plant with silver-gray leaves covered with pink flowers on trailing stems.

Sweet Garlic and Society Garlic

The genus *Tulbaghia* (named for Ryk Tulbagh, Dutch governor of the Cape of Good Hope, who died in 1771) is represented by two species, both of which are excellent houseplants blooming most of the year indoors.

Pink agapanthus or sweet garlic, botanically known as *Tulbaghia fragrans*, is a herbaceous perennial with enlarged rhizomes rather than bulbs, dependably blooming from October through April. Straplike leaves an inch wide and about a foot long, surround 1½-foot stalks that bear clusters of small, star-shaped, pink and fragrant flowers. Plants need at least four hours of full sun and an evenly moist soil consisting of potting soil, peat moss, and sharp sand, one-third each. Temperatures should be 60°F or lower. Take plants outside to the patio during the summer where they'll enjoy filtered sunlight and feed them monthly.

Society garlic, *Tulbaghia violacea*, is a larger plant with leaves that smell of onion when bruised and flowers on a 2½-foot stalk, generally blooming from April to November. Give it the same care as described above for its cousin.

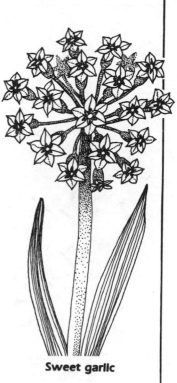

Sweet garlic

A Favorite Food for Baboons

South Africa is home to the genus *Babiana* (from the Dutch *babianer*, for baboon), which includes a number of species. *B. stricta* is the type usually found in catalogs and in plant stores. These fibrous-coated corms produce 1-inch wide, sweetly scented flowers in colors of crimson, yellow, rose, blue, violet, and white. There are usually 15 to 20 flowers on each 1-foot-tall stem.

Gardeners in very mild climates (Zone 8 and south) have the luxury of growing these flowers outside in the garden (Zone 7 gardeners stand a chance too, as long as plants are heavily mulched). For the rest of us, blooming will occur indoors.

For flowers inside start in September, planting five to six corms in a 4-inch pot using potting soil, peat moss, and sharp sand, one-third each. Cover the corms with 2 inches of soil mix. Water sparingly until growth begins, then never let the soil dry out until the foliage has withered and turned yellow. Give the plants at least four hours of sunlight a day and keep temperatures around 60° to 65°F. Fertilize babianas once a month while in active growth.

The Gardenia

A few flakes of snow are falling on this, the last night of the year. The snow won't last, for temperatures are too high and the thin clouds in the winter sky above are quickly blowing away. A rising moon makes everything look like an old engraving, but the barren landscape of brown trees and the barren earth below turns it into a sepia-tone mezzotint, not a study in black and white.

Yet in my study, one small white gardenia has opened, its perfume filling the room with thoughts of tropical nights and waving palms. The plant was a gift from a charming lady who lives down the road. She had cared for it over many years after it began its career as a small houseplant purchased at a local supermarket. Now it's a shrub, 4 feet in diameter and 4 feet high, occupying a 12-inch tub.

This particular gardenia is *Gardenia jasminoides* 'Veitchii' (named in honor of Dr. Alexander Garden of Charleston, South Carolina), often called the everblooming gardenia. Requirements are not taxing, except for a need of warmth: 60°F and up in winter and up to 80°F in summer. This plant will survive 52°F without damage, but is clear in its dislike, for leaves will turn yellow and drop if they are chilled. If the plant doesn't get temperatures of 60°F, buds will not form.

Gardenias need plenty of sunlight during the winter months and if possible, bright sun all summer. Every three weeks of active growth or flowering give them a dose of an acid fertilizer. Regular potting soil is excellent but should be cut in half with peat moss. Keep the soil moist since the roots are thin and fragile and will dry quickly without adequate water.

The Ornamental Pepper

The ornamental or Christmas pepper is a member of the edible pepper group, *Capsicum* (taken from *kapto*, to bite, a reference to the hot taste). Potted up, these plants are always popular for the Christmas and holiday seasons.

Start seeds in July and keep the young plants growing at a minimum temperature of 65°F. When a number of leaves are present, repot the seedlings to 4- or 5-inch pots. Use a soil mix of potting soil

Christmas pepper

and peat moss, one-half each. No pinching is necessary. Plants need full sun and should be fertilized only once a month. Keep the soil evenly moist.

The decorative peppers on *Capsicum annuum aurora* are about 4 inches long, begin as purple, turn tan, and then wind up a fiery red; C. 'Candelabra F1' produces crimson fruits, arranged in rows; and C. 'Red Missile' is an early-bearing type with multicolored, 1½-inch fruits that change from cream to orange, and finally red.

The Florist's Stevia

Locally, you might have to search a bit to find this plant, but at least one of the sources listed in the appendix will usually have it in stock. The botanical name is *Piqueria* (named for A. Piquer, a Spanish botanist of the 1700s) *trinervia*, and it's been used for ages as a dependable plant for late fall and winter flowering. Old references call it *Stevia serrata*. The plant is originally from Mexico and Central America. Blossoms are white, fragrant, and borne in clusters from the axils of lance-shaped and toothed leaves.

Flower buds form when the days shorten to about 13 hours. In New York State this occurs at the end of September. The normal time of bloom is December 1, if temperatures have been kept above 50°F. By placing the plants in a temperature below 50°F after the buds have formed, you can delay flowering, day by day, until you're ready.

Give the plants a mix of potting soil, peat moss, and sharp sand, one-third each. Temperatures during the winter should be between 65 and 70°F. Keep the soil evenly moist and provide plenty of winter sun, setting the plants outside for the summer in partial shade.

Florist's stevia

Outdoors: Winter Begins

Usually by mid-December the only time that I venture out into the garden is on the trip to and from the compost bins (they're located way at the end of the backyard) or when taking buckets of corn out to feed the deer. The latter chore is a continuing effort to prevent these destructive animals from entering the garden and chewing everything in sight. But other gardeners that I know—gardeners who live at the base of a mountain instead of half-way up the side like we do—receive less snow, endure less cold, and even have a few winter garden experiences to tell about.

So for those who live in a gentler climate than ours, I mention a few plants that bloom in time for the arrival of winter, and for those who don't, a suggestion that they decorate a live tree for Christmas rather than using, and then discarding, a dead tree.

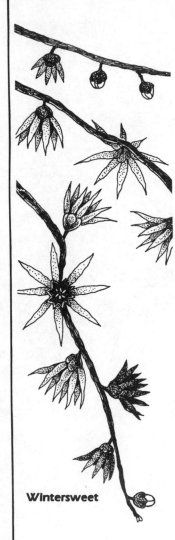

Wintersweet

A Living Christmas Tree

At holiday time what could be better to celebrate the end of one year and the beginning of another, than building your celebrations around a living Christmas tree? As the years pass by, memories will be far more than broken toys and fading greeting cards; in the yard, the remainders of pleasant times will stand fresh and green, season after season.

In autumn choose a spot for the tree before the ground begins to freeze. Call the nursery and discuss the type you wish to grow. The tree will be balled and burlaped, and the size of the hole will depend on the size and kind of tree you pick. Always dig the hole a little larger than you need.

Now put the excavated soil in plastic bags and store them in a warm spot. Cover the hole with a piece of plywood or the like.

When you pick up your tree, store it in a cool, sheltered place until the moment you're ready to bring it in to decorate. This tree should spend only the briefest time indoors, three to four days at most. Once inside don't put it near a radiator or any hot-air ducts in your house. Place the ball in a waterproof container like a galvanized tube and water every day. The root ball can never be allowed to dry out.

After Christmas, take the tree back to the garage or another cool spot for a few days. Then move it outdoors and place it in the waiting hole. Untie the burlap and pull it away from the trunk (the burlap will eventually rot and poses no threat to the roots). Water well and empty the bags of soil back into the hole. Mulch the tree and if the weather continues to be above freezing, water the tree every few days.

Wintersweet

I've never had luck with wintersweet, basically because our Zone 5 climate is just too cold. The second year in our garden the flowers appeared, but the temperature plunged and the flowers froze. But if you live in the southern part of Zone 6 or on into 7, *Chimonanthus* (from the Greek *Cheimon*, winter, and *anthos*, flower) or wintersweet is the shrub for you. Originally from China, *C. praecox* will form a mound of foliage up to 8 feet high, bearing 1-inch stemless and fragrant flowers of yellow in early winter and, as the climate warms, on into late winter. The farther north your garden, the more likelihood a sheltered position will be best. Any good garden soil will do. Plant the shrubs where they will bask in full sun. Pruning should be done in early spring.

Christmas Rose

Any book that deals with a year of flowers must mention a marvelous plant that is unfortunately always a failure in my backyard. Year after year I tried Christmas roses, in fact anything belonging to the genus *Helleborus* (from an old Greek name), and year after year they failed.

My misadventures were inspired by a quote from William Robinson's, *The English Flower Garden,* on the subject of *Helleborus:*

> "One of the most valuable classes of hardy perennials we have, as they flower in the open air when there is little else in bloom. They appear in succession from October till April beginning with the Christmas rose (*Helleborus niger*) and ending with the handsome crimson kinds."

That description fired me up and I purchased *Helleborus niger.* The leaves were nice; they lasted into the second winter and perished. I tried again, putting the plants in a well-sheltered spot away from winter winds and open to afternoon sun. Again, the plants lasted two winters, then were gone.

Since my plants never bloomed, for a description of the flowers I have to ture to M. M. Graff and her book, *Flowers in the Winter Garden:*

> "The flowers have an unearthly beauty, a matchless purity enhanced by a prominent fluff of yellow stamens. Some individuals are faintly tinted with pink or apple green, variations that add interest without altering the overall impression of crystalline whiteness."

I've never had the opportunity to enjoy these flowers in my own garden because of many bouts with very poor weather, but don't let my sad tale discourage you; for those readers in Zone 6 and south, who have a sheltered spot and a good deal of patience, try the Christmas rose.

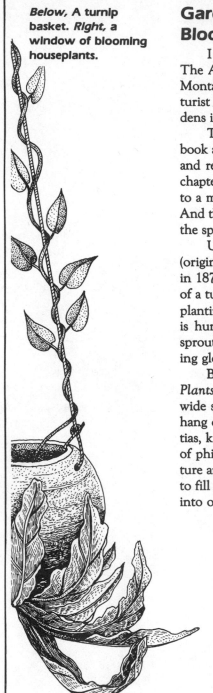

Garden Plan: A Window of Blooming Houseplants

I have a favorite book on houseplants that I bought in 1970 from The American Garden Guild. It's called *All About House Plants* by Montague Free and was written in 1946. Mr. Free was the horticulturist for the Brooklyn Botanic Garden, one of the finest public gardens in America.

Throughout the years I've written notes in various parts of the book and taped labels taken from packages of bulbs to the inside front and rear covers. For example, I tried—and forgot until writing this chapter—the hardy Chinese orchid, *Bletilla hyacinthia,* and according to a message I scrawled in the book in 1972, had reasonable success. And the Aztec lily, *Spekelia formoissiama,* bloomed in my window for the spring of 1974.

Upon rereading the preface, I rediscovered the turnip basket (originally taken from a book called *Window Gardening,* published in 1873). This marvelous affair is made by hollowing out the center of a turnip, starting at the root end, filling the hollow with soil, and planting morning-glory seed. After watering, the whole contraption is hung by cords from a bracket in a sunny window. The turnip sprouts leaves, which grow up to cover the vegetable, and the morning glories scamper up the cords.

But the thing that impresses me most about *All About House Plants* is the color photo used as a frontispiece. It is a window with a wide sill that looks out on a barren and leafless yard. Plain curtains hang on either side, and on the sill stand pots of blooming poinsettias, kalanchoes, cyclamen, a few pots of clambering ivies, long vines of philodendrons, and one Norfolk Island pine. It's a beautiful picture and any of the plants mentioned in this last chapter can be used to fill such a window in your own home and turn a white Christmas into one awash with color.

Appendix 1:
Great Spaces for
Growing Plants

My first houseplants were the result of living in Brooklyn in a railroad flat with two windows in the front that overlooked the street and two more windows in the back that surveyed narrow allies and tiny back yards, each usually having a patch of grass and some barbecue equipment. Since we lived on the third floor I was forced to concentrate my garden energies on the indoors. Within a few months the front windows were full of ferns hanging on hooks that seemed happy in the scant sunlight available from midmorning until just before noon.

When we moved to a Manhattan apartment the light was worse and the view took a corresponding drop in quality. The apartment was in such bad shape that the landlord did not object to my building a frame of wooden planks around the kitchen window, which luckily faced east. To this frame I attached an old storm window on hinges, to make what passed for a rough greenhouse. A large metal shade with a 70-watt bulb helped to improve the light, and the frame and storm window gave the plants some respite from the apartment's idiosyncratic steam heat system. Temperatures usually ran below 55°F at night (when the outside window was closed and the inside was left open) and often over 100°F during a typical winter's day (when the outside window was opened slightly and the inside was closed).

With such an installation we had plants all year long, plants to relieve the dull gray of the city streets by bringing us some semblance of green. But even if the landlord had forbidden my changes to the kitchen window and I had nothing more than a window sill, we still would have figured out a way to have flowers.

By the time we left Manhattan and moved to an old farm in upstate New York, I found that we had already built up a body of knowledge about plants from our experiences with our makeshift window in the city, and we were ready to move on to bigger and better things.

Expanding Your Plant Opportunities

Many of the indoor plants described in this book will succeed on a sunny or sometimes shady windowsill, but a number of the plants benefit from a good deal of sunlight and often require cooler temperatures than most readers would find comfortable for everyday living. Bulbs for forcing must have temperatures in the mid-40s to develop adequate root systems and many houseplants need the refreshment of cool evenings. To provide these optimal growing conditions, nothing can take the place of some kind of homemade greenhouse. A greenhouse enables you to expand your gardening horizons. You can broaden your experiences with flowering houseplants, experiment with propagating new plants from old, or try your hand at starting perennials from seed for your outdoor garden.

The following plans will show you how to build a variety of different greenhouses to fit a number of building requirements. One of them is sure to suit your situation.

My Window Greenhouse

To expand your plant collections and grow all that you can grow, nothing beats a greenhouse. And remember, such a glass house need not be 30 feet long or rival the hothouses of Kew. It can be made of everyday materials yet still be an attractive addition to your living room.

Our first bonafide window greenhouse was the result of an accident. The front door in our country farmhouse opens into a foyer with the house door on the left and the sunporch door to the right. When you enter the house proper you are in a small room with a greenhouse window on your left, a bench along the wall ahead for visitors and homeowners to sit on while removing winter boots, and a wall on the right lined with hooks that hold all the outer garments needed for a life in the country.

The greenhouse window was once a door that we decided to remove back in the mid-70s because the jamb was poorly built (the old timers were not always the consummate craftsmen we believe them to be) and the door was unnecessary.

A new window was slated to arrive on a Wednesday afternoon in November. Believing the lumber yard to be trustworthy, I tore out the door and rebuilt the frame to accept the new window, knowing that it would slip right in.

The window never came and that afternoon we had a storm of unbelievable magnitude with the clouds simply hosing down the water in direct streams and not even bothering with drops. Quickly

I stapled industrial plastic sheeting over the opening, and the lumber yard proceeded to search for the lost window.

Meanwhile I looked at that opening and thought of two large aluminum storm windows that we had yet to install in another part of the house. That cartoon electric light bulb turned on in my brain, and within a week we had our first window greenhouse.

The roof was shingled instead of glassed since the winter sun is so low in the sky we knew we could do without the extra light. The affair projected 18 inches out into the air, the two sides closed with narrower aluminum storm windows that the lumber yard agreed to rush to the site. The floor was marine plywood that I covered with black vinyl slate. Two sheets of acrylic in wooden frames were hinged to the inside of the frame and closed the greenhouse to the room during the winter. Finally the electrician installed an outlet under the window and I bought a small electric heater.

That window is now gone. We removed it when the sunporch was finished and the larger greenhouse completed. But it was the catalyst needed to throw me into a career that revolves around the plant world.

The following drawing gives the plan for that greenhouse window.

A window greenhouse

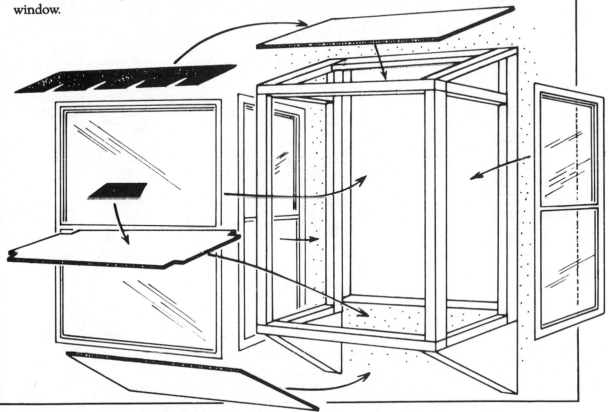

A one-sash window greenhouse

A One-Sash Window Greenhouse

The original wooden storm sashes or windows on many homes were two panes of glass in a frame that hung from two clips on the top of the window proper. By swinging that window out and adding a base plus two triangular sides, you can make a simple but effective home for plants that can easily be installed without disturbing the structure of the house.

A Basement Window Greenhouse

Anyone who lives in a house with a basement, and especially a basement with outside folding doors, has an almost made-to-order greenhouse setup.

The first opportunity is to build a small lean-to greenhouse using old wooden window sashes or a pair of aluminum storm windows from the lumber yard. Usually there is enough heat in any basement that supports a furnace to keep the greenhouse from freezing.

The second greenhouse can be built by removing the outside folding doors and replacing them with old wooden sashes or a large piece of acrylic set in a wooden frame.

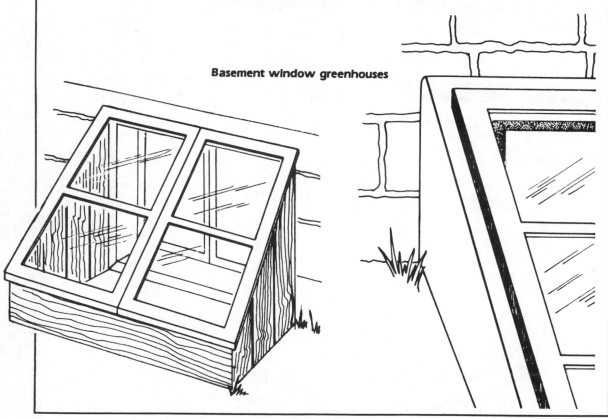

Basement window greenhouses

An Indoor Window Greenhouse

For those who cannot build a window to the outside, how about building a greenhouse on the inside of the room? The following illustration provides information for construction of such an indoor greenhouse with acrylic panels.

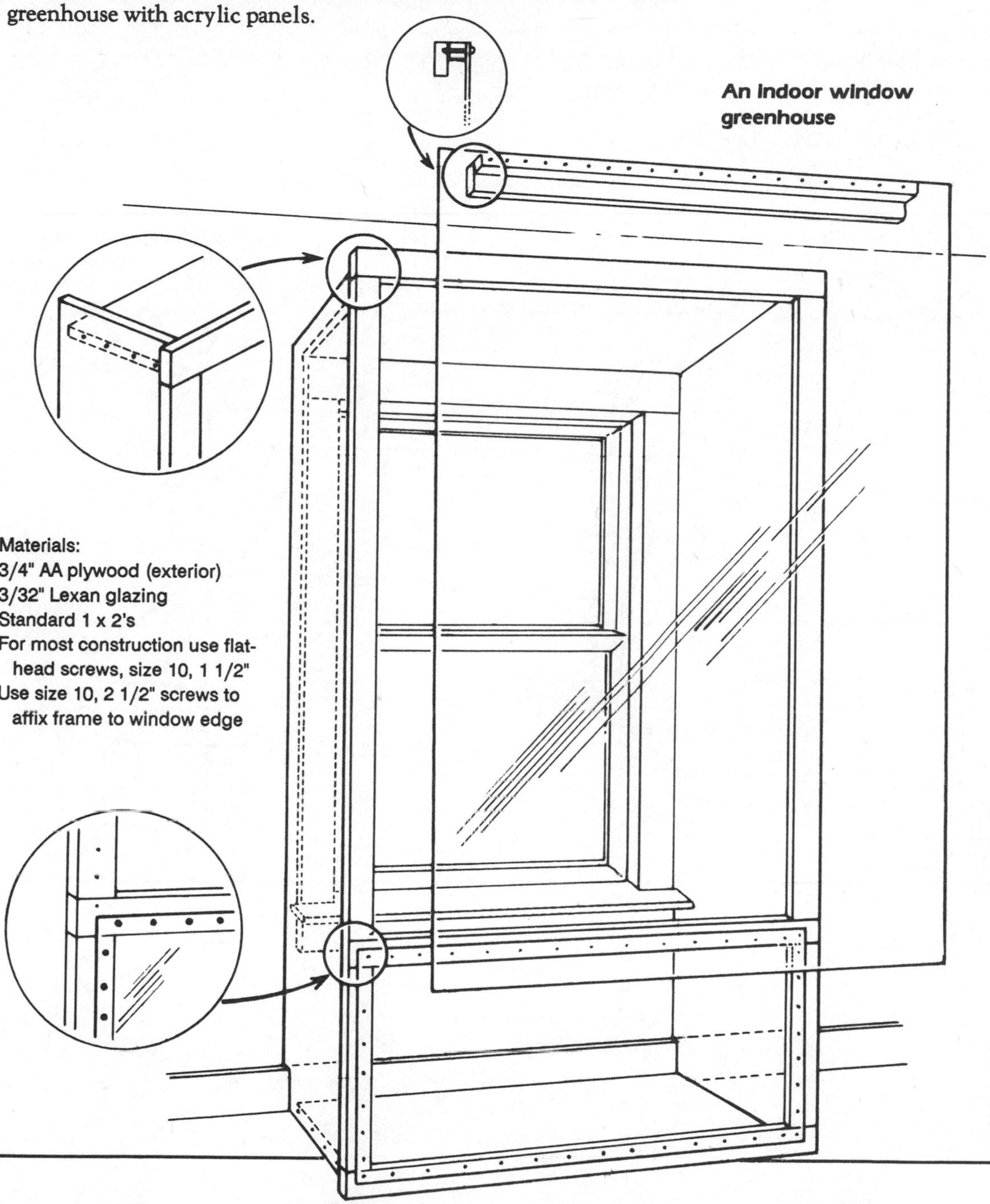

An indoor window greenhouse

Materials:
3/4" AA plywood (exterior)
3/32" Lexan glazing
Standard 1 x 2's
For most construction use flat-
  head screws, size 10, 1 1/2"
Use size 10, 2 1/2" screws to
  affix frame to window edge

A Smaller Window Garden

If you haven't the room for a large window garden how about a smaller affair? The same basic materials are used for this unit as in the previous example.

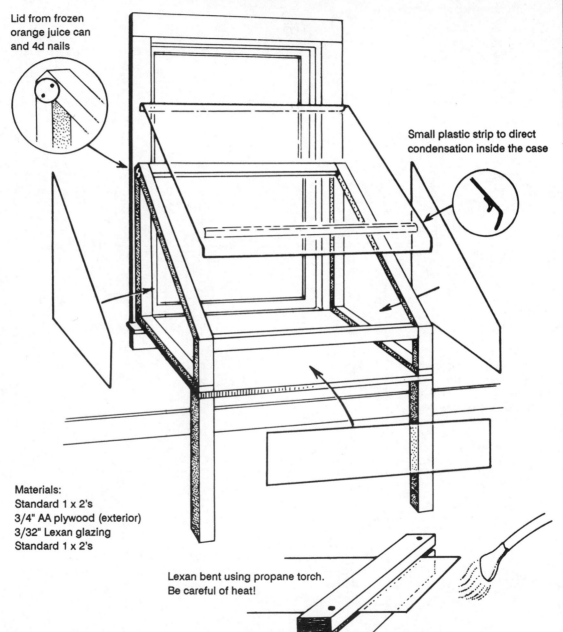

A smaller window garden

Lid from frozen orange juice can and 4d nails

Small plastic strip to direct condensation inside the case

Materials:
Standard 1 x 2's
3/4" AA plywood (exterior)
3/32" Lexan glazing
Standard 1 x 2's

Lexan bent using propane torch.
Be careful of heat!

An Inexpensive Plastic Greenhouse

For those of you who would like to test the greenhouse waters before plunging in with both feet, the answer might be the following inexpensive greenhouse made of clear polyethylene film (4 mil thick), the industrial plastic sheeting that comes in 10-foot wide rolls, and stock 2 × 4's.

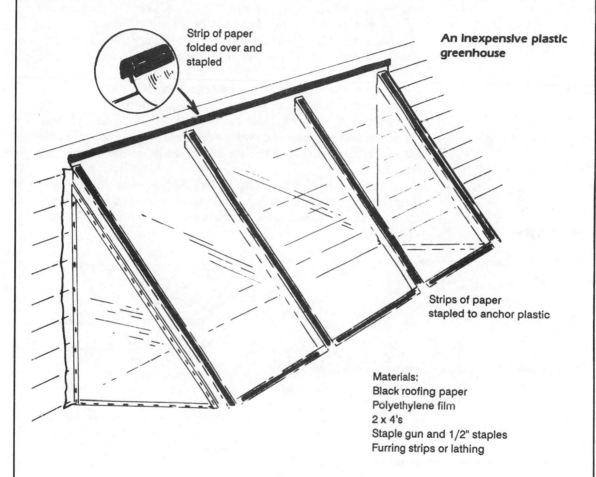

Strip of paper folded over and stapled

An Inexpensive plastic greenhouse

Strips of paper stapled to anchor plastic

Materials:
Black roofing paper
Polyethylene film
2 x 4's
Staple gun and 1/2" staples
Furring strips or lathing

The Sunporch

When we lost our front porch to carpenter ants one part survived the ravages of their chewing. It was the section to the right of our front door, measuring 8 by 14 feet. I removed the old window sashes, since they were beyond repair, and replaced them with aluminum storm windows and screens on tracks. I walled up the open-ing that joined the now rotten porch and put in a window (today that window is a door that joins the greenhouse and the sunporch). I then (with the help of my wife's cousin Fred) installed an overhead skylight and brought in a water faucet from the basement.

The happy result is a plant room that on a sunny day in January will see the temperature often reaching 75°F, yet could easily go be-low freezing on a cold February night. True, it's not the perfect place for the average houseplant, but you should see the range of plants that I do store in here over the winter. If a night is particularly cold, I have a small greenhouse heater that burns kerosene and holds the temperature around 40°F.

Out in that sunporch my cabbage palm (*Cordyline australis*) shares space with my dwarf redwood (*Sequoia sempervirens*), while my tub of cannas (*Canna* spp.) and a number of hanging baskets contain-ing my collection of orchid cactus (*Epiphyllum* spp.) all add to the jum-ble of plant material that finds a safe haven from the winter cold outside.

If you live up North and have a screened-in porch that faces any direction except north, I recommend that you consider replacing the screens with storm windows for the winter and creating your own sunporch.

A coldframe

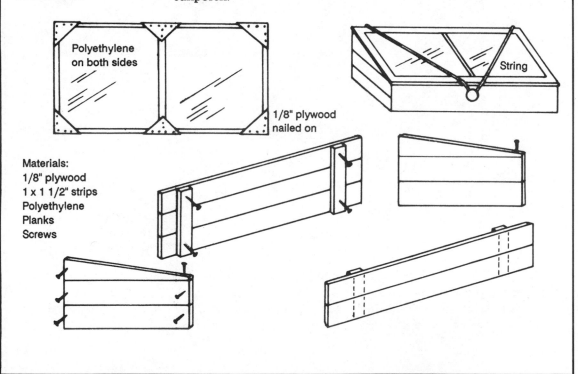

Polyethylene
on both sides

String

1/8" plywood
nailed on

Materials:
1/8" plywood
1 x 1 1/2" strips
Polyethylene
Planks
Screws

The Cold Frame and the Hotbed

Even if you have a fine greenhouse you will still find it valuable to have an outdoor cold frame. With such a structure, you can move seedlings out to a spot in maximum sunlight and make room for more plants in the greenhouse. It's a great place to store forced bulbs while they develop root systems and also a perfect spot to harden off greenhouse seedlings until they are adjusted to outdoor conditions.

A hotbed is a cold frame with a heating cable installed to warm the soil that houses the plants. Years ago, hotbeds received their warmth from the action of maturing manure, but it's not so easy to find a good supply these days and the cable is much easier to move about. A hotbed will work as a small greenhouse even in the most winter-prone parts of the country.

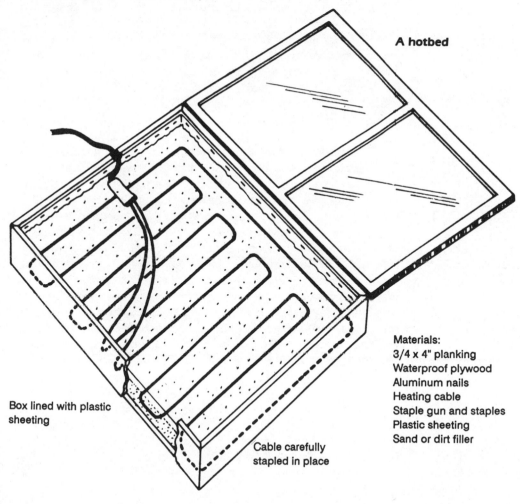

A hotbed

Box lined with plastic sheeting

Cable carefully stapled in place

Materials:
3/4 x 4" planking
Waterproof plywood
Aluminum nails
Heating cable
Staple gun and staples
Plastic sheeting
Sand or dirt filler

Appendix 2: Forcing Hardy Shrubs for Winter Flowers

One area where a gardener can feel free to experiment is forcing shrubs to bloom in the midst of winter. The usual practice is to force cut branches into bloom, but you can enjoy flowers on an even grander scale by forcing entire plants in pots into bloom. The following information on forcing shrubs is taken from volume three of *Thompson's Gardener's Assistant*, a book that dates from the turn of the century, described in the bibliography.

Large numbers of hardy shrubs are now grown solely for forcing, either for the supply of cut flowers or to be used as plants in flower for furnishing sunrooms, greenhouses, or for decorating the home.

Though shrubs for forcing can be purchased at a reasonable rate, it is more economical to set aside a piece of ground where you can grow your own supply of plants. In this way healthy young plants would be at hand to replace exhausted ones, which could be rejuvenated by giving them a rest for a year or two in a special nursery bed. This nursery is a spot with well-worked soil that is sheltered from the hot sun of a summer noon and close to the watchful eye of the gardener. In addition there should be a special place where potted plants can be buried, pot and all, for the better part of the garden year. This practice alleviates the continual worry of constant watering (exposed pots have a high rate of evaporation), and, at the same time, protects the plants from unnecessary heat. Although some shrubs require planting-out every other year (where they are unpotted and planted directly in the garden) there are others that must always be grown in pots.

For the best flowering you need healthy and mature plants with good, well-ripened wood. To encourage this growth, the ground selected for the nursery should be exposed to full sun. For the majority of shrubs a rich medium loam will be suitable, with the addition of peat moss and leaf-mold for acid-loving species. The best approach is to raise plants from cuttings, seeds, or grafts, and grow them for two years without flowering. This time should be spent in laying a good foundation for the future plants; consequently all weak, useless wood should be removed so that the plant's strength may go to the healthy parts. At three years of age most shrubs are in first-rate condition for forcing. Those grown in borders should be lifted in October, potted, plunged in light soil, and if the garden is in the colder zones of the country, heavily mulched until needed.

Use a sharp shovel when digging up the shrubs for potting. The diameter of the rootball should be about half the width of the shrub's branches at their widest point. Pot sizes will usually vary between 8 and 12 inches with an occasional 14-inch pot used for large shrubs.

February, March, and April are the three months when the shrubs are in the best condition for forcing, and for this they do not require excessive heat. As a rule it is better to place shrubs in a temperature not exceeding 50°F for the first two weeks, raising it to 60°F or more as the buds begin to swell. As flowers begin to open, the plants should be removed to a cool place to keep the blossoms in good condition.

After the flowers are over, the plants must be pruned. Cut out all weak and old flowering wood to encourage strong new growth. Keep these plants in a cool place until frost danger is past. Then those that require a year's rest go to the nursery plot where they are unpotted and replanted while the others that may be forced again the following season are plunged and kept well fed until the new flower-bearing growth is completed. Unless otherwise noted, the shrubs listed below need a year's rest between flowering.

Flowering Shrubs for Winter

Amelanchier canadensis (serviceberry or shadbush) bears white flowers in great profusion. It may be flowered early in February, and forced two successive years, after which it should spend a year in the nursery bed. Little pruning is needed.

Ceanothus species (redroots) should be grown in pots and pruned hard after flowering. They need the protection of a cold house during winter.

Choisya ternata (Mexican orange) will bloom with white, fragrant flowers for Christmas.

Clematis species, represented by a selection of the best garden varieties, should be grown in pots, to flower from the middle of February and on for several months. One-year-old plants twisted around stakes and placed in a temperature of some 50°F will produce from 12 to 20 flowers in 6 weeks. To obtain quick results plant three plants to one 12-inch pot. The plants should spend the summer outdoors. C. × *Jackmani* and C. *Viticella* are not suitable for forcing.

Corylopsis pauciflora (buttercup) and C. *spicata* (spike witch hazel) produce catkin-like inflorescences of yellow blooming in February.

Crataegus species (hawthorn) are easily forced, the most suitable being bushes from 3 to 4 feet high. During the summer pinch back shoots to produce spurs from which the white or pink flowers are produced. Hawthorns may be brought into flower in the same pots for several years but need an occasional rest in the nursery.

Cytisus (broom) is a favorite for forcing. After flowering cut them back or the plants become leggy. The most useful are C. × *kewensis*, C. *purpureus*, and C. *scoparius*.

Daphne Cneorum, D. × *hybrida*, and D. *Mezereum* will produce fragrant flowers from December to February with little forcing (meaning only moderate warmth). Flowers are pink, red, or white.

Deutzia species are excellent for forcing. If subjected to excessive heat they require a rest every alternate year; if moderately forced in

Making Branches Bloom in Winter

It can be a surprise to realize that most early blooming trees and shrubs enter the winter season with flower buds fully formed, but they do. Carefully wrapped in waxed layers of modified leaves, the fragile petals merely wait for the warming rays of the burgeoning spring sun to awaken and open. You can trick them into unfurling their flowers before the vernal equinox with a very simple procedure.

But first there are some myths to be debunked. Over the years a number of tests have been conducted on forcing woody twigs into bloom and the following practices have been found to be meaningless: It doesn't make any difference how you cut the end of the branch, just use a sharp tool; splitting or mashing the ends of the stems is not necessary; adding chemicals doesn't help; and it isn't necessary to presoak the branches in warm water.

The best time to collect branches is when the shrubs are dormant. Those twigs cut in January, then placed in water, take about two weeks for the flowers to open. When taken in February, the time for blooming is about one week.

The best shrubs or trees to force are: forsythia, *Cornus mas*, pieris, flowering quince, leucothoe, dogwoods, flowering crabapples, and blueberries.

relatively cooler temperatures they will last three successive years. *D. gracilis* and *D. parviflora* are particularly fine and both have white flowers.

Erica species (heath), especially the hardy ones, may be forced. Pot them up in September and plunge in the cold frame until December, when they may be removed to the greenhouse. Flowers last two to three months. *E. australis* bears purple flowers; *E. carnea* has red flowers; *E. lusitanica* has white flowers; and *E. mediterranea* bears flowers of deep purple.

Forsythia syspensa (golden-bells) forces well in a greenhouse with bright yellow flowers. Prune hard after flowering.

Hibiscus syriacus (rose-of-Sharon) bears white or purple flowers and can be successfully forced in temperatures of 50° to 60°F.

Hydrangea macrophylla (French hydrangea) is the species usually forced. Take cuttings in early autumn. Once they've rooted expose to full sun and allow the fledgling plants to thoroughly ripen. During early winter keep them cool and dry. In January repot into 5-inch pots and move them to flower-inducing warmth. Flowers are white, pink, or blue.

Itea virginica (sweetspire), when forced slowly so that the leaves develop with the white, fragrant flowers, is a pretty plant. They open early in March and last for several weeks.

Jasminum nudiflorum bears yellow flowers freely in mid-winter if started in December.

Kalmia angustifolia (sheep laurel), *K. poliifolia* (bog laurel), and *K. latifolia* (mountain laurel) force nicely if brought into gentle heat, to flower in April. They should be well established in pots before being asked to bloom. Flowers are red, white, and pink.

Kerria japonica (Japanese rose) bears orange-yellow flowers in February if started in January. It may be grown and forced in the same pots with liberal feeding three years in succession. All old flowering wood should be removed as soon as the flowers are past. After the third year, start again with new plants.

Laburnum species (bean tree) are easily forced for the sunporch or greenhouse. Pot plants in spring to force the following year. The flowers are yellow.

Lonicera fragrantissima and *L. Standishii* are honeysuckles that force easily in mid-winter and bear white flowers.

Magnolia species may be lifted from the open ground with care and planted in pots to be in flower for early spring. *M. heptapeta*, *M. hypoleuca*, *M.* × *Soulangiana*, and *M. stellata* are excellent subjects.

Olearia stellulata (tree aster) is an admirable plant for forcing. If kept in pots and not subjected to excessive heat, it may be used several years in succession. Flowers are white.

Paeonia suffruticosa (tree peony) is an excellent plant for forcing if grown in pots and well established before being subjected to heat. Flowers may be ready for February. Colors vary according to cultivar but range from white to pink to deep red.

Philadelphus species (mock orange) should not be subjected to high heat. *P. × Lemoinei* should have all old flowering wood removed as soon as the flowers are past. Flowers are white and fragrant.

Pieris floribunda (fetterbush), a dwarf, compact evergreen, with upright panicles of white flowers and *P. japonica* (lily-of-the-valley bush) bearing pendulous clusters of white flowers, will both bloom in February after a month's easy forcing.

Prunus species are some of the most beautiful, useful, and easily managed plants for forcing and include plums, cherries, almonds, and peaches. They can be forced into flower from January until they normally bloom outside. Plants may be potted up from the open border in October or grown in pots, given the same culture as fruit trees grown in containers. They may be used for a number of years in succession provided they are not exhausted by excessive heat. After flowering they should be pruned hard and fed liberally to induce strong growth, and placed in full sun to thoroughly ripen the wood.

Rhododendron species, either large or small plants, may be used. It is advisable to plant them out after flowering and give them a year's rest, although some will do fairly well two years in succession. Weak inside shoots should be cut out. For December and January the best are *R. × Nobleanum* with rose-pink flowers; *R. luteum* with yellow flowers; and *R. × praecox* with purple flowers. For February and March, the best are *R. caucasicum* with pink flowers and *R. × Everestianum* with rose-purple flowers.

Ribes aureum (golden current) has yellow flowers and *R. sanguineum* bears dark red flowers. Both are both easily forced.

Robinia hispida (rose acacia) may be forced for early bloom if they are established in pots and don't receive too much heat. Flowers are rose to pale purple.

Rosa species may be successfully forced but they require some preparation if good specimens and fine flowers are expected. A rose should be three years old before it is forced; after that, if properly treated, it will last for years. The plants should be on their own roots, not grafted. Cuttings of half-ripened wood, taken with a heel, and inserted in 5-inch pots filled with loam and peat moss, plunged in a greenhouse with bottom heat, will soon root. They may be wintered in a cold frame and protected from frost. Cut them back to two eyes in January, and give them no water until they begin to grow. Once they begin to put on new growth, repot, and if the weather is favorable, plunge them in the open border, making sure they get plenty of water. Pick off all flower buds. In the autumn they must be protected again in a cold frame or cool part of the house. In January, prune them by shortening the strong shoots to three or four eyes and plunge them out again in the cold frame.

About midsummer repot again (they will not require repotting until after they flower). Some of the tea roses may be allowed to flower in autumn. The plants should be pruned according to the time at which they are required to bloom. For instance, plants required to bloom at Christmas should be pruned no later than the first week in October; and they must be brought along very gradually, allowing three months for them to make their growth and flower.

Spiraea species will often force readily in a temperature of 50°F for flowering in February; with attention to pruning and feeding they may be used two or three successive years. The best are *S.* × *arguta, S. media, S. prunifolia, S. Thunbergii,* and *S.* × *Vanhouttei.*

Staphylea colchica (bladdernut) is one of the best shrubs for forcing, since it produces white flowers from Christmas onwards. It should be rested alternate years.

Viburnum Opulus (cranberry bush) is easily forced but if too great a heat is used the white flower stalks will be weak and easily broken. *V. macrocephalum* (Chinese snowball) has immense heads of white flowers. Both species should be rested alternate years.

Wisteria chinensis is particularly pleasing when encouraged to flower for March and April. Establish such plants in pots two years before they are forced. Flowers are white.

Zenobia pulverulenta, if forced, will open white flowers in early spring.

Appendix 3: Sources of Supply

Seed Exchanges

The following organizations send out seed lists to their members and everyone is given an opportunity to choose a set number of species as part of their membership. At the same time interested gardeners are asked to donate seeds from their own gardens in an effort to continually expand the collections.

The Alpine Garden Society is mainly concerned with alpine and rock garden plants. Its quarterly bulletin is stocked with valuable information and photos of rare and unusual plants. The seed exchange lists well over 4,000 species. Both are available to members for $20 per year but the price varies with the exchange rates.
—Lye End Link, St. Johns, Woking, Surrey GU21 1SW, England.

The American Horticultural Society sponsors a seed exchange for members and features a subscription to the *American Horticulturist* at a cost of $30 per year.
—American Horticultural Society, Mount Vernon, Virginia 22121.

The American Rock Garden Society publishes a fine quarterly bulletin and sponsors the biggest seed exchange in the United States and Canada. Over 3,500 different species are offered as part of the membership. Cost is $20 per year.
—15 Fairmead Road, Darien, Connecticut 06820.

The Hardy Plant Society is a fine old English organization that publishes various news bulletins and sponsors a fine and select seed exchange. Cost is $8 and varies with the exchange rates.
—Simon Wills, The Manor House, Walton-in-Gordano, Clevedon, Avon BS21 7AN, England.

The Royal Horticultural Society is one of the all-time greats. In addition to *The Garden*, the monthly magazine, a membership includes a free pass to the Chelsea Flower Show, and entry to the seed exchange, a service that covers the world with 1,200 entries. The cost is $20 per year but the exchange rate will vary.
—Vincent Square, London SW1P 2PE, England.

The Scottish Rock Garden Society publishes two fine bulletins a year that deal with alpine plants and also includes interesting garden perennials. The seed exchange has over 3,200 entries. Membership is $12 per year but the exchange rates will vary.

Commercial Seed Companies

The catalogs listed below are issued by seed companies that usually deal with flowers (although a few also stock vegetables). Because of fluctuating costs, I've not included any charges incurred with receiving these publications, so if in doubt, write first.

The Banana Tree, 715 Northampton Street, Easton, Pennsylvania 18042. Exotic seeds: bananas, trees, and flowers.

Burpee Seeds, Warminster, Pennsylvania 18974. One of the oldest seeds companies around. They now stock live plants, too.

Chiltern Seeds, Bortree Stile, Ulverston, Cumbria LA12 7PB, England.

The Cook's Garden, Box 65, Londonderry, Vermont 05148. Unusual gourmet vegetable seeds.

The Country Garden, Route 2, Box 455A, Crivitz, Wisconsin 54114. A very large collection of annuals and perennials both for cutting and the border.

Far North Garden, 16785 Harrison, Livonia, Michigan 48154. A fine collection of seeds, many rare. They also have primrose plants.

The Fragrant Path, Box 328, Fort Calhoun, Nebraska 68023. A wonderful collection of fragrant plants.

Gurney's Seed & Nursery Co., Yankton, South Dakota 57079. An old-fashioned catalog with old-fashioned pictures and many interesting varieties.

J. L. Hudson, Seedsman, PO Box 1058, Redwood City, California 94064. A huge selection of seeds from around the world.

Johnny's Selected Seeds, Albion, Maine 04910. Mostly vegetables but a few good flowers and many herbs.

Jung Quality Seeds, Randolf, Wisconsin 53956. Another fine American seed house with many flowers.

Maver Rare Perennials, Route 2, Box 265B, Asheville, North Carolina 28805. A large selection of unusual seeds including many ornamental grasses.

Moon Mountain Wildflowers, PO Box 34, Morro Bay, California 93442. Seeds for wildflowers native to and naturalized in North America.

Nichol's Herb and Rare Seeds, 1190 N. Pacific Highway, Albany, Oregon 97321. A large number of special seeds: herbs, flowers, and bulbs.

Geo. W. Park Seed Company, Greenwood, South Carolina 29647. One of the most famous seed houses in America.

Pinetree Garden Seeds, Lewiston Road, New Gloucester, Maine 04260. An excellent seed house with a number of unusual plants.

Plants of the Southwest, 1570 Pacheco Street, Santa Fe, New Mexico 87501. An interesting catalog with many wildflowers and grasses.

Clyde Robin Seed Company, PO Box 2855, Castro Valley, California 94546. One of the major dealers in wildflower seeds.

Seeds Blüm, Idaho City Stage, Boise, Idaho 83706. They only sell open-pollinated seeds, including many heirloom varieties.

Stock Seed Farms, Route 1, Box 112, Murdock, Nebraska 68407. Flowers and grasses native to the Midwest.

Thompson & Morgan, PO Box 100, Farmingdale, New Jersey 08527. One of England's oldest seed houses, now with offices in America.

Live Plants and Supplies by Mail

The following suppliers grow and sell live plants to be shipped: You order by mail and they ship by United Parcel. Over the years I've ordered hundreds of plants and almost everything has arrived in fine fettle—and when it has not, the nurseries have rectified the mistake. They know how to wrap the plants so that they arrive alive. Like seed suppliers, no two nurseries are alike. Each firm will have a few unusual things to offer. Included in the list are greenhouse and equipment suppliers. The catalog fees—if any—are not listed.

Alpenglow, 13328 King George Highway, Surrey, B.C., Canada V3T 2T6. A large variety of alpines, perennials, and shrubs.

Bernardo Beach Native Plant Farm, Star Route 7, Box 145, Vesquita, New Mexico 87062. Perennials, vines, and others for south-western gardens.

Kurt Bluemel, Inc., 2543 Hess Road, Fallston, Maryland 21047. World's largest nursery of ornamental grasses.

The Bovees Nursery, 1737 S. W. Coronado, Portland, Oregon 97219. Rhododendrons, azaleas, and companion plants.

Camellia Forest, 125 Carolina Forest Road, Chapel Hill, North Carolina 27516. Camellias and other shrubs.

Charley's Greenhouse Supplies, 1569 Memorial Highway, Mount Vernon, Washington 98257. A major supplier of greenhouse-related items.

Dutch Gardens, Inc., PO Box 200, Adelphia, New Jersey 07710. Many, many bulbs.

Endangered Species, Box 1830, Tustin, California 92681. Bamboos, grasses, flax, and unusual plants.

Gardener's Supply Company, 133 Elm Street, Winooski, Vermont 05404. Many garden tools.

Garden Place, 6780 Heisley Road, PO Box 83, Mentor, Ohio. Large selection of perennials.

Glasshouse Works, Church Street, PO Box 97, Stewart, Ohio 45778. Plants for indoors and out.

Greenlife Gardens, 101 County Line Road, Griffin, Georgia 30223. A large collection of orchid cactus and other epiphytic cactuses.

Holbrook Farm, Route 2, Box 223B, Fletcher, North Carolina 28732. Wide range of perennials.

Klehm Nursery, Route 5, Box 197, South Barrington, Illinois 60010. Peonies, daylilies, hosta, and iris.

A. M. Leonard, Inc., 6665 Spiker Road, Piqua, Ohio 45356. A large supplier of horticultural tools.

Lilypons Water Gardens, 6800 Lilypons Road, Lilypons, Maryland 21717. Plants for pool and pond.

Logee's Greenhouses, Danielson, Connecticut 06239. A vast selection of plants for home and greenhouse.

McClure & Zimmerman, 108 W. Winnebago, PO Box 368, Friesland, Wisconsin 53935. Major supplier of bulbs.

Milaeger's Gardens, 4838 Douglas Avenue, Racine, Wisconsin 53402. Large collection of perennials.

Walt Nicke Company, 36 McLeod Lane, PO Box 433, Topsfield, Massachusetts 01983. A houseplant and garden supermarket of supplies.

Niche Gardens, Route 1, Box 290, Chapel Hill, North Carolina 27516. Many nursery propagated southeastern native plants.

Prairie Nursery, PO Box 365, Westfield, Wisconsin 53964. American grasses and wildflowers.

Steve Ray's Bamboo Gardens, 909 79th Pl., South, Birmingham, Alabama 35206. Huge selection of bamboos.

Rocknoll Nursery, 9210 U.S. 50, Hillsboro, Ohio 45133. Rock garden plants and perennials.

Sandy Mush Herbs, Route 2, Surrett Cove Road, Leicester, North Carolina 28748. Herbs and garden perennials.

John Scheepers, Inc., Phillipsburg Road, RD 6, Middletown, New York 10940. A large selection of lilies and other bulbs.

Smith & Hawken Tool Company, Inc., 25 Corte Madera, Mill Valley, California 94941. Tools and fancy items for the garden.

Andre Viette Farm & Nursery, Route 1, Box 16, Fishersville, Virginia 22939. Daylilies, hostas, ornamental grasses, and others.

Wayside Gardens, Hodges, South Carolina 29695. A tremendous selection of perennials, shrubs, and trees.

We-Du Nurseries, Route 5, Box 724, Marion, North Carolina 28752. Many unusual and American wildflowers.

White Flower Farm, Litchfield, Connecticut 06759. A large selection of perennials.

Woodlanders, 1128 Colleton Avenue, Aiken, South Carolina 29801. Many fine wildflowers and native shrubs and trees.

Bibliography

Abraham, George (Doc) and Katy. *Organic Gardening Under Glass*. New York: Van Nostrand Reinhold Company, 1984. Instructions on growing a number of unusual plants under glass by two time-honored garden writers.

Blanchan, Neltje. *Nature's Garden*. New York: Doubleday, Page & Co., 1904. Full of wonders about wildflowers, how they grow and survive, and the bees who flit from blossom to blossom.

Crockett, James Underwood. *Greenhouse Gardening as a Hobby*. New York: Doubleday & Company, Inc., 1961. Mr. Crockett was one of the horticultural leaders in the United States and for anyone who is contemplating a greenhouse, this is a must book. Unfortunately, it is probably long out of print. Check your local library or firms that sell used garden books.

Dictionary of Gardening. The Royal Horticultural Society. 4 vols. and supplement. Oxford: Clarendon, 1965. Next to *Hortus Third*, these volumes are the most used in my library. Fascinating not only for advice on plants and planting, but for history, too.

Encyclopedia of Organic Gardening. The staff of *Organic Gardening* magazine. Emmaus, Pennsylvania: Rodale Press, 1978. For all the information needed to grow a fine garden of flowers without resorting to artificial chemicals, this is the reference book to use.

Free, Montague. *All About House Plants*. New York: Doubleday & Company, Inc., 1946. To my mind, one of the most valuable books on houseplants ever written. Mr. Free was for 30 years the horticulturist at the Brooklyn Botanic Garden and a most knowledgeable gentleman.

———. *All About the Perennial Garden*. New York: Doubleday & Company, 1955. Mr. Free's contribution to planning a perennial garden including excellent advice in laying out and installing a garden full of perennials.

Genders, Roy. *Bulbs: A Complete Handbook*. Indianapolis/New York: Bobbs-Merrill, 1973. Full cultural instructions for most bulbs, corms, and tubers being grown today.

Hortus Third. New York: Macmillan, 1976. This is the monumental revision of L. H. Bailey and Ethel Zoe Bailey's original work of nomenclature for the American gardener and horticulturist, overseen by the staff of the L. H. Bailey Hortorium at Cornell University. Very expensive but worth talking your local library into acquiring, if they haven't already.

Loewer, Peter. *Bringing the Outdoors In.* Chicago/New York: Contemporary Books, 1988. A reprint of a book I wrote in 1974, that deals with growing and flowering all sorts of plants indoors.

Lovejoy, Ann. *The Year in Bloom.* Seattle: Sasquatch Books, 1987. A most literate discussion of growing and flowering plants in the Pacific Northwest.

Miles, Bebe. *Wildflower Perennials for Your Garden.* New York: Hawthorne, 1976. A classic book on wildflowers for the garden, written by a fine American gardener and writer.

Moir, May A. *The Garden Watcher.* Honolulu: University of Hawaii Press, 1983. A month-by-month diary of growing plants in Hawaii.

Paul, Anthony and Yvonne Rees. *The Water Garden.* New York: Penguin Books, 1986. A comprehensive guide to both installing and planning a water garden from hot tubs to waterfalls.

Pizzetti, Ippolito, and Henry Cocker. *Flowers: A Guide for Your Garden.* 2 vols. New York: Harry N. Abrams, 1975. Using the fine color plates from the great eighteenth- and nineteenth-century botanical periodicals for a starting-off point, these books cover both history and culture of a host of plants for the garden.

Taylor, Norman, ed. *The Practical Encyclopedia of Gardening.* New York: Garden City Publishing Company, Inc., 1936. This edition is the book to look for, not the fourth which turned into a "cut and paste" job that edited out the marvelous asides that the older edition was famous for. A book for dipping into when you cannot go out to the garden but the muse is sitting on your shoulder.

Thompson's Gardener's Assistant. 4 vols. London: The Gresham Publishing Company, N.D. Although there is no publishing date for this wonderful set of books, there is an inscription on the flyleaf: Ernestine M. Smith, September 9, 1909. I paid $4.00 for the complete set in the mid 70s. Although English, much of the information is usable, the engravings are beautiful, and like many old garden books, far more fun to read than most of today's.

Index

Bold type denotes illustration

Rodale Press, Inc., publishes RODALE'S ORGANIC GARDENING,
the all-time favorite gardening magazine.
For information on how to order your subscription,
write to RODALE'S ORGANIC GARDENING, Emmaus, PA 18098.